Real Resumix & Other Resumes for Federal Government Jobs

...including samples of real resumes used
to apply for federal government jobs

PREP Publishing
1110½ Hay Street
Fayetteville, NC 28305
(910) 483-6611

Library of Congress Cataloging-in-Publication Data

McKinney, Anne, 1948-
Real resumix & other resumes for Federal Government jobs : including samples of
real resumes used to apply for Federal Government jobs / Anne McKinney.
       p. cm. -- (Government jobs series)
     ISBN 1-885288-35-2
     1. Civil service positions--United States. 2. Resumes (Employment)--United
States. 3. Applications for positions. I. Title: Real resumix and other resumes for
Federal Government jobs. II. Title. III. Series.

  JK716.M35 2003
  650.14'2--dc21   2003042932
                                                                          CIP

Printed in the United States of America

By PREP Publishing

Business and Career Series:

RESUMES AND COVER LETTERS THAT HAVE WORKED

RESUMES AND COVER LETTERS THAT HAVE WORKED FOR MILITARY PROFESSIONALS

GOVERNMENT JOB APPLICATIONS AND FEDERAL RESUMES

COVER LETTERS THAT BLOW DOORS OPEN

LETTERS FOR SPECIAL SITUATIONS

RESUMES AND COVER LETTERS FOR MANAGERS

REAL-RESUMES FOR COMPUTER JOBS

REAL-RESUMES FOR MEDICAL JOBS

REAL-RESUMES FOR FINANCIAL JOBS

REAL-RESUMES FOR TEACHERS

REAL-RESUMES FOR STUDENTS

REAL-RESUMES FOR CAREER CHANGERS

REAL-RESUMES FOR SALES

REAL ESSAYS FOR COLLEGE & GRADUATE SCHOOL

REAL-RESUMES FOR AVIATION & TRAVEL JOBS

REAL-RESUMES FOR POLICE, LAW ENFORCEMENT & SECURITY JOBS

REAL-RESUMES FOR SOCIAL WORK & COUNSELING JOBS

REAL-RESUMES FOR CONSTRUCTION JOBS

REAL-RESUMES FOR MANUFACTURING JOBS

REAL-RESUMES FOR RESTAURANT, FOOD SERVICE & HOTEL JOBS

REAL-RESUMES FOR MEDIA, NEWSPAPER, BROADCASTING & PUBLIC AFFAIRS JOBS

REAL-RESUMES FOR RETAILING, MODELING, FASHION & BEAUTY JOBS

REAL-RESUMES FOR HUMAN RESOURCES & PERSONNEL JOBS

REAL-RESUMES FOR NURSING JOBS

REAL-RESUMES FOR AUTO INDUSTRY JOBS

REAL RESUMIX AND OTHER RESUMES FOR FEDERAL GOVERNMENT JOBS

REAL KSAS--KNOWLEDGE, SKILLS & ABILITIES--FOR GOVERNMENT JOBS

REAL BUSINESS PLANS AND MARKETING TOOLS

Judeo-Christian Ethics Series:

SECOND TIME AROUND

BACK IN TIME

WHAT THE BIBLE SAYS ABOUT...Words that can lead to success and happiness

A GENTLE BREEZE FROM GOSSAMER WINGS

BIBLE STORIES FROM THE OLD TESTAMENT

Table of Contents

A WORD FROM THE EDITOR:
ABOUT THE GOVERNMENT JOBS SERIES

Welcome to the Government Job Series. The Government Job Series is a series of books which have been developed based on the experiences of real job hunters and which target specialized fields or types of resumes. As the editor of the series, I have carefully selected resumes and cover letters (with names and other key data disguised, of course) which have been used successfully in real job hunts. That's what we mean by "Real-Resumes." What you see in this book are *real* resumes and cover letters which helped real people get ahead in their careers.

The Real-Resumes Series is based on the work of the country's oldest resume-preparation company known as PREP Resumes. If you would like a free information packet describing the company's resume preparation services, call 910-483-6611 or write to PREP at 1110½ Hay Street, Fayetteville, NC 28305. If you have a job hunting experience you would like to share with our staff at the Real-Resumes Series, please contact us at preppub@aol.com or visit our website at http://www.prep-pub.com.

We hope the superior samples will help you manage your current job campaign and your career so that you will find work aligned to your career interests.

The resumes and cover letters in this book are designed to be of most value to people already in a job hunt or contemplating a career change. If we could give you one word of advice about your career, here's what we would say: Manage your career and don't stumble from job to job in an incoherent pattern. Try to find work that interests you, and then identify prosperous industries which need work performed of the type you want to do. Learn early in your working life that a great resume and cover letter can blow doors open for you and help you maximize your salary.

Real Resumix & Other Resumes for Federal Government Jobs

Anne McKinney, Editor

PREP PUBLISHING

What is a resumix?

This strange new word is a term which describes a popular tool used to apply for federal government positions. A resumix is a special type of resume which is, in general, more detailed than an ordinary "civilian resume." A civilian resume is often on one or two pages and is accompanied by a cover letter. On the other hand, a federal resume is usually lengthier -- usually between two to five pages long, with three pages being the most standard length at this time. A federal resume contains data which is often not shown on a civilian resume; for example, a federal resume reveals your salary history and provides your employers' names and addresses as well as supervisors' names and phone numbers.

How do you know how to apply for federal government jobs?

Most of the time, a federal job is "announced" through a position vacancy announcement which you can usually obtain online through www.govjobs.com or other websites. The first thing you should do is download and print out the position vacancy announcement or announcements which interest you. Then read it carefully. Usually four or more pages long, the position vacancy announcement will tell you exactly what you need to do to apply for the job. You may be instructed to put your resume online using Resume Builder or another electronic tool.

Putting your resume online using Resume Builder or another electronic tool

This book will be very helpful to you even if you plan on applying for federal jobs electronically -- that is, by posting your resume or resumix online through Resume Builder or another electronic method suggested in the job vacancy announcement. It is not in your best interest to simply sit down at a computer and just "think up" your resume impulsively and submit a written product which is your first draft. It's important that you create a draft and "get it right" before you actually post your resume. In that way, you will make sure you have a carefully thought-out resumix which is fully descriptive of your skills and abilities. It's best to create a solid draft on paper first before you sit down to the computer to post your resumix online. The samples in this book will be a rich source of inspiration for you as you create a draft of your resumix prior to mailing it or posting it online.

ACCOUNTING & SUPPLY TECHNICIAN

OLIVER A. JERRY
SSN: 000-00-0000
Mailing Address: 8759 Buies Street, Warren, MI 56871
Home Telephone: (111) 111-1111
Work Telephone: (222) 222-2222
oliverjerry@earthlink.net

Highest permanent play plan or grade held: grade, month/year from ___ to month/year
Position, Title, Series, Grade: Accounting Technician, GS-09
Announcement Number: DN-00-000

EXPERIENCE

ACCOUNTING and SUPPLY TECHNICIAN. Cherry Bekaert & Holland, LLP, 1860 Hannover Square, Warren, MI 56845, Charles Adams, Supervisor, phone: (333) 333-3333, hours worked: 45-50, (2004-present). Excelling in handling diverse responsibilities, have been credited with making changes which have significantly improved operating procedures while supervising three people including accounting clerks and office staff for a business with five separate plant locations.

- Streamline operations in the accounting department and implement changes which have reduced the time needed to complete support activities; for instance, payroll processing which had taken three days is now completed in one.
- Apply knowledge in database creation to establish a new system for tracking equipment purchases and status of computers, printers, vehicles, and other equipment.
- Prepare payroll for up to 36 Cherry Bekaert employees in the company's five plants.
- Manage Workmen's Compensation claims and yearly audits, preparation of forms for OSHA, and monthly approval of employee health insurance; prepare daily bank deposits; post payroll and accounts payable check numbers; issue and then post manual checks; prepare the petty cash sheet; process state and federal tax payments.
- Verify data between the general ledger, accounts payable, and accounts receivable.

ACCOUNTS PAYABLE AND PAYROLL TECHNICIAN. Pechmann-Ellis & Associates, 2583 Ravenhill Circle, Warren, MI 56845, Charles Adams, Supervisor, phone: (444) 444-4444, hours worked: 45-50, (2001-04). After my retirement from the U.S. Army, was recruited by this commercial construction company to handle accounts payable for multimillion-dollar projects and to process payroll for 200 employees.

- Assisted in purchasing support for large projects; prepared weekly and monthly reports for Project Managers and Supervisors.

Other experience gained in the US Army:
BATTALION PROPERTY ACCOUNTING TECHNICIAN. U.S. Army, 37th Finance Division, Fort Rucker, AL, 77646. Supervisor: MAJ Edgar Nixon, (555) 555-5555, hours per week: 40, (1998-01). As a Property Book Officer and senior logistician for a logistics battalion, was commended in writing for "excellent performance in superbly

performing all assigned missions" while directing management and accountability procedures for supplies, property and equipment worth over $105 million. Worked closely with the subordinate companies to assure smooth transfers of excess equipment out of the battalion. Identified over $750,000 of excess items for turn-in with 63%+ redistributed throughout the corps. Acquired shortage items and force modernization equipment. Expertly utilized both manual and automated property accounting procedures, including VLOS and TAQlS. Exercised staff supervision of the battalion logistics low-density program. Supervised one NCO and one soldier. Ensured all M35A2 cargo trucks were turned in through supply channels. Executed the M4 carbine fielding to the battalion. Achieved "zero defects" in hand-controlled inventory. This battalion's supply and property accountability ranked among the best at Fort Rucker. Provided the leadership for a drive to reduce excess property and became the "go-to" manager for all companies in the battalion seeking guidance in reducing excess property.

PROPERTY BOOK OFFICER. U.S. Army, 151st Finance Division, FA Bn, Stuttgart, Germany, APO, AE 564, Supervisor: MAJ David N. Butler, (666) 666-6666, hours per week: 40, (1996-98). Supervised 11 people as Property Book Officer for a Finance Division in Stuttgart. During this time, played a key role in the operation of the Battalion's Finance office in Germany for 2 years, and maintained accountability of one Battalion fuel point, maintaining formal property book records through the use of the Standard Property Book System. Redesigned (SPBS) property valued at $2.1 billion. Provided technical expertise to the chain of command on logistical and budget policies and procedures. Ensured the battalion maintained a rating consistent with its Authorized Level of Organization. My performance was rated as "absolutely outstanding" in this position Maintained 100% accountability of the organization's property. On my own initiative, developed training and orientation procedures which ensured smooth transition when new personnel assumed control of property. Provided leadership in fielding new modernized equipment including SINCGARS radios, data transfer devices, squad automatic weapons, and radio meters. Was described in writing as "without a doubt the subject matter expert on property management."

PROPERTY BOOK OFFICER. U.S. Army, 43rd Intelligence Brigade, Fort Riley, KS 46323-5442. Supervisor: SSG Larry Norris, (555) 555-5555, hours per week: 40, (1993-96). Responsible for all administrative matters pertaining to the Property Book of the Intelligence Brigade, a 1,000-man independent combat team. Maintained organizational hand receipts for eight companies and one battery, including associated shortage annexes and documents supporting files in excess of $70 million. Supervised two enlisted personnel to ensure cyclic and sensitive item inventories were properly conducted and hand receipts reassigned in a timely manner. In this position, constructed a property accounting system using the Standard Property Book System (SPBS-R). In May 1994 during Operation Mission Relief, ensured the brigade's supply requirements were met, coordinating support for two other bases in Fort Campbell, KY, Fort Myer, VA, and Fort Wainwright, AK. Yielded a zero deficit accounting record for all equipment on hand. Also oversaw the transfer of well over 100 railcars of equipment from inactivating intelligence units into the command and the fielding of new equipment. In a formal performance evaluation, was described thusly: "his knowledge, long-range vision, and desire to conduct all property and supply transactions properly have had a significant impact on the battalion."

BATTALION PROPERTY BOOK TECHNICIAN. US Army, B-253rd Intelligence Division, Fort Hood, TX, 87646, Supervisor: SFC Scott Grenald, (666) 666-6666, hours per week: 40, (1990-93). Property Book Officer for this Intelligence division. Once assigned to the unit, maintained organizational and installation hand receipts for five batteries to include associated shortage annexes and document supporting files in excess of $50 million. Managed excess property by coordinating and monitoring turn-in and lateral transfer directives.

Monitored training programs and supervised 11 enlisted personnel. Directed and supervised the fielding of several Force Modernization items of equipment including SINCGARS radios, M40 protective masks, M16A2 rifles, and Mobile Subscriber Equipment (MSE). Developed a plan for the turn-in or transfer of excess equipment in the battalion totaling 27 LIN items. Maintained 100% property accountability for two separate books.

PROPERTY BOOK TECHNICIAN. HHC-535, Artillery Brigade, APO AE 13856, Supervisor: MAJ Nathan Jennings, (777) 777-7777, hours per week: 40, (1988-90). Brigade Budget Officer/Supply Technician responsible for monitoring and advising the brigade commander, battalion commanders, and the brigade S4 on the status of budget operations and expenditures. Assisted four battalion property book officers in maintaining property book accountability and providing technical advice and assistance. As the HHC Brigade Property Book Officer, responsible of the accountability of $9 million worth of equipment, property, and supplies. Ensured proper codes and fund cites were placed on unit requisitions to ensure the brigade would receive proper credit, resulting in over $585,000 of funds reimbursed. Instrumental in the development of the brigade's FY 89 budget. Monitored the budget accounts for the brigade and tracked the battalion's budget expenditures and recording procedures. Ensured excess property was identified, redistributed when possible, or disposed of in accordance with standard regulations. Communicated with outside agencies to obtain essential equipment that critically short with in the Army supply system. Ensured all classes of supply were obtained to sustain a field artillery brigade consisting of 5 battalions, 3,000 soldiers, 90 155mm howitzers, 18 rocket launchers, and over 960 wheeled vehicles for 6 months in the Panama and during combat operations against Panamanian forces.

Excelled in a "track record" of promotions with the US Army at Fort Polk, LA:
1986-88: **DIVISION PROPERTY BOOK TEAM CHIEF.** HHC, 67th Artillery, Fort Polk, LA 76307, Supervisor: SSG James A. Hennegan, (888) 888-8888, hours per week: 40. As Property Book Team Chief for Property Book Teams One and Two, provided property accountability for the 1st and 2nd Brigades. Managed the over $89 million of assets for the 82d Signal Bn, 307 Engineer Bn, and 618th Engineer Company. Ensured all authorized property was on hand or on requisition. Verified CBS-X asset reporting, unit readiness output, and ensured all records, forms, and printouts were accurate. Responsible for installation and training of a new automated cross-leveling/redistribution program which resulted in saving the Division hundreds of thousands of dollars. From Jan to Jul, served as the Government Accountable Officer (GAO) in Korea prior to being Team Chief for two Property Book teams consisting of 40 units. As GAO, brought all measures of supply performance above DA standards.

1984-86: **SUPPLY TECHNICIAN,** 7th Division Infantry, Supervisor: SGT Harold G. Nicholls, (999) 999-9999, hours worked: 40. Maintained organization hand receipts for 19 units, to include associated shortage annexes and supporting documentation files. Provided an audit trail for all supply transaction, and ensured that cyclic and sensitive item inventories were properly conducted and hand receipts signed. Verified CBS-X asset reporting; established and monitored training programs and supervised four enlisted personnel. utilized state-of-the art equipment to manage $4.6 million worth of deployable equipment of the 1/504th Parachute Infantry Regiment and the 73d Signal Battalion. Personally cited by GAO auditors and given praiseworthy comment by the Brigade Commander for the timely support and management of supplies and equipment in Honduras.

1982-84: **SUPPLY TECHNICIAN.** HHS, 321st Logistics, Supervisor: SGT Wesley K. Combs, phone unknown. hours worked: 40. Was team chief in charge of maintaining organization and installation of hand receipts for 23 units, including associated shortage annexes and supporting documentation files. Managed excess property by coordinating and monitoring turn-in and lateral transfer directives. Verified equipment on-hand asset reporting, unit readiness output, and ensured all cards, form, and printouts were accurate. Established and monitored training programs and supervised team operations consisting of three enlisted personnel.

EDUCATION

Bachelor of Science Degree in Accounting, Detroit College of Business, Dearborn, MI, 2000.
Associate of Science degree in Business Administration, Central Texas College, Killeen, TX, 1993.

SPECIALIZED TRAINING LICENSES CERTIFICATES

Military courses include: Unit Level Logistics System Operator Course, 2001; Property Accounting Technician, 1999; Depot Inventory Reconciliation, 1998; Physical Inventory Management, 1998; Standard Property Book System, 1998; General Supply Technician, 1997; Warrant Officer Entry Course, 1997; NCO Officer Logistics Course, 1996; Supply NCO Advanced Course, 1996; Division Logistics Course, 1995; Unit and Organizational Supply, 1995, and Organizational Maintenance of Radio Field Equipment, 1994.

AWARDS

Humanitarian Service Medal, Noncommissioned Officer's Professional Development Ribbon, Army Service Medal, Overseas Service Ribbon (2nd award), Germany Liberation Medal, Legion of Merit, Bronze Star Medal, Meritorious Service Medal, Army Commendation Medal (2nd award), Army Achievement Medal (3rd award), Army Good Conduct Medal (4th award), National Defense Service Medal (2nd award), European Service Medal with 3 bronze Service Star.

ADMINISTRATIVE ASSISTANT

LAURA C. BRYANT
Address: 3030 Uppergate Avenue, Trenton, NJ 22634
Home number: (111) 111-1111
SSN: 000-00-0000
E-mail: lcbryant@cs.com
Position, Title, Series, Grade: Human Resources Coordinator, GS-8888-88
Announcement Number: DN-00-000

ADMINISTRATIVE ASSISTANT

Here you see a resumix of a woman who is seeking a position in the human resources field.

EDUCATION

Currently pursuing a **Bachelor of Arts degree in Human Resources**, Essex County College, Trenton, NJ.
- Am only one Economics course short of completing my degree.
Completed two-year program at Mercer County Community College, Trenton, NJ 1996.
Graduated from E.A. Burnes High School, Trenton NJ, 1994.

EXPERIENCE

ADMINISTRATIVE ASSISTANT. Maxwell Properties, 698 Wallace Trail, Trenton NJ 22678 (07/2004-present). Supervisor: Thomas Deaver, Executive Manager: (222) 222-2222. Provide administrative support to 4 top-selling real estate executives.
- Manage finances for more than 25 membered staff.
- Act as the Human Resources representative for personnel pay, travel, and recruitment issues.
- Manage a $100,000 travel budget for real estate executives because of company property in various national locations.
- Manage financial, administrative, and travel records also coordinating efforts with our home office in New York.
- On formal performance evaluations, was evaluated as "a hard charger who is willing to do whatever it takes to get the job done;" and "an individual with unique ability to coordinate group efforts toward common goal in any given situation" and as "an individual whose advice and technical knowledge is regularly sought by subordinates, peers, and superiors alike."
- Routinely write and deliver press releases which have been praised for their articulate and concise style; communicate via e-mail and the Internet while also communicating extensively through telephone, meetings, and written correspondence.
- Utilize computers regularly, and develop specialized expertise with Excel while using that program to manage the monthly supplied budget. Am skilled in database management.
- Maintain daily statistical records for annual reports.
- Continuously seek new methods of improving internal efficiency while maintaining administrative and personnel files.

ADMINISTRATIVE ASSISTANT. Wachovia Bank, 6644 Garner Road, Baltimore, MD 29845 (04/2001-07/2004) Supervisor: Allison Malone, Bank Manager (333) 333-3333. In this administrative position, performed numerous phases of human resource duties.
- Reviewed and corrected evaluation reports.
- Prepared reports related to personnel strength, promotions, branch transfers, staff actions, evaluation reports, and various banking personnel assignments.
- Assisted in preparing, coordinating, and monitoring personnel accountability actions.

ADMINISTRATIVE ASSISTANT. Department of Defense, 1548 Faxton Avenue, Baltimore, MD 29887 (05/1999-04/2001). Supervisor: Carlton M. Busch: (444) 444-4444. Assisted 3 managers supporting 45 staff members; was involved in managing the full range of personnel administration activities.

- Typed military and non-military correspondence used notes, drafts, verbal instructions, or other courses to prepare documents.
- Prepared suspense control documents and maintained suspense files.
- In an ongoing process once a month, acted as supervisor in charge of training and managing soldiers in administrative and combat duties; developed lesson plans and gave formal classes; counseled soldiers about personal and career matters.
- Researched, prepared, and processed retirement packets, reclassification packets, early out request packets, and other specialty actions.
- Acted as Customer Service Representative for the battalion.
- Analyzed and resolved any problems soldiers and civilians were experiencing related to their promotions, awards, personnel records, and financial matters.
- Handled duties which included filing, writing, and preparing reports and documents.
- Utilized computers for word processing and statistical analysis, and became skilled in database management. Played a key role in providing humanitarian aid and disaster relief for victims of Hurricane Floyd, and received the Humanitarian Service Award.

CLERK TYPIST. Jones & Martin Law, 1168 Cool Springs St., Baltimore, MD 13546 (11/1996-05/1999). Supervisor: Carolyn Heyward: (555) 555-5555. Processed legal documents; performed transcription and dictation duties for memorandums and managed records of oral briefings and conversational notes.

- Maintained database of client evidence, court records, and hearing documentation; distributed copies to lawyers, clients and court attendees. Conducted briefings which included question-and-answer sessions which refined my ability to "think on my feet."
- Used computer databases, files, typed, prepared training reports and documents, and maintained statistical information and records used to compile annual reports.
- Nominated for Employee of the Month for September 1997.

PHOTO-LAYOUT SPECIALIST. Photo Design, 346 Second Street, Trenton, NJ 22877, (7/1995-11/1996). Supervisor: Michael Rowan: (666) 666-6666. Produced photographs, processed and developed film, opaque, and revised maps.

COMPUTERS	Highly proficient in utilizing a variety of software and operating systems.

- Used Microsoft Office including Word, Excel, Access, and Powerpoint.
- Have used Adobe Acrobat Reader when dealing with Internet and HTML software.
- Have automated thousands of files; produced numerous graphics for briefing presentations; produced and maintained administrative files and databases; wrote and produced hundreds of written reports of oral briefings and conversational notes.

TRAINING
Administrative Specialist Course, September 2001
Management Development and Leadership Course, April 2002
Business Management Course Phase I, February 2002
Business Finance Course Phase II, July 2002

CLEARANCE
Hold Top Secret security clearance; SCI in progress

HONORS & AWARDS
Achievement Awards (2); Humanitarian Award; Good Conduct Medal; Joint Meritorious Unit Award, Certificate of Appreciation

PERSONAL
Outstanding personal and professional references upon request. Strong work ethic.

ADMINISTRATIVE ASSISTANT

BRYAN TIMOTHY
SSN: 000-00-0000
1910 Lamb Road
Tacoma, WA 88325

Home: (999) 999-9999
Work: (888) 888-8888
E-mail address: bryan123@hotmail.com
Position, Title, Series, Grade: Administrative Assistant, GS-08
Announcement Number: DN-00-000
Veteran's Preference:

ADMINISTRATIVE ASSISTANT & DATA PROCESSOR

This military veteran has a 10 point preference derived from his military service.

SUMMARY of SKILLS

Knowledge of several **administrative operations** and **automated data processing** as well as strong **motivational, leadership, and counseling** skills.

EXPERIENCE

ADMINISTRATIVE ASSISTANT and **DATA PROCESSOR.** Tacoma Medical Center, 11635 Long Branch Road, Tacoma, WA 88987-9611 (December 2003-present).
Supervisor: Julian Stephenson (777) 777-7777
Pay grade: **Hours worked per week:** 40
Duties: Provide clerical and logistics support for chaplains at a major medical center; assist in programs which provide for the free exercise of religion; administer to the spiritual, moral, and ethical needs of patients, their families, and staff members.
Accomplishments:
* Described as a highly resourceful professional, was cited for my contributions during a ten-day training exercise designed to prepare medical students for field duty; provided support for the religious program and in other functional areas.
* Was awarded the Employee of the Month during the month of August of 2003 and August 2004 and selected for special training in providing instruction, technical writing, and blueprint reading.

ADMINISTRATIVE ASSISTANT TO THE MAYOR. Mayor's Office, 3654 Grimble Circle, Tacoma, WA 88265 (Feb 2001-Dec 2003).
Supervisor: Mayor Terrence Herriott (666) 666-6666
Pay grade: **Hours worked per week:** 40
Duties: Supported city officials and other mayoral personnel and attended councilmen meetings, and handled the processing of regular performance reports and other administrative actions.

Other experience gained in the US Navy:
SENIOR ADMINISTRATIVE ASSISTANT TO THE CHIEF OF CHAPLAINS. U.S. Navy, USS Garrett #535, Jackson, MS, 56775-4688 (May 1998- February 2001).
Supervisor: Commander Fredrick Ranalli (555) 555-5555
Pay grade: **Hours worked per week:** 40
Duties: Learned administrative skills in the fast-paced, multi-task environment of the office of the Chief of Naval Operations.
Accomplishments:
* Was awarded a Navy Achievement Medal for my contributions

which included coordinating the reorganization of office work space for increased productivity. Handled multiple responsibilities in ADP security, training, and career counseling.

- Was entrusted with numerous functional duties ranging from trainer to ADP system security specialist, to career counselor, to financial counselor.
- Held the additional special duty assignments as Career Counselor, member of the quality assurance/quality control board, and member of the Command Assessment Team.

MATHEMATICS STUDENT. U.S. Navy, USS Garrett #535, Jackson, MS, 56775-4688 (July 1995 - May 1998).
Supervisor: Captain Jeffrey V. Quimby (444) 444-4444
Pay grade: RP2   **Hours worked per week:** 40
Duties: Earned an A.S. in Mathematics in a military-sponsored education program for active duty personnel—the Academic Advancement Program.
Accomplishments:
- Volunteered as a tutor for students at a high school for math and science.
- Was accepted for membership in the Honor Society with a 3.7 GPA.

ADMINISTRATIVE ASSISTANT TO THE CHAPLAIN. U.S. Navy, USS Carter, Naval Operations, Okinawa, Japan, FPO AE 77684-4644 (September 1992 - July 1995).
Supervisor: LTC Matthew L. O'Connor (333) 333-3333
Pay grade: RP 1   **Hours worked per week:** 40
Duties: Was cited for numerous contributions to the effectiveness of the ship's religious programs and support for personnel requiring counseling and support services during crisis and emergency situations.
Accomplishments:
- Was described in official performance evaluations as "intelligent, impressively articulate, and refreshingly conscientious."
- On my own initiative, developed a cross-training program.
- Utilized my computer skills to create a database of all books and video tapes as well as a tracking system for library materials.

EDUCATION

A.S. in Mathematics, Tacoma Community College, Tacoma, WA, 1997.

TRAINING

Attended US Navy training schools which included basic infantry and basic administration as well as the "Class A and Class F" career courses. Completed nonresident training courses which included the following subjects:

religious program operations	inventory control
safety	customer service
human behavior	administrative assistance
engineering administration	electricity/electronics
computer programming	educational services

CLEARANCE

Was entrusted with a secret security clearance.

COMPUTERS

Am experienced with FORTRAN, C++, Microsoft Word, Excel, Access, and PageMaker.

AIR OPERATIONS SPECIALIST

JANICE DEANENE BRADY

4511 Drake Lane, Travis AFB, CA 91567

(111) 111-1111 Home (222) 222-2222 Work (333) 333-3333 Cell

jandeane@lycos.com

SSN: 000-00-0000

Country of Citizenship: United States

Veteran's Preference: 2-point preference

Contact current supervisor: Yes

Vacancy Announcement Number: 00-000-00

Job Title: Air Operations Specialist, GS-0000-00

EXPERIENCE

AIR OPERATIONS SPECIALIST, OPERATIONS CENTER. Start and End Dates: March 2003-present. **Hours worked per week:** 40+. **Current Salary:** E-8. **Employer's Name and Address:** AF02847475 (AFPA) Data Masked. **Supervisor's Name and Phone Number:** Lt Col Edgar Dalton, Phone: (444) 444-4444. Have received the highest ratings on all measured areas of duty performance while also receiving a National Defense Service Medal for providing distinguished support for a classified, sensitive mission in support of U.S. policies and objectives. The citation for the Joint Service Medal cited my "remarkable ability to lead others to excellence under pressure" and praised my "personal vision" which led to the renovation of the Travis AFB flight line procedures that significantly increased launch reliability.

Knowledge of DOD and USAF policies on special access programs controls and procedures, document control and accountability. Lead a section tasked as U.S. Policy Administrators (USPA) focal point for all operational command and control (A16) issues impacting "must succeed" special access program supporting DOD's most elite forces. Lead teams implementing A16 policies and procedures to insert and extract clandestine forces and remove weapons of mass destruction from denied areas across the globe. Manage A16 requirements for 13 unique weapon systems at six geographically separated locations. Optimize performance of six controllers to meet the demands of highly modified A16 procedures through classified training programs. Solely responsible for extremely urgent recall and launch of battle staff personnel and all aircrew members.

- Was evaluated in writing as a "Administration Ambassador" Was praised for "brilliantly revising group NOTAMS reporting procedures" and for "enterprisingly designing a communication-out recall system to ensure 100% verbal and physical contact."
- Was praised on a formal performance evaluation for "outstanding leadership" and was praised for saving a member from suicide through my "flawless A16 deployment team."
- A formal performance evaluation recognized me for "superior judgement" and described an incident in which I "saved the day" through rapidly accessing headquarters A16 equipment failure and taking control of radios.
- I was described in writing as "innovative" after designing a A16 process preventing aircraft interception by drug enforcement which was hailed as a "safety milestone."

Expert writing and oral communication skills. Have been described on a formal performance evaluation as "an expert writer" and was praised for authoring all new command, control, and communications training techniques. Continuously generates and submits time-critical USPA operational reports while also performing as the most trusted advisor to the commander. As acting First Sergeant for 24 enlisted personnel, interacted skillfully with subordinates and superiors. Instituted a Leadership Training Instruction schedule for junior NCOs and aggressively executed the hottest contingencies. Updated quick reaction checklists, rewrote operations instructions, and authored policy letters.

Knowledge of developing, implementing, and employing ground and airborne communications systems while conducting training and world missions. Single-handedly developed backup communication procedures for airborne assets, thereby ensuring 100 connectivity. Procured communication equipment from headquarters to provide all airborne assets with Communications Security (COMSEC) material in the event of emergency supersession. Designed procedures for subordinate unit to use Ops Center's alert crew database. Was cited as a "key leader in major aircraft accident exercise", and a formal performance evaluation said that my security procedures protected sensitive mission details. Have expertly managed the operations center during multiple major exercises as well as numerous real world operations. During exercises and operations, managed crew alert posture and coordinated air refueling, air traffic control, deception, and ground support. On one occasion, increased aircrew combat readiness after researching, coordinating, and publishing procedures to test the readiness and response capability of the alert aircrews of three different classified aircraft.

NONCOMMISSIONED OFFICER IN CHARGE (NCOIC), OPERATIONS CENTER.

Start and End Dates: Sep 2000-Mar 2003. **Hours worked per week:** 40+. **Salary:** E-7. **Employer's Name and Address:** UH0XAF876 (USPA) Data Masked. **Supervisor's Name and Phone Number:** MSgt Clifton McClamara, Phone: (555) 555-5555. Supervised ten enlisted personnel while establishing policy and procedures governing daily activities of a one-of-a-kind Operations Center. Developed policies and procedures for the preparation and execution of weekly briefings provided to headquarters, unit senior leadership, and staff members. Assisted in the development, coordination, and implementation of command and control (A16) policies and procedures for a selectively manned, classified organization performing U.S. Policy Administrators (USPA) tasked combat missions.

- Was praised as "the key to a successful A16 Conference" and was described in writing as an "outstanding NCO with unequalled leadership skills."
- Through resourceful problem solving, saved an already-airborne asset threatened by an air refueling tanker ground alert by rapidly coordinating a divert location.

NCOIC, REPORTS BRANCH.

Start and End Dates: Sep 1996-Sep 2000. **Hours worked per week:** 40+. **Salary:** E-7. **Employer's Name and Address:** 51st Air Operations (AOP), USAFB Eareckson AS Shemya, Alaska. **Supervisor's Name and Phone Number:** MSgt. Jesse Britt, Phone: DSN (666) 666-6666. Maintained certification as a Special Air Mission (SAM) controller while developing and presenting training on standard air operation requirements for 11 reporting commanders, their deputies, and 29 unit monitors. Developed reporting procedures and analyzed operational reports for the wing commander and his staff. Kept data reflecting capability of the wing and base tenant units.

Refined my knowledge of all aspects of worldwide sensitive air support and employment mission requirements, including fixed wing, ground refueling, air refueling, navigation, and offensive/defensive employment operations for air assets.

- Provided clear, concise monthly briefings to the Wing Commander and senior wing leaders on all aspects of the complex programs. Provided leadership during an aircraft nose landing gear malfunction which led to the successful landing of the aircraft. Was recognized in writing for "superbly coordinating the launching of the entire SAM fleet" for a Memorial Day Tribute which involved the movement of 103 senators, congressmen, Joint Chiefs of Staff, and Air Force One. Also orchestrated the launching of all special mission aircraft during Desert Storm/Desert Shield.

NCOIC, QUALITY.

Start and End Dates: Jun 1994-Sep 1996. **Hours worked per week:** 40+. **Salary:** E-7. **Employer's Name and Address:** 51st Air Operations (AOP) USAFB Eareckson AS Shemya, Alaska. **Supervisor's Name and Phone Number:** MSgt. Donald Kropp, Phone: (777) 777-7777. Designed, implemented and managed Quality Air Force (QAF) Program within the Objective Wing Command Post, and ensured that 38 people were properly trained and utilizing QAF principles. Assisted in scheduling aircraft missions, dispatched special mission aircrafts, and performed associated air control duties. Fostered an award program which provided incentive for continuous improvement and creativity within the command post.

- Contributed to the air mission training in Shemya, Alaska. Also designed new AMC airlift movement boards for daily and contingency use in the primary and alternate command post. Assisted in the development of checklists and procedures for controlling and flight following all Department of Defense(DOD) fixed wing aircraft operating in Eareckson AFB, Alaska.
- Knowledgable of FAA regulations; coordinated flight plans with related agencies; maintained current file on aircraft flying regulations and navigational aid information.

Highlights of other experience:

SPECIAL AIR MISSIONS CONTROLLER. Apr 1992-Jun 1994. Provided direct command and control and worldwide flight following for Special Air Mission (SAM) aircraft carrying the President, Vice President, Cabinet members, members of Congress, and foreign heads of state. Coordinated several humanitarian relief missions into Texas and Mexico in the aftermath of hurricane and tornado disaster events. On numerous occasions, tracked and recovered lost aircraft parts.

COMMAND POST CONTROLLER. Aug 1990-Apr 1992. Was involved in missions supporting the President and Vice President of the U.S. Coordinated 120 Presidential support missions, 58 Vice Presidential support missions, and 48 aeromedical evacuation channel missions. Was specially selected for this position normally held by a more senior professional.

EMERGENCY ACTIONS CONTROLLER. Dec 1989-Aug 1990. Acted in an executive capacity for USCINCEUR, SACEUR, CINCUSAFE, and the wing commanders in execution of emergency war orders (EWO) and plans for both US and NATO alliance combat forces. A formal performance evaluation said that my "error free actions and multi-position qualifications" lead me to be named Actions Controller of the Year. Was selected as NCO of the Quarter. Performed emergency actions training for over 100 users located in 15 basewide work centers.

TRAINING NCO COMMAND POST. Jan 1987-Dec 1989. Established all training requirements for officer and enlisted controllers. Provided leadership during the aftermath of several plane crashes, bombing attacks and air show disasters.

EMERGENCY ACTIONS CONTROLLER. Oct 1985-Jan 1987. Received, validated, and took required actions on Joint Chief of Staff (JCS) and U.S. Air Forces in Korea while relaying emergency action messages. Performed as Shift Supervisor during countless aircraft emergencies, vehicle accidents, and unusual incidents. Disseminated threat condition directions to mission operation units during a period of increased terrorist activity.

UNIT COMMAND AND CONTROL SPECIALIST. Feb 1982-Jul 1984. Was responsible to the NCOIC of the Live Flying Section. Prepared and maintained detailed activity logs and forms to record and track missions flown by Ninth Air Force. Maintained Fighter Status Boards. Received a Letter of Appreciation for "flawless reporting."

EDUCATION	**Associate of Science degree in Information Systems Technology**, Illinois Central College, East Peoria, IL, Jun 2001.

Senior Noncommissioned Officer, Sep 2000
Air Force Trainer Course, 1999
DOD Hostage Survival Training, Jan 1999
DOD Information Security Orientation Course, Oct 1998
Noncommissioned Officer Academy, 4 weeks, 1998
Introduction to Special Operations, May 1998
Noncommissioned Officer Orientation Course, Dec 1996
Dynamics of International Terrorism, Oct 1995
Status of Resources and Training Systems Data Handlers Course, Oct 1992
Noncommissioned Officer Leadership School, 6 weeks, 1992
Supervisor Development Course, Dec 1986
Technical School, 6 weeks, Nov 1983
Basic Military Training School, 6 weeks, May 1982

CLEARANCE   Top Secret/Sensitive Compartmented Information.

COMPUTERS   Proficient with software including Word, PowerPoint, Outlook, Access, Excel and PageMaker; have utilized supply, inventory control, purchasing, and logistics software. Experienced in using Windows 95, 98, 2000, and NT.

Have operated the following communication systems:
- Command and Control Information System (CCIS)
- Computer Assisted Force Management System (CAFMS)
- Special Air Mission Andromedia System
- Global Decision Support System (GDSS)
- Command and Control Information Processing System (C2IPS)
- Secure Satellite Communication Radio (SATCOM)
- Ultra High Frequency Radio (UHF)
- Very High Frequency Radio (VHF)
- Defense Message System (DMS)
- Secure Telephone Unit III (STU-III)
- Automatic Digital Network (AUTODIN)

HONORS &   Air Force Good Conduct Medal, 5 devices; National Defense Service Medal, 1 device; Air Force
AWARDS   Overseas Long Tour Ribbon, 1 device; Air Force Longevity Service Award Ribbon, 4 devices; Non Commissioned Officer Professional Military Education Graduate; Ribbon, 2 devices; Air Force Training Ribbon; Defense Meritorious Service Medal; Joint Service Commendation Medal; Air Force Commendation Medal, 1 device; Joint Service Achievement Medal, 1 device; Air Force Outstanding Unit Award, 1 device; Air Force Outstanding Unit Award, 2 devices.

ASSISTANT INSPECTOR GENERAL

LUTHER T. SCOTT
3360 Lovette Drive
Cincinnati, OH 54876
111 111-1111 H
222 222-2222 W

SSN: 000-00-0000
Source: EXTERNAL
Highest Grade Held: N/A
Vacancy Announcement Number: 000AB00-000
Position Title: Assistant Inspector General, GS-0000-00

ASSISTANT INSPECTOR GENERAL

This is a city chief of police who has decided that he wishes a federal position.

EXPERIENCE

2004-present: CHIEF OF POLICE. $80,500.00. Cincinnati Police Department, 4846 Ward Avenue, Cincinnati, OH 54885. Supervisor: Mayor Robert Lamkin 333-333-3333. As Chief of Police, exercise authority over the operations and administration of a 68-person police force. Have modernized and rebuilt the entire department which includes computerizing operations and developing a system for wireless computers in the city's fleet of squad cars which allows officers to obtain assignments in their car via computer as well as to prepare reports and check status on individuals from squad cars. Have negotiated with the Ohio House of Representatives for over $2.8 million in funding for the police department and city operations; that funding was used for modernization and was in excess of the $2 million dollar annual police budget. Have written numerous successful federal and state grants for improvements and upgrades to police equipment as well as for funding for additional officers. Have instituted a community policing strategy that includes a police department-run Youth Intervention Center which takes teenagers off the streets. Have started a Senior Citizens Program which provides a trained investigator to deal solely with problems encountered by "senior citizens." Frequently serve as a popular guest speaker for various "at risk" groups and at local schools. Have gained wide respect and have been elected to serve on the executive board of the city's computerized Law Enforcement Dispatching Center which serves 8 police departments, 8 fire departments, and serves a 250,000-person population. Work closely with federal law enforcement agencies, and have assigned two detectives to work full-time with DEA and Customs, which has enabled the police department to play a key role in drug and immigration investigations worldwide.

1988-2004: SERGEANT MAJOR. Army Reserve. $4,000.00. Support Operations Reserves Center, Cincinnati, OH. Col. Brad Kreiton Apt. Phone: 444-444-4444. While simultaneously serving in the Reserve, served on active duty from 2002-2003 and was extensively involved in disaster relief coordination with the New York terrorist attacks. Worked with organizations including the Federal Emergency Management Agency (FEMA) and the United Nations. In September 2001 was assigned to Afghanistan to a forward deployed task force, and was responsible for the movement of troops and engineer equipment between Afghanistan and Bosnia while coordinating with line haulers and vendors for engineer equipment.

1997-2001: DEPUTY CHIEF OF POLICE. $68,000. Cincinnati Police Department, 4846 Ward Avenue, Cincinnati, OH 54885. Mayor Maurice L. Peterson, 555-555-5555. As Deputy Chief of Police, supervised four Commanders while overseeing operations and administration of a 52-person department with a $2 million annual budget. Provided outstanding police services to a community with 17,500 residents and three large school districts including the College of Mount St. Joseph which has a 16,450-student population. Negotiated all police department labor contracts. Served as Project Manager of the Police Accreditation Program.

1995-1997: PATROL DIVISION WATCH COMMANDER. $57,000. Cincinnati Police Department, 4846 Ward Avenue, Cincinnati, OH 54885. Mayor Maurice L. Peterson, 666-666-6666. Was responsible for all uniformed patrol functions occurring on assigned shifts. Simultaneously from 1996-1997 in the Army Reserve, was Operations Sergeant for a Military Police physical security unit; supervised operations of select teams of Military Police inspectors who traveled all over the U.S. inspecting the physical security of fixed and temporary military sites. From 1995-1996, served as Platoon Sergeant in charge of 45 people.

1993-1995: DETECTIVE DIVISION SERGEANT. $46,000. Cincinnati Police Department, 6574 Odum Cove, Cincinnati, OH 55190. Jack B. Pruitt, Chief of Police 777-777-7777. Supervised four Detectives and one Police Psychologist while leading the division to conduct in-depth criminal investigations including undercover narcotics operations, white collar crime investigations, and investigation of serious juvenile offenses.

1989-1993: SPECIAL AGENT. $43,520. Ohio Protection Agency, 8745 Carthage Avenue, Canton, OH 54365. Daniel E. Vainwright, Group Supervisor. 888-888-8888. Was detailed to work as an Undercover Narcotics Agent throughout Canton County and other areas in Ohio. Investigated the sale of controlled substances, infiltration of motorcycle gangs, and underworld criminal organizations engaged in the sale of large quantities of narcotics.

1986-1989: DETECTIVE. $37,580. Canton Police Department. 17899 Elliott Road, Canton, OH 54433. Mayor Dennis Shaw. 999-999-9999. Investigated crimes, controlled crime scenes, initiated crime prevention programs, involved in stakeouts, body guard.

EDUCATION	**B. S. degree in Criminal Justice**, Xavier University, Cincinnati, OH, 1997.
SPECIALIZED TRAINING LICENSES & CERTIFICATES	1996, Southern Police Institute, Command Officer Development Course. 1991, International Association of Chiefs of Police, Internal Affairs Course. 1991, Successful Grantsmanship Course. 1990, Legal Aspects of Department Discipline. 1989, Hazardous Materials Course. 1988, Police Liability Course. 1982, 1981 and 1977, Narcotics and Dangerous Drug Instructors Course. 1976, Criminal Investigators Course. 1974, Police Training Academy.
PROFESSIONAL ASSOCIATIONS	5TH District Chiefs of Police Association. International Association of Chiefs of Police. Ohio Association of Chiefs of Police. South Suburban Association of Chiefs of Police. International Narcotic Enforcement Officers Association. Fraternal Order of Police. Police Hills Police Association. Chamber of Commerce. Noncommissioned Officers Association of the U.S. Army. Veterans of Foreign Wars. Association of the United States Army. Army Engineer Association.
AWARDS	Numerous medals including Joint Task Force Commendation Medal, Legion of Merit, Bronze Star. Recipient of FBI and Department commendations for arrest of kidnappers and others. Received Officer of the Year Award in 1982. Numerous letters of appreciation from citizens and groups.
CLEARANCE	Secret security clearance

BIO-MEDICAL EQUIPMENT TECHNICIAN

CARLTON S. MOORE
SSN: 000-00-0000
3594 Wilshire Cove
Ft. Stewart, GA 31452
home: (111) 111-1111
work: (222) 222-2222
E-mail: CSMoore@aol.com

**BIO-MEDICAL
EQUIPMENT
TECHNICIAN**

Vacancy Announcement Number: 000-000-00
Country of Citizenship: U.S.A.
Veterans' Preference: 10-point preference
Reinstatement Eligibility: NA
Highest Federal Civilian Grade Held:

SUMMARY

Offer well-developed skills in training development. Am a technical **subject-matter expert on bio-medical equipment.** Am experienced in calibrating sensitive equipment including anesthesia equipment. Have expertly serviced and trained others to service specific medical equipment with the aid of various test, measurement, and diagnostic equipment to include volt-ohmmeters, multi-trace oscilloscopes, logic probes, analyzers, and computers. Experienced in fielding, adjusting, and modifying state-of-the-art equipment.

EXPERIENCE

LEAD BIO-MEDICAL EQUIPMENT TECHNICIAN. Winn Army Hospital, Medical Equipment Center, Ft. Stewart, GA (2004-present).
Supervisor: Kenny Johnson, Telephone number:
Pay grade: $22 hour   **Hours worked per week:** 40+
Duties: Was recruited for this position by a former military colleague who was familiar with my reputation as a subject matter expert on bio-medical equipment. At this state-of-the-art medical facility which is scheduled to open in May 2003, am supervising four Bio-Medical Equipment Technicians while reviewing government contracts in excess of $8 million to assure that the government is receiving the goods and services it contracted for.

- Work with vendors including Compaq, Bell-Medical, and DICON to oversee the fielding and installation of their equipment and troubleshoot any problems in this computer-driven equipment.
- Perform expert calibration, if needed, and document all activities according to government, hospital, and federal regulations.
- Have developed specialized knowledge of government contracting procedures. Continuously train the four personnel I supervise in advanced techniques of calibration; train personnel in advanced skills related to repair and modification.
- Ensure that new medical equipment is installed in the proper area, is fully operational, and is properly tagged and added to the property book in accordance with government regulations.

SENIOR BIO-MEDICAL EQUIPMENT TECHNICIAN. Columbus Regional Veterans Hospital, Columbus, GA (1999-04).
Supervisor: James Garrison, Telephone number:
Pay grade: E-7   **Hours worked per week:** 40+
Duties: While operating independently as Technical Representative of the Surgeon General, provided extensive training in theory,

electronics, electro-mechanical, pneumatics, hydraulics, and x-ray as they relate to medical equipment repair. Provided instruction in the methods and procedures associated with inspection, installation, operation, calibration, and repair of a wide range of medical equipment. Instructed others in the use and servicing of medical equipment using volt-ohmmeters, multi-trace oscilloscopes, logic probes, analyzers, and probes.

- Performed installation, repair, modification, calibration, testing, and training on mobile and fixed medical and scientific equipment in mobile and fixed facilities.
- Conducted final acceptance on x-ray systems for adherence to contract specifications.
- Conducted on-site audiometric calibration of equipment at over 150 different audiometric equipment servicing sites. As Technical Representative for the Office of the Surgeon General, assured the maintenance of satellite telecommunications equipment to be utilized at veteran hospitals worldwide.
- Conducted extensive training sessions with operators of medical equipment to ensure that they could proficiently operate and maintain medical equipment; conducted training sessions with personnel at dozens of hospitals.
- Saved more than $70,000 by troubleshooting and resolving excessive air leaks on 500 portable ventilators/respirators; corrected the problem so that the respirators could be returned to inventory.
- Functioned routinely as an Inspector and Quality Assurance Supervisor; on my own initiative, designed and implemented a comprehensive quality assurance test system utilizing state-of-the-art Test, Measurement, and Diagnostic Equipment to effect the calibration of audiometric equipment. Was a regular instructor of classes of all sizes, and coordinated several manufacturers' training schools to improve operator proficiency.

SENIOR BIO-MEDICAL EQUIPMENT TECHNICIAN. Delta Company Medical Clinic, Camp Humphries, Korea (1997-99).
Supervisor: Craig Evanston, Telephone number:
Pay grade: Starting: E-6; Ending: E-7   **Hours worked per week:** 40+
Duties: Was extensively involved in training as I held the position of Training Non-Commissioned Officer. Coordinated with the commander on issues pertaining to planning, coordinating, and implementing all training associated with the Medical Maintenance Shop. Was promoted to the position of Detachment Sergeant during this period.

- Was directly responsible for the training of 10 people and indirectly responsible for the training of hundreds of others.
- Scheduled and published a Training Schedule so that all personnel were aware of training opportunities and requirements.
- Used formal lectures, practical exercises, and computer programs to instruct students.
- Administered practical exercises as well as written and practical exams.
- **Special Project: 06/97-12/98:** On a special assignment in Seoul, Korea, established a comprehensive preventive maintenance and safety program which was eventually adopted for use by all field medical units which is still in use today. Established an oxygen purity program for a hospital in Korea which ensured that all medically related gases purchased from local vendors was of the highest quality. Trained U.S. and Korean soldiers through in-service training programs which I developed.
- Provided periodic scheduled service and repair on all types of medical equipment employing mechanical, hydraulic, and radiological principles.

EDUCATION   Completed **Medical Equipment Repair Course (Advanced)**, U.S. Medical Equipment Training Center, Winn Army Hospital, Savannah, GA, 2003.
Completed **Medical Equipment Repair Course (Basic)**, U.S. Army Medical Equipment and Optical School, Winn Army Hospital, Savannah, GA, 2003.
Associate of Science degree in Bio-Medical Equipment Maintenance degree, Cardinal Stritch University-Fort McCoy, Wisconsin, 1996.

BUDGET ANALYST

SUE L. JAMESON
7521 Currin Lane,
Little Rock, AR 36545
(111) 111-1111
SSN: 000-00-000
E-mail: suejames@earthlink.net
Position, Title, Series, Grade: Budget Analyst (GS-0000-00)
Announcement Number: DN-00-000
Veteran's Preference:

BUDGET ANALYST

EXPERIENCE

BUDGET ANALYST (GS-1111-11). Department of Defense, Finance Department, Little Rock, AR (06/04-present). Supervisor: Mr. Curtis Strickland, phone (333) 333-3333. Transferred from Cleveland, MS to support the formulation, execution, and reporting of multiple funds which are direct, reimbursable, multiple appropriations as well as multi-year appropriations.

- Gather, extract, review, and consolidate narrative statistical data.
- Prepare input for various financial reports to include Budget Estimate Submissions (BES) and Amended Budget Estimate Submissions (ABES).
- Assist in compiling and gathering data for budget presentations to the Senior/Working Program Budget Advisory Committee and for Mid Year Review.
- Establish and maintain commitment and obligation control ledgers for assigned areas which have direct and reimbursable fund accounts with established ceilings.
- Post amounts and assign accounting and/or document control numbers prior to transmittal to appropriate offices: ensure accounting codes correspond with the correct account in order to ensure funds control and correct balances.
- Reconcile ASIMS reports to guarantee accuracy of their content and that committed and obligated funds are controlled and accounts are operating within their budgets.

OFFICE SUPPORT CLERK (GS-2222-22) and SUPPLY CLERK (GS-3333-33). Department of Defense, Finance Department, Cleveland MS (07/01-06/04). Supervisor: Mr. George Gary, phone (444) 444-4444. Performed multiple, diverse duties related to tracking expenditures of funds by utilizing cost data received daily from the center's budget analyst and obtained from the Database Commitment Accounting System (DCAS).

- Prepared status reports pertaining to budget matters.
- Processed fuel issue tickets and checked for proper accounting data for payment; prepared daily and monthly inventory records, accountability records, and DD 871 delivery documents.
- Maintained administrative functional files for Base Operations and prepared a variety of memoranda and correspondence.
- Managed database software, files, and maintenance records.
- Was entrusted as the office's credit card holder with authority to make purchases outside the normal military supply channels.
- Prepared and maintained files which assured monthly statements of accounts were correct and submitted prior to deadlines.

BUDGET ASSISTANT (E-5). Naval Air Station Whiting Field, Milton, FL (11/98-07/01). Supervisor: Captain Delaina Clarkston, phone: (555) 555-5555. Maintained separate travel and transportation fund control records and provided budget development, managers, and higher headquarter executives with reports on the status of travel expenditures.

- Input data into spreadsheet format and was tasked with reviewing travel orders for authority and conformance with policies and procedures.
- Developed cost estimates for individual travel expense reports, group training, large conferences and other events. Contacted supported units and nine supporting institutions by telephone or written correspondence when dealing with budgetary issues and problems. Resigned to pursue civilian employment.

BUDGET ASSISTANT (E-4). Naval Weapons Station, Seal Beach, CA (01/95-11/98). Supervisor: LTC Michael H. Hubbard, phone: unknown. Originally hired as a supply clerk, was selected for training and promotion and to hold duties in both functional areas until 1990 when I became solely tasked in this area

- Monitored the budget for the Commanding Officer while actively participating in the budget formulation process. Compiled, consolidated, checked, and arranged funding data to cover projected annual operating expenses.
- Maintained commitment ledgers for accounts which included reimbursable funds.
- Reviewed documents and made adjustments to civilian pay, TDY, supplies and equipment, contracts and force protection accounts.
- Input expenditures into the finance system using various spreadsheet programs and tracked obligation and expenditures using information supplied from Finance and Accounting Office. Prepared recurring reports which reflected account balances.

Highlights of earlier experience: Mid-South Communications, Gatlinburg, TN (10/92-01/95). Supervisor: Mr. Rick H. Caldwell, phone (888) 888-8888.

- Was promoted to receive orders for new service or changes to existing service; entered information into computers; answered billing questions while working with an average of 60 customers a day.

EDUCATION & TRAINING	**B. A. in Business Administration with a concentration in Finance,** Delta State University, Cleveland, MS, 1995. Have completed professional education and correspondence courses which include: 80-hour Finance School program emphasizing Planning, Programming, Budgeting, and Execution, 1994. **A. A. in Business Technology**, Hinds Community College, Raymond, MS, 1992. • Completed computer the following computer courses: Graduated from **Hillcrest High School**, Raymond, MS, 1991.

MILITARY TRAINING

Information Systems Security, 2001	Activity and Major Activity Budgeting, 2001
Military Correspondence, 2000	Installation Budget Officer Course, 1996
7 Habits of Highly Effective People, 1996	Intro to Special Operations Command, 1995
PowerPoint, 1995	Appropriated Funds – Intermediate, 1994

CLEARANCE Secret security clearance; Top Secret in progress.

COMPUTERS Offer extensive experience with software including the Microsoft Office Suite (Word, PowerPoint, and an emphasis on preparing a high number of spreadsheets using Excel).

HONORS & AWARDS Have received numerous Certificates of Achievement, Certificates of Appreciation, Letters of Commendation, and Exceptional Performance Awards.

PERSONAL Outstanding personal and professional references upon request. Strong work ethic.

CAPTAIN & FIREFIGHTER

JUAN J. ONSTOTT
SSN: 000-00-0000
ADDRESS: 5729 Ivanhoe Ct, Scottsdale, AZ 87966
HOME PHONE: (111) 111-1111
TELEPHONE: (222) 222-2222

Position, Title, Series, Grade:
Announcement Number: DN-00-000
Veteran's Preference:

CAPTAIN/FIREFIGHTER

This firefighter is seeking a federal position in his field.

EXPERIENCE

Am excelling in four simultaneous positions:
April 2002-present. **CAPTAIN & FIREFIGHTER.** Up to 40 hours per week (2-3 days a week on 12-hour shifts). $8.75 per hour. Scottsdale Fire Department. Scottsdale, AZ. Eric Simmons, Supervisor, (333) 333-3333. Began as a Firefighter in April of 2002 and was promoted in April of 2003 to Shift Captain. Serve as a **member of a firefighting crew** engaged in the protection of life and property. Respond to major emergencies, and respond to alarms. Combat fires while performing the full performance of firefighting tasks involving structures, equipment, facilities, as well as fuel and chemical fires. When combating structural fires, wear self-contained breathing apparatus and move through dark interior corridors and stairways to locate the origin of the fire. Control and extinguish fires while performing rescues.

- **Management Responsibilities as Shift Captain:** Responsible for the supervision of all daily, weekly, and monthly activities of shift members. Establish and document public fire awareness programs. Supervise live fire/rescue calls and conduct after-action debriefings of firefighters. Supervise up to 30 personnel on small and large-scale emergency situations.

- **Hazardous Material Incident Management:** As Shift Captain, handle supervisory responsibilities related to medical emergencies, fire suppression related emergencies, and Hazmat incidents. Respond to hazardous material incidents. Detect and identify hazardous materials. Make proper risk assessments. Understand and interpret basic hazards of a chemical incident. Identify safety and health hazards encountered at hazardous materials incidents. Play a key role in determining and implementing response plan and termination of the incident. Utilize advanced control containment and/or confinement procedures, cleanup, decontamination, and related operations.

- **Crosstraining:** On as needed basis, am skilled in performing the duties of hoseman, ladderman, hydrantman, rescueman, nozzleman, salvageman, and hand lineman. Am skilled at technical duties including unreeling connects, laying and operating hose lines, placing and raising ladders, and operating portable and stationary firefighting apparatus.

- **Safety, First Aid, and Rescue Operations:** Evacuate and rescue occupants. Administer first aid and protect fellow firemen during firefighting.

- **Detection, Reduction, and Elimination of Potential Fire Hazards:** Perform fire protection inspections. Check fire alarms and sprinkler systems in buildings to ensure operability. Prepare reports of fire inspections.

- **Operation of fire communications equipment:** Operate

communication alarm center and monitor sprinklered buildings and alarm systems. Operate computerized telecommunications equipment. Receive administrative and emergency telephone calls.

May 1999-present. **SEARCH AND RESCUE (S.A.R.) TEAM MEMBER.** Maricopa County Sheriff's Department, Glendale, AZ. Up to 10 hours per week (am on call, 24 hours a day for two weeks at a time). $11.00 per hr. Issac McDouglas, Supervisor (444) 444-4444. Am a member of a highly skilled search and rescue team. Assist with all tactical search and rescue operations. Provide swiftwater and dive rescue operations. Play a key role in land searches and high angle rescues on statewide response areas. Was instrumental in planning and implementing all aspects of rescue training for S.A.R. team members.

- **Emergency Services Coordinator:** Was honored by selection as Glendale Emergency Services Seminar Equipment Coordinator in May of 1999. Was the youngest person ever chosen for this role which involved setting up classes for law enforcement and public service officials. Planned and managed the Glendale Emergency Services Seminar in September 2001 which was attended by hundreds of people from many states. Work closely with more than 45 instructors at Glendale Community College to coordinate training in fire protection, counterterrorism, Hazmat, and public fire education.

December 1996-May 1999. **CAPTAIN & TRAINING OFFICER (Volunteer).** Up to 10 hours per week as a volunteer, Flagstaff Volunteer Fire Department, Flagstaff, AZ. Rudolph, Dugle, Supervisor (555) 555-5555. Am the Officer in Charge in the absence of the chief and deputy chiefs. Responsible for recordkeeping of all training and continuing education hours for firefighting personnel. Schedule and instruct classes pertaining the state certifications.

February 1994-December 1996. **EMERGENCY MEDICAL TECHNICAN (DEFIBRILLATION).** 48 hours per week. $10.00 per hour. Flagstaff Emergency Medical Services, Flagstaff, AZ. Jimmy Bullock, Supervisor (666) 666-6666. Function as primary care giver in basic and advanced life support. Responsible for defibrillating and intubating patients in an attempt to sustain life. Take steps to prevent further head, neck, and c-spine injuries.

- **Extensive medical knowledge:** Became knowledgeable of subjects including trauma and wound care.

VOLUNTEER RESCUER. January 1993-February 1994. 15 hours per week. Pinal County Rescue, La Palma, AZ. Katie Fadden, Supervisor (777) 777-7777. Assisted with all BLS/ALS medical calls. Assisted with all heavy and technical rescue operations.

- **Advanced lifesaving skills:** Became skilled in advanced lifesaving techniques.

HONORS & AWARDS

September 6, 2003: Named **Glendale Emergency Services Seminar Equipment Coordinator** for Maricopa County. Was the youngest person ever to receive this honor.
April 14, 1999: Flagstaff Fire Department Chief's Award. For outstanding service to the firefighting field "above and beyond the call of duty."
September 12, 1998: Flagstaff Fire Department Chief's Award. For outstanding service and in recognition of contribution to the firefighting field.
July 5, 1998: Flagstaff Distinguished Service Award. Volunteered to go to Colorado to assist in fighting fires caused by natural wildfires.

CERTIFICATIONS:

Fire Officer Level I, October 15, 2004, 180 hours
Arizona Public Fire Educator, July 12, 2004, 80 hours
Arizona Firefighter Level II, February 23, 2003, 260 hours
Arizona Hazardous Materials Level I, January 3, 2003, 40 hours
Arizona Basic Rescue Technician, November 9, 2002, 160 hours

CAPTAIN/FIREFIGHTER

Arizona Emergency Rescue Technician, March 19, 2002, 180 hours
National Registry Emergency Medical Technician, October 2, 2002, 230 hours
Arizona Driver/Operator Pumps, April 11, 2001, 30 hours
Arizona Driver/Operator Aerials, April 11, 2001, 50 hours
Incident Command (NFPA), August 21, 2000, 20 hours
Arizona E.M.T. Defibrillation, January 17, 2000, 48 hours
Arizona Arson Investigation, March 28, 1999, 40 hours
National Fire Academy Radiological Emergency Management, June 7, 1998, 40 hours
Arizona Forestry Wildland Fire Suppression, May 28, 1998, 40 hours

EDUCATION

Graduated from D.E. Lakes High School, 1997.
- Made the decision to become a firefighter when I was a youth. Spent all my spare time in the evenings and on weekends during my junior and senior year of high school earning certifications in the firefighting field.

At institutions which included the Arizona Justice Academy, Maricopa Technical College, Scottsdale Community College, Arizona National Fire Academy, the University of Arizona, and Glendale Community College, completed courses and training programs including these:
Fire Officer I, Oct 2003
A.R.F.F., Oct 2003
Driver/Operator (Aerials), Sep 2001
Driver/Operator (Pumps), Sep 2001 Emergency Medical Technician (Defibrillation), Jun 2001
Emergency Rescue Technician, Jun 2001
Emergency Medical Technician (National Registry), Aug 2000
Arson Investigation, Aug 2000
Radiological Emergency Management (National), Aug 2000
Wildland Fire Suppression, NC Forestry, Jun 1999
Arizona Firefighter Level I & II, Jun 1999
Hazardous Material Responder Level I, Jan 1998
Basic Rescue Technician, Jan 1998 Incident Command (NFPA), Dec 1998

COMPUTER SKILLS

Proficient with software including Microsoft Word, Excel, and PowerPoint. Have utilized databases used in law enforcement. Use Firehouse software.

CLEARANCE

Nonsmoker and nondrinker. Can pass the most rigorous background investigation.

CIVIL ENGINEERING GENERAL MANAGER

ANTHONY I. SAMPSON
SSN: 000-00-0000
Arroyo #515/22 Box 455
Muniz, Puerto Rico ANGB
Home: (111) 111-1111
Work: (222) 222-2222
Vacancy Announcement Number:
Position:

Country of Citizenship: U.S.A.
Veterans' Preference: Veterans Readjustment Appointment
Reinstatement Eligibility: N/A
Highest Federal Civilian Grade Held:

SUMMARY   Offer strong leadership and technical skills, well-developed planning and organizational abilities, and a track record of accomplishment in programming and design of construction projects, supervision and training, and project management.

EXPERIENCE   **CIVIL ENGINEERING GENERAL MANAGER.** Muniz Air National Guard, Puerto Rico ANGB (2003-present)
Supervisor: Lt. Colonel Mitchell Rollins (333) 333-3333
Pay grade: Major (O-4)
Hours worked per week: 40+
Duties: Supervise and train up to four managers and as many as 96 personnel. Oversee all aspects of facility maintenance and repair, while also handling the duties of the Deputy Civil Engineer, directly handling programming and design of essential facility construction projects, including a critical design for a new $11.8 million hangar. As Senior Engineer, hold final accountability for a 32-facility physical plant covering more than 410,000 square feet with a value in excess of $85 million. Direct planning and programming of construction programs totaling $37 million, while single-handedly managing a design and construction program comprising 15 major projects totaling more than $17 million. Exceptional staff development and training resulted in 32 personnel under my supervision receiving promotions.
Accomplishments:
- Due to my specific leadership and execution as Civil Engineering Commander during the Wing's Operational Readiness Inspection, we achieved an overall rating of excellent.
- Negotiated for and obtained a third of the Air National Guard's entire $17 million Real Property Maintenance (RPM) budget for 2004 in order to provide funding for essential repairs at Muniz ANGB.
- Described in official evaluations as "the finest officer in the Support Group."
- Received Air Force Achievement Awards for April to June 2004 in recognition of my exemplary performance as General Manager of this Civil Engineering Organization.
- From August 2003 to September 2004, the organization was honored with the Air Force Outstanding Unit Award for exceptionally meritorious service under my leadership.

CIVIL ENGINEERING OPERATIONS MANAGER. Pennsylvania Air National Guard, 193rd Special Operations Wing, Harrisburg, PA (2000-03)
Supervisor: Lt. Colonel Rodney Fuller (444) 444-4444
Pay grade: Major (O-4)
Hours worked per week: 40+
Duties: Provided supervisory oversight and training to 52 engineering personnel. Interviewed and hired all employees. Conducted negotiations with officials from those companies to arrive at a more favorable price and obtain required modifications to their design specifications.

Identified and programmed required maintenance and repair for a 15,000 acre, 295 facility physical plant comprising more than 375,000 square feet. Managed the programming, design, and construction of 22 projects totaling more than $31 million, including a complex, environmentally sensitive $2.3 million project to remove and replace underground fuel storage tanks. Reviewed and evaluated cost proposals and designs submitted by architectural and engineering firms.

Accomplishments:

- Effectively executed critical fast-track construction when facilities were not in use, completing all necessary projects during the winter and keeping construction on schedule in spite of adverse building conditions and temperatures as low as -25° Fahrenheit.
- Projects completed included a 11,500-foot runway repair, an addition to and replacement of the refueler haul road, an $11.5 million aircraft ramp refurbishment, as well as construction of a $3.4 million Radar Control facility, design and construction of a $1.9 million Communications facility, and construction of a $1.1 million Vehicle Maintenance facility.
- Created and developed computerized scheduling, programming, and documentation programs, streamlining the process of obtaining project approval and funding.

PROGRAM MANAGER. California Air National Guard Base, Fresno ANGB, Fresno, CA (1996-2000).
Supervisor: Major William Jagger (555) 555-5555
Pay grade: Captain (O-3)
Hours worked per week: 40+
Duties: Oversaw all phases of technical management for a unique five year, $93 million contract providing quick-reaction critical support to Space Systems Division launches, launch-related facilities, and satellite operations and tracking facilities. Coordinated and directed complex planning and funding from three separate operating locations using five different appropriations channeled through 22 different using organizations. Expertly managed the transition to a new contractor from an organization that held this contract for 30 years, ensuring continuous support to space systems ranging from meteorological, surveillance, and global positioning satellites to organizations such as the Aerospace Expeditionary Force Center at Langley Air Force Base in Virginia.

Accomplishments:

- Reviewed and evaluated a proposal for a fast-track repair of USAF Demonstration Squadron's "Thunderbirds" in Nevada; approved the project at a cost of only $866,000, saving the government more than $2.2 million dollars from the contractor's original cost projection while ensuring the project was completed in time to meet the Thunderbird's launch window.
- Evaluated and processed more than 23 time-critical, mission-essential design and construction projects totaling $9.1 million within a six-month period.
- Analyzed the contractor's accounting and reporting system, detecting and correcting errors that resulted in approximately $325,000 in savings to the government.
- Developed and implemented a new Total Quality Management

CIVIL ENGINEERING
GENERAL MANAGER

(TQM)-based metric measurement system designed to clarify critical issues to upper management and eliminate bureaucratic delays in the processing system for putting work on the contract.

COMMUNITY PLANNER. California Air National Guard Base, 146th Airlift Wing, Channel Islands, CA (1992-96).
Supervisor: Captain Richard Fortney (666) 666-6666
Pay grade: Captain (O-3)
Hours worked per week: 40+
Duties: Managed planning activities for the largest military community in California, developing and maintaining detailed plans for future development of the facilities and structures of the National Guard Base and 18 satellite areas. Oversaw design, construction, repair, and maintenance as well as fire protection for 974 facilities and nearly 5,800 housing units. Created traffic management and land use plans, performed preliminary site selection of new facilities, and ensured compliance with explosive safety and airfield and airspace clearance requirements.
Accomplishments:
- Programmed and site developed in excess of $33.3 million dollars in future facilities and utilities within the constraints of space, environment, and existing utilities.
- Recognized for my "knowledge of surveying, engineering design, and explosive safety criteria," which "were key in gaining approval for a $1.87 million base security upgrade."
- Provided training to the Civil Engineering airfield recovery team and the airfield damage assessment team, resulting in a rating of "excellent" during a mission tactical evaluation.
- Under tight deadlines, created a new Force Reduction Plan to provide higher headquarters with an aid to mission changes, and consolidations within U.S. and abroad.

MECHANICAL DESIGN ENGINEER. California Air National Guard Base, 222nd Combat Communications Squadron, Costa Mesa ANGS, CA (1992).
Supervisor: Captain Benjamin Foster (777) 777-7777
Pay grade: 1LT (O-3)
Hours worked per week: 40+
Duties: Supervised program management of more than $66 million in facilities construction projects and $42 million worth of design work. Created and developed mechanical engineering designs as well as managing the design team for both in-house projects and those produced by outside architectural or engineering firms. Acted as liaison between the Military Airlift Command, using agencies, Programming Section, and the Base Contracting Office during the design and construction process. Performed additional duties as the Petroleum, Oils, and Lubricants (POL) Officer and Heating, Ventilation, and Air Conditioning (HVAC) officer for the installation.
Accomplishments:
- Described as an "unsurpassed technical expert;" provided mechanical design for 22 projects worth $3.4 million, completing this work under deadline in order to facilitate contracting action during the current fiscal year.
- Improved the selection process for Heating, Ventilation, and Air Conditioning by introducing Life Cycle Economic Analysis techniques resulting in an overall savings of more than $1.8 million.
- Worked 16-hour days in order to correct design errors made by the civilian architectural and engineering firms on a $368,000 passenger terminal renovation with tight deadlines.
- Received the highest possible evaluations; evaluated as "well above standards" in every single measured proficiency.

**CIVIL ENGINEERING
GENERAL MANAGER**

MECHANICAL ENGINEER. Arizona Air National Guard, 162nd Fighter Wing, Tucson, AZ (1988-1992).
Supervisor: Mr. Marcus Pendleton (888) 888-8888
Pay grade: 2LT (O-2)
Hours worked per week: 40+
Duties: Provided Civil Engineering support and technical assistance, including but not limited to preparation of construction drawings, specifications, and estimation of material and labor costs. Designed plumbing, electrical, HVAC, and other systems, providing a variety of professional engineering services required in programming and in the design for construction, modification, and maintenance of facilities.
Accomplishments:

- Provided technical assistance during the negotiation phase and follow-on engineering assistance in the design phase of more than $15.3 million in construction projects that were bid on by outside architectural and engineering firms.
- Recognized by the Command Center of the Arizona ANG office for my "superb technical input to the Energy Conservation Initiative."
- Received the highest possible evaluations; evaluated as "well above standards" in every single measured proficiency.

**EDUCATION &
TRAINING**

Master of Science in **Mechanical Engineering**, California State University, Fresno, CA, 1998.
Bachelor of Science in **Mechanical Engineering**, The University of Arizona, Tucson, AZ, 1992.
Completed numerous leadership and management development courses sponsored by the United States Air Force, including:

- **Air Command & Staff College**, Harrisburg, PA, July 2001.
- **Squadron Officer School** – Distinguished Graduate, June 1992; member of the squadron Eagle League flight for top performance in academic and leadership competition.
- **Officers Training School**, June 1988.

HONORS

Received numerous prestigious awards and honors from April to June 2003, including:

- Outstanding Officer of the Quarter, April 2003.
- The Air Force Commendation Medal (4) May 2003.
- The Air Force Achievement Medal, May 2003.
- The Air Force Outstanding Unit Award, June 2003.

LICENSES

Registered Professional Engineer for the state of Arizona, certificate #D-662387 (September 1990).

PERSONAL

Excellent personal and professional references are available upon request.

DATABASE ADMINISTRATOR SYSTEMS ANALYST

ERIC NEIL DIXON
SSN: 000-00-0000
Mailing Address: 1353 Manning Drive, Mansfield, PA, 98871
Home Telephone: (555) 555-5555
Work Telephone: NA
ENDixon@cs.com

Highest permanent play plan or grade held:
Position, Title, Series, Grade: , GS-8888-88
Announcement Number: DN-00-000

SKILL SUMMARY To offer expertise in information technology to an organization that can benefit from my technical skills as well as proven management abilities.

EDUCATION **Bacholor of Scienco dogroo** in Administrative Office Management (Systems Management), Mansfield University, Mansfield, PA, 1998; was Vice President of the 30-member Computer Science Club.

HIGHLIGHTS OF TRAINING Courses in **Oracle SQL** and **PL/SQL, JavaScript, Microsoft Visual Basic 6.0, Oracle Developer/2000, UNIX Programming,** and **C++ Programming**, Pittsburgh Technical College, 1997; **DataPlan version 1.5.9** project management, McColl, 2001.

Training programs included an advanced management and **computer science** emphasizing system hardware, design, Local Area Network (**LAN**) management, and programming languages with an emphasis on **Visual Basic and Ada95.**

Courses in **A+ Microcomputer Support and Service, Windows NT Server 4.0** Core Technologies, **Microsoft Exchange Server 5.5** Concepts and Administration, **Unified Modeling Language (UML)** Concepts and Analysis, and **Rational Rose.**

COMPUTERS Proficient with **Oracle8i** and **Rational Rose**, additionally use Embarcadero Rapid SQL 5.6, ER/Studio, DBArtisan and Describe Visio 5.0 Technical Drawing software, **The Oracle Application Developer (TOAD)**, Allround Automation's PL/SQL Developer, **Oracle Developer2000**, McColl DataPlan Enterprise Project Management software, versions 1.6.4 and 2.0, **Microsoft Project 2000, Visual Basic 6.0** as well as Front Page 2000, Hot Metal Pro version 4; basic knowledge of DreamWeaver, Oracle JDeveloper, Oracle9i Forms Developer, IBM Visual Age for Java; Proficient in database modeling techniques such as, IDEF1X and **UML**, Proficient in Computer Associate's **ERwin** database modeling software, Web design and development. Basic knowledge of **XML** and **XSLT**; Completed a resident course on the Powerbuilder 5.0 application language utilized by the ASAT and SATS system development teams.

- Extensive experience in enterprise database application development.
- Knowledge of data communications, hardware construction and design, LANs, WANs.
- Extensive knowledge and of the following software development methodologies: **Rational Unified Process (RUP), waterfall, spiral and Rapid application development (RAD),** Agile Programming Methodologies such as **Extreme Programming.**
- Knowledge of N-Tier application architectures; J2EE concepts; object development concepts. Knowledge of SEI Capability Maturity Model (CMM). Basic knowledge of web services; SOAP, UDDI.
- Extensive knowledge of the Project Management Body of Knowledge (**PMBOK**) and Software Engineering Body of Knowledge (**SWEBOK**); knowledge of project controls such as Earned Value Management.

EXPERIENCE Have excelled in the following track record of promotion with Intel, Inc., a Pennsylvania firm which develops state-of-the-art solutions to some of the world's most puzzling problems

firm which develops state-of-the-art solutions to some of the world's most puzzling problems in the information arena:

2004-present: DATABASE ADMINISTRATOR and SYSTEMS ANALYST. 1786 Bingham Dr, Mansfield, PA, 98871. Arron Platter, Supervisor, phone: (111) 111-1111. Have worked on a nine-month medical systems project for the Mansfield Medical Center which had the mission of providing the local medical community with a solution that will allow health care providers to track and monitor the clinical preventive services for needed patients.

- **Project management:** Took over this project when the initial vendor failed to meet delivery requirements; assumed control of the project when it was two months old with little progress made toward source code and other documentation. Provided leadership to a project team comprised of two software engineers, one programmer, and one functional analyst. We made decisions to utilize Java and developed PMS based on Java. Therefore, we were rebuilding a product using another programming language late in the development process.

- **Risk and budget management:** Establish risk management techniques, and demonstrate commitment to keeping the project within the $350,000 budgeted cost.

- **Team management:** Manage the team members as they implemented tasks I assigned them. Developed the metrics to track the progress of the project. Am responsible for the implementation of the database, and work closely with engineers to assure that proper security measures were put into place that would minimize the chances of intrusion.

- **Status and delivery management:** Conduct regular project status reviews with the client. Deliver the product on time and under budget.

- **Follow-on phase:** Was successful in obtaining additional funding for a follow-on phase which has the mission of transitioning the previous product from a client server application into true web architecture based application that would meet the needs of thousands of users globally. For the follow-on phase, we decided to change the engineer development process from a traditional waterfall approach to the Rational Unified Process (RUP), which employs an industry standard UML to visually model a system's architecture and components.

- **Project management of the follow-on phase:** Served as Project Manager of the follow-on phase, and facilitated numerous modeling meetings that resulted in the creation of robust object model that accurately captured the functionality of the application. Assisted engineers in the development of the data representation models used to created the supporting database. Have been involved in all aspects of the development of the supporting framework based on the concept of enterprise component based solution.

2001-04: SENIOR SYSTEMS ANALYST. Worked on two major projects for the Regency Information Systems Agency in Philadelphia—the Capital (OJTB) and the Intel-System Compulation Module (ISCM) for the Department of Energy.

- Acted as **Database Administrator** for the Enterprise Project

Management database for the Capital (OJTB) project. This database served as the central repository for all projects managed within OJTB, and the database contained more than 2500 projects valued at $40 million and used by over 1300 people. Gained respect for my expertise in implementing the enterprise-wide project management database and DataPlan project management tools which have resulted in significant improvements in tracking and managing projects. I oversaw all aspects of database design and development integrating with other systems with the result that there was a seamless information flow through separate departments and agencies.

- Acted as **Database Developer** and **Developer** for the database segment of the ISCM project. Was responsible for the design, development, and integration of the physical database, which included installation and Configuration of the Oracle 8I RDBMS and addressing of DII COE compliance issues. As Application Developer, I created procedures using Java to store, retrieve, and manipulate data from database. Gave briefings in how the database would meet business objectives. Earned respect for my knowledge of Oracle objects and Java stores procedures.

In the following track record, advanced to the position of Systems Analyst with McColl DD, Philadelphia, PA:

1999-01: SYSTEMS ANALYST. 721 North Main Street, Philadelphia, PA, 11881. Michelle Kreitz, Supervisor, phone: (111) 111-1111.

Was the key architect of the McColl's Systems Approach to Training (ASAT), a $10 million application supporting a $1 billion learning program; this state-of-the-art training and policy development and production tool for XQE XII was the major generator of information for the McColl's Systems Training seminar.

- Commended for leadership as well as hardware infrastructures and IDEF modeling knowledge.

1997-99: PERSONNEL ADMINISTRATION ADVISOR. 322 Ireland Hwy, Pittsburgh, PA 11222. Molded eight personnel specialists into a team which supported a 1,500-person center training in 11 career fields; developed program which resulted in 99% on-time document processing.

1995-1997: GENERAL MANAGER. 6063 Parkton Road, Pittsburgh, PA, 11155. Phil Wallace, Supervisor, phone: (222) 222-2222.

Oversaw training, performance, and logistics for 340 people and $1 million in assets. Automated routine tasks.

1994-1995: LOGISTICS MANAGER. Calihan Court 1822, London, England. Richard Hightower, Supervisor, phone: (011) 888-888-8888.

Planned and supervised supply, maintenance, and transportation while tracking expenditures/trends for a 2,500-person organization. Automated logistics review and budget programs. Was cited for technical skill in translating complex statistics.

- In a previous job as Project Manager, was involved in planning, coordinating, reviewing, and analyzing logistics support for the fielding of new telecommunications equipment.

PERSONAL   Self-starter with strong personal initiative. Held Secret security clearance. Strong references.

DENTAL ASSISTANT

BOBBIE E. TOUSSAINT
SSN: 000-00-0000
Home Address: 1283 Main Street, Decatur, IL 54870
Home: (888) 888-8888
Vacancy Announcement Number: DN-00-0000
Position: DN-00-0000

Country of Citizenship: U.S.A.
Veterans' Preference:
Reinstatement Eligibility:
Highest Federal Civilian Grade Held: GS-000-000

SUMMARY

Offer exceptional **patient care, organizational, and communication skills** and a thorough knowledge of **medical terminology** as well as **versatile clinical experience in a wide variety of medical and dental environments.**

EXPERIENCE

DENTAL ASSISTANT. Richland County Medical and Dental Clinic, 685 Valleygate Drive, Decatur, IL 54887 (2001-present).
Supervisor: Carl Holmes, D.D.S., P.A. (777) 777-7777
Salary:
Hours worked per week: 40
Duties: Serve as a Clinical Assistant in the Pediatric Dentistry department at this busy dental clinic. Perform chair-side assisting, including the use of four and six-hand dentistry to pass and retrieve materials and instruments needed for the procedure to and from the dentist. Prepare patients for various surgical and dental procedures. Gain experience in orthodontic, general dentistry, restorative, and endodontic procedures. Develop the ability to work effectively with special needs and behavior management children. Provide patient education in areas ranging from correct brushing and flossing techniques, to proper care of prosthodontic and orthodontic appliances, to post-surgical care for oral surgery patients.

- Described as an "outstanding self-starter and motivator," was credited with being a quick learner who was very knowledgeable in all aspects of my assigned duties.
- Am recognized for outstanding communication and interpersonal skills that allowed me to put the most difficult patients at ease.

Surgical Procedures: Work in the Operating Room; set up surgical materials, instruments, and medications as well as assisting in oral surgery and other surgical procedures; skilled at working with patients who are sedated as well as those who have been given nitrous oxide. Operate high speed evacuator, suction tip, and irrigation to keep the intra-oral area of operation clear of obstructions. Maintain and disinfected all equipment and instruments necessary for procedures, using both cold and hot sterilization methods.

- Cited in an official evaluation for my "exceptional skills while performing in the operating room," as well as for "exceptional coordination of hospital Operating Room cases with medical staff."
- Praised for maintaining all equipment in a high state of readiness and maintaining adequate supply levels in the operating room.

Radiological Skills: Skilled in operating x-ray equipment to produce intro-oral and extra-oral radiographs, including but not limited to full mouth series, panoramic, temporal mandibular, joint series, sinus series and cephalometric x-rays, as well as periapicals, bite wings, and occlusal x-rays. Develop radiological views using the automatic processor as well as both the dip tank method and the fixer tank method.

Administrative Skills: Respond to a large number of patient inquiries regarding scheduling, billing, and insurance questions, both over the phone and in person. Update and maintain the clinic's appointment schedule to reflect cancellations, changes, and new appointments. Coordinate with outlying clinics concerning patient care. Update patient charts and took patient histories from new patients. Verify insurance information.

DENTAL ASSISTANT. Kettering Dental Care, 9774 Gateview Road, Decatur IL 54988 (1999-01).
Supervisor: Mark Eggerson, D.D.S. (666) 666-6666
Salary:
Hours worked per week: 40
Duties: Received training and gained experience in chair-side dental assisting; performed restorative, prosthodontic, endodontic, periodontal, and oral surgery procedures. Provided administrative support to the clinic, managing the appointment calendar, answering patient inquiries regarding scheduling and billing; as well as conducting inventory of and ordering supplies needed for the office. Performed the same essential duties as described in the position above.

NURSING ASSISTANT. Primary Medical Care Plus, 2687 Meed Lane, Decatur IL 54887 (1997-99).
Supervisor: Gladys Platt, RN (555) 555-5555
Salary: G-2
Hours worked per week: 40
Duties: Provided total patient care for preoperative and postoperative patients in the Critical Care Unit/Intensive Care Unit (CCU/ICU), as well as in the Medical/Surgical and Ambulatory Care Units. Performed venipuncture to draw blood for laboratory testing and to start IVs for medication, liquid nutrition, and hydration of the patient. Administered medications through a variety of delivery methods, including but not limited to orally, intravenously, and subcutaneously. Provided pain management and wound care, changed dressings, and collected samples for urinalysis testing. Bathed patients and assisted with personal hygiene for patients with limited mobility. Familiar with telemetry monitoring.

Medical Clerk: Served as a clerk, taking patient histories and making charts for new patients as well as breaking down discharge charts and scheduling follow-up appointments for patients being discharged. Made arrangements for and scheduled X-rays, laboratory tests, EKGs, and other special tests for patients. Ordered patient meals, ensuring that special diet patients received the correct tray according to their nutritive requirements. Utilize my extensive knowledge of medical terminology and experience in a wide range of medical environments to ensure the accuracy and completeness of patient charts.

MEDICAL TECHNICIAN. Richland County Medical and Dental Clinic, 685 Valleygate Drive, Decatur, IL 54887 (1993-97).
Supervisor: Tara C. Kosterman, RN (333) 333-3333
Salary: G-1
Hours worked per week: 40
Duties: While stationed at Beaufort Naval hospital, provided medical care to patients in a number of different areas, including the hospital's Emergency Room, Obstetrics/Gynecology

Clinic, and Eye, Ear, Nose, and Throat (EENT) Clinic. Performed triage on all incoming patients, categorizing and prioritizing each patient based on the severity of their medical condition. Utilized my exceptional communication skills to tactfully and diplomatically obtain vital medical information for patient medical histories from individuals who were frequently upset, injured, or in pain. Prepared medical charts for new patients, and assisted doctors in a wide variety of medical procedures. Took patient vital signs, weighed patients, and filed, maintained, and updated charts.

DENTAL ASSISTANT

Opthalmology: During my tenure at the hospital's Eye, Ear, Nose, and Throat (EENT) clinic, frequently performed or assisted in the full range of diagnostic testing procedures. Conducted triage on clinic patients, prioritizing cases according to the nature and severity of the patient's condition. Checked eyes for corneal abrasions and other types of eye trauma; disinfected the area of examination and changed dressings. Performed opthalmalogical pre-screening, comprised of tests for visual acuity, depth perception, and color-blindness. Used the auto-refractor to measure nearsightedness and/or farsightedness and provide an estimate of the prescription needed for the patient's corrective lenses, and conducted NCT testing for glaucoma. Assisted the doctor in various minor surgeries. Removed sutures for the doctor during follow-up appointments for surgical patients.

Audiology: Visually inspected the patient's ear to check for fluid discharge or excessive buildup of wax. Conducted hearing tests to determine if the patient was experiencing any loss of hearing. Instructed the patient listen to a series of high and low tones through headphones and raise their right or left hand when they heard the tone. Evaluated their responses to determine the nature and extent of any hearing loss, as well as which ear was effected, if the hearing loss was not bilateral. Assisted the doctor in various minor surgeries. Worked with children, using probes to remove items lodged in the ear canal. Performed lavage, flushing the ear canal with saline solution to cleanse the ear. Placed medication in the ear canal.

EDUCATION

A. A. in Dental Technology, Richland Community College, Decatur IL, 1999.
- Dental Specialist Correspondence Course, 2001
- Intra-oral Radiography Course, 2000
- Patient Relations Course, 2000
- Infection Control, 1999

CERTIFICATIONS Medical Technician Certification course, Richland Community College, Decatur IL, 1993.
- Completed a three-month internship at Richland Medical and accepted a full-time position as a Medical Technician, 1993.
- Completed approximately 160 hours of medical instruction, Richland Community College, 1994.
- Courses included: Medical Terminology, Pharmacology, Emergency Patient Care, and Anatomy & Physiology
- Completed extensive training courses related to various medical and dental disciplines, including the following:

- Advanced Cardiac Life Support (ACLS), American Heart Association, expires 2004.
- Community CPR (adult, child, and infant), American Red Cross, expires 2004.
- Advanced Cardiac Life Support (ACLS), 1999
- Professional Development for Nurses Assistants, 1999
- Sexual Harassment, 1998
- Sterilization, 1998
- Customer Service, 1996

HONORS

Throughout my career in the medical and dental profession, have consistently received numerous annual and special awards for Outstanding Work Performance.

Received four Certificates of Appreciation for my outstanding performance in a variety of medical environments.

TECHNICAL SKILLS

Performed sterilization and setup of and utilized the full range of dental instruments and surgical equipment, including but not limited to the following:

mouth mirrors	explorers	cotton pliers	periodontal probe
saliva ejectors	pulp testers	dental chisels	root elevators
aspirating syringes	extracting forceps	spoon excavators	

rubber dam instruments (holder, punch, clamp, and forceps)

dental burs, both excavating and surgical

periodontal instruments (curetts, hose, files, probes, and knives)

endodontic instruments (broaches, reamers, files, and pluggers)

prosthodontic instruments (impression trays, dental casts, articulators, and the alcohol)

PERSONAL

Exceptional personal and professional references are available upon request.

DEPUTY SHERIFF (CAREER CHANGE)

CHARLES F. EVERMAN
3239 McLean Avenue,
Philadelphia, PA 11129
111-111-1111 H
222-222-2222 W
E-mail: cfeverman@hotmail.com
SSN: 000-00-0000
Country of Citizenship: United States
Veteran's Preference:

DEPUTY SHERIFF

Vacancy Announcement Number:
Position Title: Deputy Sheriff

EXPERIENCE

JAN 2003-present: **DEPUTY SHERIFF.** Burlington County Sheriff's Office, Browns Mills, NJ. Salary: $27,500. Hours per week: 40. Supervisor: LT Stephen Lewis, 777-777-7777. Manage security and administration for 45 inmates in a linear facility. Process, fingerprinted, and classified inmates for housing assignments. Act as Instructor for Emergency Vehicle Operations and represented the Sheriff's Office on numerous occasions at civic events while enforcing traffic and criminal codes of the State of New Jersey while simultaneously serving my country in the U.S. Army Reserves.

- Instruct classes on Emergency Vehicle Operations.
- Conduct investigations of traffic violations, misdemeanor criminal cases, and violations of municipal and criminal codes of Burlington County and the State of New Jersey.

MAR 1992-present: **OPERATIONS SERGEANT MAJOR.** U.S. Army Reserves, E 282nd Special Operations, Military Freefall and Underwater Operations Division, Fort Dix, NJ 19548, Salary: $78,500. Hours per week: 40. Supervisor: Captain Ramon Washington, DSN 444-444-4444. Handle a wide range of administrative and operations management responsibilities while serving as Operations Sergeant Major for a major Joint Task Force (JTF) element. Was promoted from Master Sergeant to Sergeant Major.

- Hold one of the nation's highest security clearances. Am engaged in activities which are classified in nature.
- Oversee management, safety, and accountability of 212 military and civilian personnel in three locations. Control $3.2 million in assets which include vehicles, housing, and equipment.
- Have supervised the efficient coordination among the Central Intelligence Agency (CIA), Federal Bureau of Investigation (FBI), and other agencies as well as the Combined Task Force (CTF) Chief of Staff and principals.
- Supervised bimonthly 9mm weapons familiarization and live fire courses.
- Trained junior enlisted managers in preparing evaluation reports, awards documents, and other paperwork. Trained and motivated 215 personnel in hazardous duty/high risk environments.

Highlights of other U.S. Army Reserve experience: 1992-2002 Locations worldwide. JAN 2002-MAR 2002: **SPECIAL FORCES OPERATIONS SERGEANT.** For three months, served as Assistant Instructor for an Infantry Battalion Briefing. Assisted Primary

Instructors on Marksmanship, Close Quarters Battle, Demolitions, and Vehicle Ranges.

JAN 2000-FEB 2000: TRAINING NCO. During a four-week period, developed a Program of Instruction for Hazard Control Course. Created a curriculum which prepared Special Forces officers for military and diplomatic tasks.

APR 1999-JUL 1999: EXERCISE CONTROL NCO. During a three-month period, played a key role in supervising receipt of operational information on maps and aerial photos. Was involved in an Initial Planning Conference in Atlantic City, and was considered the "internal expert" on security policies and procedures.

SEP 1998: ADMINISTRATIVE NCOIC. For 18 days, managed an Exercise Control Group for the JCS directed Workout Control Group Charlie 98.

OCT 1996: SPECIAL OPERATIONS COMMUNICATIONS NCO. For 14 days, served as Electronics Technician Chief, and was responsible for the installation, operation, and maintenance of command, control, communications, and computer (C4) information systems including FM, AM, VHF, UHF, and HF secure and nonsecure voice and data systems.

DEC 1994: SPECIAL OPERATIONS COMMUNICATIONS NCO. For 22 days, installed, operated and maintained FM, AM, VHF, UHF, and SHF radio communications in voice, CW and burst radio nets.

JUN 1992: OPERATIONS SERGEANT. For 16 days, was the focal point for tracking information pertaining to foreign and domestic units participating in a Joint Chiefs of Staff Exercise.

CIVILIAN LAW ENFORCEMENT EXPERIENCE

AUG 2000-JAN 2003: CAPTAIN, ADMINISTRATION & TRAINING. Burlington County Sheriff's Office, Browns Mills, NJ. Salary: $49,200. Hours per week: 40-plus. Supervisor: Major Edwin Wilson, 555-555-5555. Provided input into the Sheriff's Office's annual budget for submission to the Board of Supervisors while managing five sections including the Finance section, Quartermaster section, Computer section, Policy and Procedure section, Sheriff's Office, and the Burlington County Training Academy. Held various positions and "hats" within the Sheriff's Office.

- Served as Range Master for the Sheriff's Office and the Training Academy.
- As Internal Affairs Investigator, investigated violations of Sheriff's Office policies and procedures as well as civil and criminal violations of the Code of the County of Burlington and state of New Jersey.
- As Police Sergeant, supervised and trained 16 deputies responsible for 450 inmates.
- As Police Lieutenant, supervised and evaluated two Sergeants and 18 Deputies. Developed and implemented the Emergency Center Operational Plan for the Jail East facility—the plan received public commendations.
- As Police Captain, established a new personnel structure for the Training Academy which resulted in more highly trained graduates.

DEC 1999-AUG 2000: REGIONAL SECURITY DIRECTOR. Bank of America, 21 Atkinson Road, Cookstown, NJ. Salary: $34,500. Hours per week: 40. Supervisor: Randy M. Burke, General Manager, phone: 66-666-6666. Provided oversight for 375 people in 23 separate locations in the eastern region of New Jersey. Was in charge of security clearances, security training, first aid/CPR training, and the Executive Protection Program.

- Performed liaison with federal, state, and law enforcement agencies.

FEB 1996-DEC 1999: PATROL OFFICER & BURGLARY DETECTIVE & SNIPER, SWAT TEAM. Philadelphia City Police Department, 1445 Ivey Street, Newark, NJ 11124. Salary: $38,600. Hours per week: 40. Supervisor: Lt. Stuart Morgan, 333-333-3333. Investigated violations of burglary, narcotics, and pawn shop violations while also serving as a Sniper on the SWAT Team.

JUN 1993-FEB 1996: **PATROLMAN & DETECTIVE.** Crestwood County Police Department, 11464 Catawba Hwy #684, Crestwood Village, NJ. Salary: $24,650 hours per week: 40. Supervisor St. Martin Berkowicz, 888-888-8888. Started as a rookie in 1993 and later excelled in a track record of promotions while serving my country in the U.S. Army Reserves. Enforced traffic and criminal laws of the State of New Jersey, and was a member of the High Intensity Target Team providing intelligence and surveillance of targeted business areas.

DEPUTY SHERIFF

- As a member of the SCUBA team, recovered evidence leading to a murder conviction.
- Authored the Canine Projection Report that led to development of the police department's K-9 Section; Received a special award for valor.

ACTIVE DUTY MILITARY EXPERIENCE

MAR 1989-FEB 1992: **INSTRUCTOR & WRITER.** United States Army, B 44th Special Forces, Fort Rucker, AL. Salary: $41,600. Hours per week: 40-plus. SGM Chad W. Henderson, 555-555-5555. Was promoted to Noncommissioned Officer in Charge of the Advanced Skills Department for Special Forces Training. Performed research, developed lesson plans, managed training, and assured that schools were prepared to teach skills related to Strategy Reconnaissance, Military Freefall, and SCUBA. Planned and implemented missions involving counter narcotics operations.

AUG 1986-MAR 1989: **RADIO COMMUNICATIONS SUPERVISOR.** United States Army, B 349th Special Forces, Fort Gordon, GA. Salary $27,450. Hours per week: 40-plus. Supervisors: Walter T. Moore and Phillip Hastings. Was Senior Communications Supervisor for a Special Forces team which was later deployed to Germany. Led a small reconnaissance element in intelligence and observation activities.

EDUCATION

Completed one year of university coursework towards a **Master of Arts degree in Sociology**, University of Pennsylvania, Philadelphia, PA, 2004.
Bachelor of Arts degree in Criminal Justice, Crestwood College, Crestwood Village, NJ, 1996.
Diploma from Willingboro High School, Willingboro, NJ, 1986.

SPECIALIZED TRAINING LICENSES CERTIFICATES

1996, Burlington County Sheriff's Academy, Graduate and recipient of the Law Enforcement Excellence Award.
1994, SCUBA Course.
1993, Law Enforcement Instructors Course.
1993, Honor Graduate, Crestwood County Police Academy.
1993, Crestwood County Police Academy (recipient of the Academic Excellence Award).
1993, Defense Driving Course.
1993, Crestwood County Police Academy. 1990, New Jersey Law Enforcement SWAT School.
1991, US Army Security Managers Course.
1989, Special Forces Strategic Reconnaissance.
1989, Military Instructors Course.
1987, Special Forces Advance Urban Combat.
1986, Special Forces Communications

LICENSES & CERTIFICATES	Law Enforcement Firearms Instructor, State of New Jersey.
	Law Enforcement General Instructor, State of New Jersey.
	State of New Jersey Hazardous Materials Handler.
	Law Enforcement Emergency Vehicle Operations Course Instructor, State of New Jersey.
	Law Enforcement Special Weapons and Tactics Course, State of New Jersey.
	Certified in SCUBA and SWAT
PROFESSIONAL ASSOCIATIONS	Northern Society of Security, Philadelphia Diamond Chapter of the Philadelphia Masonry Lodge, International Divers, Inc., Black Hawk Association, and the Noncommissioned Officers Association.
AWARDS	Meritorious Service Award for Valor from the Philadelphia City Police Department, Excellence in Patrol Investigations Award from the Crestwood County Police Department, as well as academic awards from the Burlington County Sheriff's Academy.
CLEARANCE	Top Secret with SCI

EQUAL OPPORTUNITY ADVISOR

WILLIAM M. CAGE
SSN: 000-00-0000
6677 Winchester Road
Washington D.C. 17194
E-mail: sagattao@compuserve.com
Home: (999) 999-9999
Work: (888) 888-8888
Vacancy Announcement Number:
Country of Citizenship: U.S.
Veterans' Preference:
Reinstatement Eligibility:
Highest Federal Civilian Grade Held:

SUMMARY

Offer well-developed **management, staff development, planning, and organizational abilities**, a reputation as a **gifted instructor** and **natural leader**, and a background in **equal opportunity counseling, and human resource management and supervision.**

EXPERIENCE

EQUAL OPPORTUNITY ADVISOR. Department of State, Human Resources Division, 11273 Rennert Road, Washington D.C. 17180 (2004-present).
Supervisor: Anthony Perry (777) 777-7777
Pay grade:
Hours worked per week: 40+
Duties: Promote and transfer to the Human Resources Division in Washington, DC. Assist in designing, planning, and implementation of Equal Opportunity Programs, as well as planning and conducting special/ethnic observances. Train personnel to assume Equal Opportunity leadership roles throughout the organization. Receive, analyzed, and initiated appropriate action in response to individual Equal Opportunity complaints. Review and analyze existing policies, procedures, and practices, recommending modifications where necessary to prevent discrimination and sexual harassment. Conducted organizational-level Affirmative Action meetings and interpreted, explained, and presented Department of State Equal Employment Opportunity policies. Execute sensing sessions and human relations surveys to determine areas where the Equal Opportunity program needed to improve, contributing to personal growth throughout the organization.
Accomplishments:
*   "Flawlessly" design, plan, and establish "from scratch" the creation of the Equal Opportunity program and office for the organization; authored an 85-page organizational-level Affirmative Action Plan (AAP) that was adopted for use by higher headquarters.
*   Successfully initiate and develop a Unit Facilitator instruction program which produced more than 65 trained facilitators throughout the organization.
*   Earn certification as a Department of State Personnel Training Facilitator.
*   Train and certify all 38 general managers and supervisors within the organization, including over 175 Department of State personnel facilitators.
*   Personally train, produce, and facilitate more than 400 personnel

during the organizations "Consideration for Others" training sessions.
- Designed, constructed, and implemented the organization's Equal Opportunity Web page, including a 24-hour automated hotline to facilitate easier access to personnel with Equal Opportunity issues.
- Planned, organized, and executed the celebration of eight Special/Ethnic observances, serving more then 2,750 personnel from diverse backgrounds.

HUMAN RESOURCES MANAGER. Department of State, Human Resources Division, 6174 Alva Avenue, Richmond, VA 22244 (1999-04).
Supervisor: Casey T. Hollingsworth (666) 666-6666
Pay grade: G-9
Hours worked per week: 40+
Duties: Provided assistance in designing, planning, and implementation of Equal Employment opportunity Programs at the installation level, as well as planning and conducting special emphasis programs. Managed, led, and implemented special emphasis programs, to include planning, organization, and execution. Trained newly assigned Equal Opportunity Advisors/Counselors on installation, the Richmond office of the Department of State equal opportunity policies and procedures. Processed, determined the validity of, and initiated appropriate action on individual EO Issues/Equal Employment Opportunity pre-complaints. Reviewed and analyzed existing policies, procedures, and practices, recommending modifications where necessary to prevent discrimination and sexual harassment. Taught Prevention of Sexual Harassment (POSH) to employees. Conducted installation-level Affirmative Action meetings; interpreted, explained, and presented the Department's policies concerning EO to personnel throughout the installation.
Accomplishments:
- Successfully orchestrated the Department of State Sexual Harassment visit, involving over 1,000 personnel as well as developing and implementing instructional programs at the installation level designed to prevent sexual harassment.
- Utilizing personal knowledge of automation technology, provided instruction on computer applications to Equal Employment Specialists, increasing productivity in the office and generating savings both in labor hours and in money.
- Enhanced and refined the installation's Equal Employment Opportunity Counselor Course.
- Credited in an official evaluation with "flawlessly developing the General Manager's quarterly Equal Employment Opportunity presentation," and "masterfully constructing a slide show briefing on the Special Emphasis Program for the Director."
- Personally initiated actions that resulted in revision of Standard Operating Procedures (SOPs) and equal opportunity policies already in place on the installation.
- Developed an exhaustive training program on extremist groups that was adopted at the higher headquarters level.
- Provided instruction in the knowledge and skills required of an Equal Opportunity leader to hundreds of personnel; mentored Equal Opportunity leaders throughout the installation.
- An articulate communicator, was selected ahead of other Equal Opportunity officers to serve as guest lecturer at an advanced management course.

Officially cited as a "self-starter with natural ability and aptitude for demanding, sensitive tasks," and a "high-performing, top notch supervisor; articulate and insightful with judgment beyond reproach."

Other military experience:
QUALITY CONTROL SUPERVISOR and AVIATION MAINTENANCE SUPERVISOR.
U.S. Army, 389th QM CO, Fort Eustis, VA 22505 (1993-96).
Supervisor: LT Jim N. Lucas (555) 555-5555

Pay grade: Starting: SSG/Staff Sergeant, Ending: SFC/Sergeant First Class **Hours worked per week:** 40+

Duties: Supervised as many as 58 personnel, directing their training, safety, and overall readiness while managing an Aviation Intermediate Maintenance Company. Oversaw support maintenance and quality assurance for all aircraft assigned to personnel under my supervision. Planned, directed, and executed all phases of aircraft systems maintenance, coordinating the work load and assigning personnel to specific tasks to ensure safe and efficient completion of necessary repairs. Provided backup organizational quality assurance for the division's aircraft. Ensured strict compliance with all quality control practices and procedures. Was responsible for the maintenance, accountability, and operational readiness of more than 20 million dollars worth of rotary-wing aircraft and related support equipment.

Accomplishments:

- Developed and implemented monthly safety inspections that resulted in zero organizational accidents.
- Chosen as representative to the organization's Military Resource Management organization (MRMO).
- Identified and reported procedural problems which resulted in 17 changes in Department of the Army Procedures for Aviation Maintenance, increasing safety and efficiency.
- Exceeded readiness standards for all ground support equipment and flawlessly maintained 100% accountability for all assigned equipment.

LOGISTICS SUPERVISOR. U.S. Army, D. Co. 29th AVN 5th REGT, Fort Shafter, HI, 00144 (1990-93).

Supervisor: SFC Barry Collier (444) 444-4444

Pay grade: SSG/Staff Sergeant

Hours worked per week: 40+

Duties: Directed supply personnel in establishing supply and inventory control management functions in support of aviation maintenance operations. Assisted in developing equipment requirements and other logistics reports. Reviewed all requests for major, large expenditure, or controlled items to ensure that proper authorizations had been obtained and to verify the correct stock numbers or prepared items or authorized substitutes. Reviewed the property book for accuracy, adjusting documents as necessary to correct errors. Trained supply personnel in all aspects of logistics and support operation.

Accomplishments:

- Oversaw the successful turn-in of more than 3.1 million dollars worth of aircraft and equipment when the unit's Aviation brigade was decommissioned.
- Known as a gifted instructor, supply personnel that I trained consistently scored 90% or better during common skills testing.
- Demonstrated strong technical competence during on-hand evaluations and inspections as well as during Annual Qualification testing, where I maintained a high proficiency level.

OPERATIONS SPECIALIST. U.S. Army, C Company 107th Supply and Service, Ft. Stewart, GA 31404 (1988-90).

Supervisor: Sgt Paul R. Gibson (333) 333-3333

Pay grade: E-4 Specialist

Hours worked per week: 40+

- **Duties:** Supervise 45 employees while leading, directing, and advising the executive staff on the daily operations of the organization, assisting with development of the annual budget, and preparing daily and monthly personnel reports. Maintained accountability for more than $32 million in equipment, including 8 rotary-wing utility aircraft, vehicles, equipment, and supplies.

Highlights of earlier military experience:

Won respect for my accomplishments, was promoted ahead of my peers, and earned a reputation as a natural leader and gifted trainer while excelling in earlier positions as a **TRAINING MANAGER, MAINTENANCE SUPERVISOR,** and **HELICOPTER CREW CHIEF.**

CERTIFICATIONS   Certified as an Equal Employment Opportunity Counselor by the Director of the Equal Employment Opportunity Review Board, 2003.
Certified as a Department of State Training Facilitator, 2002.
Certified as a Department of State Equal Opportunity Advisor, 2004.

EDUCATION & TRAINING   **Bachelor of Arts degree in Human Resource Management,** Virginia Commonwealth University, Richmond, VA, 1996.
Completed numerous military training and development courses, which included:

- Equal Opportunity Counselor Training Course, 1993; Defense Equal Opportunity Management Institute Equal Opportunity Staff Advisor Course, 16 weeks, 1994.
- Sergeant First Class Course, 1 week, 1992; Advanced Management Course for enlisted supervisors, 8 weeks, 1993; Basic Management Course for enlisted supervisors, 3 weeks, 1993; Primary Leadership and Development Course, 4 weeks, 1992.
- Small Unit Instructor Training Course, 2 weeks, 1992; Platoon Training Workshop, 1 week, 1991.
- Automated Unit Level Logistics System Course, 2 weeks, 1990.
- Aircraft Battle Damage Repair Course, 4 weeks, 1988; Aircraft Maintenance Senior Management Course, 3 weeks, 1988; Aircraft Maintenance Junior Management Course, 5 weeks, 1988; Scout Helicopter Repairer Course, 8 weeks, 1988.

HONORS   Recognized with numerous prestigious honors, including three Army Achievement Medals, the Combat Air Medal, the Armed Forces Expeditionary Medal with Bronze Arrowhead, four Meritorious Service Medals, six Army Commendation Medals, and the Joint Meritorious Unit Award, as well as the Order of Saint Michael Medal, one of the highest Aviation honors.

PERSONAL   Excellent personal and professional references are available upon request.

EQUIPMENT SPECIALIST

ALBERT CALCUTTA
549 2ND Street
McConnell Air Force Base, KS 63355.
111 111-1111 W
222 222-2222 H
SSN: 000-00-0000
Source: EXTERNAL
Highest Grade Held: N/A
Vacancy Announcement Number: 00000-0000
Position Title: EQUIPMENT SPECIALIST (AIRCRAFT) GS-000

EXPERIENCE

2003-present. **Equipment Specialist.** Lockheed Martin, McConnell Air Force Base, Kansas 63379. Supervisor: Roger Clemmons (333) 333-3333. Oversee and control receipt, issuance, inspection, modification, maintenance, and performance of major repairs on air crew life support equipment. Prepare Summaries of Performance (SOPs) and Quality Performance Summaries (QPSs) to provide command headquarters with essential information on equipment reliability, maintainability, and support ability. Provide rotary wing pilots with instruction in the use and care of protective and survival equipment. Order critical and routine aircraft parts while controlling a tool crib and stockroom with an inventory of aircraft repair parts as well as hand and power tools. Operate equipment which includes motor vehicles weighing less than 25,000 pounds, 3-1/2 ton tractors, and a 25,000-pound forklift.

2001-03. **Mechanic and Driver.** ALL Core, Inc., Wichita, KS 63330. Supervisor: Vincent Parkerson (444) 444-4444. Performed safety inspections, services, and maintenance on five mixer trucks, a tanker truck, Core Mill machinery, and the concrete plant.

2001. **Vehicle Maintenance and Inspection Specialist/Bus Driver.** Sedgwick County Bus Company, Wichita, KS Supervisor: Edward Martin (555) 555-5555. Performed safety inspections twice daily and transported 55 children as operator of a passenger bus. Earned my Class "B" Driver's License.

1998-01. **General Maintenance Manager.** CDT Construction, Inc., 4886 Rockford Road, Wichita, KS 63845 Curtis Dumar (666) 666-6666. Provided management, supervision, and advice on issues which impacted on the health, welfare, training, productivity, administrative support, and professional development of a 98-person organization with equipment valued in excess of $14.5 million. Provided guidance for resolving problems related to maintenance, supply, repair arts, equipment logs, proper records, and report procedures. Coordinated production support for departments in three locations. Assisted contract managers of subordinate units in making determinations of basic parts and support loads for authorized equipment. Supervised proper handling/maintenance of equipment; presented weekly safety briefings.

Other experience in the U. S. Army:
1996-98. **Production Control NCOIC.** U.S. Army, 83th Main Support, Fort Wainwright, AK, CPT Gene R. Pinckney, (777) 777-7777. Planned and supervised maintenance and administrative support for a unit

with ten helicopters and five vehicles valued at $32 million. Supervised the professional development of a 28-person organization in a forward-deployed aviation unit operating in a desert environment.

1994-96 Aviation Maintenance Shop Foreman. U.S. Army, 282nd Maintenance Shop, Fort Monroe, VA 21464. Supervisor: Calvin Singletary (888) 888-8888. Directed maintenance for more than 315 air mobility wing aircrafts from different design series in an intermediate maintenance company. Provided maintenance and logistical support for four organic and eight operational float aircraft and for Aviation Unit Maintenance (AVUM), Aviation Intermediate maintenance (AVIM), and supply facilities. Monitored the flow of repairable returns of critical, intensively managed or selected secondary items at collection points to assure timeliness of packing, preservation, and evaluation.

1992-94. Production Control Supervisor. U.S. Army, E Company, 3-51st 90 AVN, Stuttgart, Germany. Supervisor: LT. David J. Eisenhower (999) 999-9999. Advised personnel in diagnosing complex malfunctions and assisted in determining maintenance requirements while coordinating production and maintenance control for more than 198 refueling wing aircrafts. Assisted in preparation of work orders, recurring reports, and correspondence. Advised program managers on the feasibility of maintenance procedures required for prototype aircraft components. Represented command at Active Army, Reserve, and National Guard conferences and other top-level meetings to discuss operational and maintenance characteristics of systems.

1990-92. Aviation Maintenance Supervisor. U.S. Army, 1-385th Aviation Brigade. Ft. Carson, CO Supervisor: CPT Kent Warrick (111) 111-1111. Supervised 55 aviation maintenance personnel while directly overseeing intermediate maintenance for equipment valued at $6.3 million which included four organic Apache helicopters and ten float aircrafts. Determined maintenance requirements in order to ensure helicopters and associated equipment were repaired. Coordinated work assignments and assigned duties.

Highlights of earlier experience:
1988-90. OH-58 Crew Chief, U.S. Army, Fort Hood, TX.
1986-88. Recruiter, U.S. Army, Ft. Carson, CO.
1984-86. Battalion XO Driver, Korea.

EDUCATION Pursuing an **Associate of Science degree in General Studies**, Wichita State University, Wichita, KS.
Completed 44 semester hours, Wichita Community College, Wichita, KS, 2000.
Graduated from R. E. Shepherd High School, Wichita KS 1982.

SPECIALIZED TRAINING LICENSES CERTIFICATES 1994, Certificate Aviation Life Support Equipment Repair, 40 hours, Germany. Diploma, Senior Enlisted Advisor Course, Ft. Campbell, KY. 1994, Advanced Aviation Maintenance Course, Germany. 1989, Basic Aviation Maintenance Course, Ft. Stewart, GA. 1989, Apache Helicopter Repair Course, Ft. Stewart, GA.
1988, Primary Leadership Management Course, Ft. Hood, TX 1988.

LICENSES Commercial Drivers License – Class B with endorsements for double, triple trailer, tanker, hazardous material, passenger bus, and school bus.

AWARDS The Meritorious Service Medal (1997), The Army Commendation Medal (three awards – 1996, 1994, and 1993), The Army Achievement Medal (1999, 1997, and 1988).

CLEARANCE Secret security clearance

FEDERAL CRIMINAL INVESTIGATOR

JACK W. BRITT
SSN: 000-00-0000
84 Woodcreek Road
Indianapolis, IN 47953
Home: (999) 999-9999
Work: (888) 888-8888
Vacancy Announcement Number:

Country of Citizenship: U.S.A.
Veterans' Preference: 10-point
Reinstatement Eligibility: N/A
Highest Federal Civilian Grade Held: GS-12

SUMMARY

Offer well-developed planning and organizational abilities, natural leadership, supervisory experience, and a reputation as a skilled investigator and dedicated law enforcement professional with exceptional communication skills.

EXPERIENCE

FEDERAL CRIMINAL INVESTIGATOR. Department of Justice, Federal Investigation Division, 1522 W. Broad Street, Indianapolis, IN 47953 (2003-present).
Supervisor: Arnold McLaney, (777) 777-7777
Pay grade: GS-8
Hours worked per week: 50
Duties: Plan, organize, and conduct criminal and noncriminal investigations, performing mobile and stationary surveillance to observe the activities of individuals involved in the investigation. When sufficient evidence is obtained to justify such action, prepare requests for and obtain search warrants. Process crime scenes to obtain such physical evidence as latent fingerprints, hair and skin samples, fibers etc. Operate concealed cameras, audio and videocassette recorders, directional microphones, and other technical investigative aids. Conducted and documented interviews with victims, witnesses, and suspects, using learned interrogative techniques to obtain corroborative statements to support the physical evidence. Delivered sworn testimony before courts of law as well as in administrative hearings.

Prepare arrest warrants and other judicial actions. Obtain and serve arrest warrants, detaining and incarcerating criminal suspects in accordance with Federal and Indiana state laws. Collect and analyze criminal intelligence information obtained through interaction with other law enforcement agencies as well as through electronic means, to include the Internet. Build coalitions and perform liaison with other law enforcement agencies to facilitate the exchange of criminal intelligence between organizations, especially as related to matters which directly or indirectly affect the mission of the GSA. Have developed and currently maintain highly effective working relationships with Federal, State, and local law enforcement agencies in Indiana.
Accomplishments:
- Selected to serve as point/lead for Federal Investigation Division in Indiana, assuming many of the duties of a Supervisory Law Enforcement and Security Officer until that position is filled.
- Train and direct the assignment of all contract security personnel

for the entire state of Indiana, instructing them in the use of X-ray machines, magnetometers, and other electronic security equipment, as well as on FID policies and procedures.

- Successfully conducted a criminal investigation into the theft of thirteen pieces of South African Artwork which took place in January 2003, but was not reported to Federal Investigation Division until September 2004. Despite a 1 ½ year time lag between the commission of the crime and the beginning of the investigation, all of the stolen items were recovered and a suspect was identified and charged with felony theft of government property.
- Serve as a member of the Indiana Crime Prevention Group, the Northeast Criminal Intelligence Network, and the Eastern States Information Network.

LEAD FEDERAL INVESTIGATION DETECTIVE. Department of Justice, Federal Investigation Division, 8348 Denmark Hwy, Dallas TX 77456 (2000-03).
Supervisor: Richard D. Chandlier, (666) 666-6666
Pay grade: GS-7
Hours worked per week: 40
Duties: Supervised four or more Federal Investigation Detective per shift, overseeing their performance of the full range of law enforcement duties, including conducting initial and follow-up investigations, processing crime scenes to obtain physical evidence, and processing search and arrest warrants. Served as a Leader/Trainer and uniformed Federal Investigation Police Officer in the Federal Investigation Division, ensuring the safety and protecting the civil rights of individuals on Federal property owned or under the control of the GSA or one of its tenant agencies. Maintained order, preserved the peace, and protected Federally owned or controlled property. Conducted initial and follow-up investigations of reported thefts, burglaries, assaults, and threats, as well as instances of vandalism and narcotics violations. Interviewed victims, witnesses, and suspects during the investigative process.

FEDERAL INVESTIGATION POLICE OFFICER. Department of Justice, Federal Investigation Division, 1544 Desert Hill Road, Reno, NV 64106 (1998-00).
Supervisor: Norman G. Lancaster, (555) 555-5555
Pay grade: GS-5
Hours worked per week: 40
Duties: Served as a uniformed Federal Investigation Police Officer with the Department of Justice, Federal Investigation Division. Preserved the peace and prevented crime by providing a visible law enforcement presence through conducting mobile vehicular and foot patrols of the property. Served as designated shift commander in the absence of the Federal Police Sergeant or Federal Police Corporal, performing and supervising four or more Federal Investigation Police Officers per shift in performing the full range of law enforcement duties and responsibilities, to include conducting initial and follow-up investigations and processing crime scenes to obtain physical evidence. Interviewed victims, witnesses, and suspects during the investigative process, using proper interrogative techniques while obtaining and recording their statements. Prepared written reports documenting the findings and conclusions of my investigative efforts, which were then presented to the U.S. Attorney General's office to determine if the cases should be prosecuted.

POLICE OFFICER. Storey County Police Department, Patrol Division, 4860 Bain Avenue, Reno, NV 87588 (1995-98).
Supervisor: Tyrone D. Vandepool, (444) 444-4444
Pay grade: $1,950 per month
Hours worked per week: 40
Duties: While serving as a Patrol Officer with the Story County Police Department, I responded to all calls for assistance, conducting investigations of crimes which included

FEDERAL CRIMINAL INVESTIGATOR

thefts, burglaries, robbery, arson, assault, and rape. Protected the integrity of the crime scene, ensuring that no evidence was intentionally or inadvertently damaged, destroyed, or removed from the scene. Produced photographs, video recordings, and other visual documentation of the crime scene, using 35MM cameras and videocassette recorders. Processed crime scenes to locate and document such evidence as latent fingerprints, hair and skin samples, fibers, and other types of trace evidence for later use in court proceedings. Using learned interviewing techniques and interrogation practices, conducted and documented interviews with victims, witnesses, and suspects, obtaining corroborative statements to support the physical evidence. Frequently testified before a court of law, using proper courtroom demeanor and comporting myself with the dignity expected of my position as a law enforcement officer. Collected and processed lost or stolen property ranging from electronics equipment to motor vehicles. Apprehended and detained individuals suspected of violations of state and federal law, both felony and misdemeanor.

Highlights of earlier military experience: Was promoted ahead of my peers and advance to positions of increasing responsibility as a while serving my country in the U.S. Army, 1991-95:

TEAM SUPERVISOR. U.S. Army, 42nd Artillery/1st Bn, Fort Lewis, WA.
Supervisor: CPT Christopher M. Thomas (333) 333-3333
Pay grade: E-5
Hours worked per week: 40+
Duties: Managed up to nine personnel while leading and providing supervisory oversight and training to a nuclear weapons team. Oversaw training schedules for all personnel under my supervision, in addition to personally teaching some training courses. Provided both formal and informal counseling of employee performance, to ensure that each member of the team was fully proficient. Directed the personnel under my supervision in the assembly and disassembly of a small tactical nuclear device as well as leading the team on numerous training exercises.

EDUCATION & TRAINING

Bachelor of Science in **Criminal Justice**, with concentrations in **Sociology**, minor in **Correctional Administration**, University of Nevada Reno, Reno, NV 2000.
- Inducted into Kappa Lamda Nu, the Nevada Chapter of the National Criminal Justice Honor Society.

Completed numerous additional training and development courses at the Las Vegas Federal Law Enforcement Training Agency in Las Vegas, NV, which included:
- Advanced Physical Security Training Course, 120 hours, 1998.
- Data Recovery and Analysis Training Course, 80 hours, 1998.
- Financial Investigations Practical Skills Training Course, 80 hours, 1998.
- Nevada Basic Criminal Investigation Course, 240 hours, 1996.
- Nevada Basic Police Course, 160 hours, 1996.
- Criminal Intelligence Analyst Training Course, 180 hours, 1996.
- Nevada Personnel Security Adjudication Training Course, 60 hours, 1996.

Completed supervisory training courses sponsored by the GSA, Reno, NV, including:
- Supervising: A Guide for All Levels, 12 hours, 1995
- Constructive Discipline for Supervisors, 12 hours, 1995
- Nevada Basic Supervision Course, 18 hours, 1995

SPECIAL QUALIFICATIONS   Am a qualified Crime Scene Investigator.

AFFILIATIONS   Member, Association of Law Enforcement Professionals
Member, Leadership Development Organization

PERSONAL   Excellent personal and professional references are available upon request.

FOOD SERVICE MANAGER

TRAVIS KEITH EVANS
SSN: 000-00-0000
Mailing Address: 6522 Waterdown Drive, Huntsville, AL 44593
Home: (111) 111-1111
Work: (222) 222-2222

Vacancy Announcement Number:
Position and grade:
Country of Citizenship: U.S.A.
Veterans' Preference: 10-point
Highest Federal Civilian Grade Held: GS-07

EXPERIENCE

FOOD SERVICE MANAGER. 2002-present $12.50 per hour; 40+ hours per week. Ryan's Steak House, 4987 Haven Way Road, Huntsville, AL, Paula Gadson, Supervisor, phone: 333-333-3333. For a facility which services 275 people, assist in managing 13 cooks and up to 10 food prep workers. Also perform kitchen prep as needed. Also act as a Baker and Cook. When the Restaurant General Manager was out, I was in charge. From March 2002-August 2004, I acted as General Manager until a new Restaurant General Manager was assigned in August 2004.

- Coordinate and participate in inventory control operations, working in the warehouse and storeroom while unloading rations and storing them in the supply room.
- Sometimes work on the loading dock to unload and load food service supplies and equipment.

COOK–FD-0000-00. 1999-02. $11.45 per hour; 40 hours per week. Marshall County Hospital, 77441 Hillmon Drive, Huntsville, AL 44587. Callie Ross, Supervisor, 444-444-4444 Ext 555. Perform a variety of cooking and food service duties to support this major Huntsville medical facility. Received cash award recognizing dedication to my service during the relocation of the hospital in July.

- As a Warehouse Worker in a recent special project (September 2004), received a cash award for playing a major role in establishing a new warehouse for food service supplies and equipment. This project was in support of moving from the Old Marshall County Hospital to a totally new state-of-the-art medical center. Lifted heavy parcels routinely as we relocated to a new facility.
- In my capacity as a cook, also work in the warehouse and storeroom, unloading rations and storing them in the supply room, sometimes working on the loading dock to unload, load, and transport supplies.

FORKLIFT OPERATOR/LABORER. 1998-99. $7.85 per hour; 40 hours per week. Calhoun Distribution Center, 8434 Oxford Lane, Huntsville, AL 44593, Dean Harrison, Supervisor, phone: 555-555-5555. For a brief period of two months prior to accepting my current position, worked as a Warehouse Worker and Laborer at WAL-MART. Worked in the layaway department and assisted customers in obtaining goods.

- Operated a 2-1/2 ton vehicle and carried merchandise from the main store to the warehouse. Merchandise included such items as TVs, bicycles, furniture, stereo equipment, and appliances as well as other similar bulky and/or heavy items. Issued items to customers and assisted them in loading them.

Other experience in the US Army:
ASSISTANT DINING FACILITY MANAGER. E-6 1996-98. $26,460. 40 hours per week. U.S. Army, Dining Facility (DFAC), Special Forces, Fort Rucker, AL, SFC. Gavin Pringle, Supervisor, phone: 666-666-6666. For a facility which served 295 daily in two dining facilities provided leadership in staff in serving breakfast, lunch, and dinner. Managed 5 military and three civilian cooks. Acted as Manager of both facilities when the manager was on leave. Maintained accountability of foodstuffs.
- In my capacity as a dining facility manager, also coordinated and participated in inventory control operations, working in the warehouse and storeroom while unloading rations and storing them in the supply room. Sometimes worked on the loading dock to unload and load food service supplies and equipment.
- Performed allied work essential to bakery department operations such as assisting in the perpetual inventory of staple goods on hand in bakery storeroom and preparation of lists showing items and amounts needed for replenishment; stored bakery supplies in storeroom; stored leftover ingredients in proper places. Operated a motor vehicle to drive supplies as needed.
- Resigned in July 1998 because the post was scheduled to close in late 1998 by mandate of Congress, and I wanted to seek employment in the U.S. as a Cook or Baker or Food Service Manager.

COOK, NIGHT BAKER, AND SHIFT LEADER; MOTOR VEHICLE OPERATOR–FD-1913-533. E-5 1994-96. $23,000. 40 hours per week. U.S. Army, DFAC 3rd and 2nd Field Artillery, Fort Sill, OK. SSG Rick C. Grover, Supervisor, phone: 777-777-7777. Was a Cook and Shift Leader in a facility serving 210 people a day, and also worked in a major facility managing up to 22 cooks and food prep workers serving 420 customers daily.
- In recognition of my skills as a Motor Vehicle Operator, was honored with a Certificate of Achievement from the Commanding Officer in the Nicaragua in 1995. The award stated in part "his dedication to duties and constant care of his assigned vehicle, resulted in no accidents or vehicle breakdowns during his tenure at South American Ammunition Control."
- Operated a 2-1/2 ton vehicle in order to transport rations to various sites.
- Received a special award for leadership in helping this food service program become a finalist in the Commander Terrence Jakes Award for Excellence in Army Food Service. Received a Special Army Achievement Award in 1995.

MOTOR VEHICLE OPERATOR. FD-24-6877-85. E-4 1992-94. $19,000. 40 hours per week. U. S. Army, D Co. 233rd HHC Motor Pool, Fort Campbell, KY, SGT Lee R. Brown, Supervisor, phone: 888-888-8888. Operated a 2-1/2 ton vehicle while also providing assistance in fabricating Target Frames and Range Markers for Range facilities. Drove trucks in order to transport supplies to and from various warehouses and sites. Loaded and unloaded supplies from trucks. Assured cargo was properly loaded and secured and that maximum load capacity was not exceeded. Completed trip tickets and preventive maintenance service records. Filled out proper forms in case of an accident. Performed driver maintenance in accordance with established rules and regulations. Performed a variety of tasks in the receipt, storage, issue, and removal of supplies including picking up and tallying or counting items. Sorted items and stored them in the appropriate location. Moved items from one location to another in order to maintain prescribed stockage levels. Signed administrative forms which documented item counts. Assisted in maintaining and cleaning warehouse facilities and vehicles. Made sure the stockage of targets did not fall below a ten-day level. Replaced all broken wooden targets and frames within 24 hours of notification. Inspected range facilities daily for target frame serviceability. Was responsible for making minor repairs and maintaining pole ranges and signs. If any deficiencies were found, I provided concise information to my supervisor.

- Pulled proper (PMCS) operator maintenance on assigned daily vehicle daily before and after operation, and reported all deficiencies in writing to the Motor Pool Dispatcher.
- On a formal performance evaluation, was commended for my dedication an constant care of my vehicle. Maintained a perfect driving record and perfect safety records.
- Made sure the stockage of targets did not fall below a ten-day level. Replaced all broken wooden targets and frames within 24 hours of notification. Inspected range facilities daily for target frame serviceability. Was responsible for making minor repairs and maintaining pole ranges and signs. If any deficiencies were found, I provided concise information to my supervisor.
- Demonstrated the ability to exert strenuous physical effort in unloading, loading, and arranging materials and routinely handled items weighting more than 70 pounds and pushed carts weighing over 400 pounds.

FOOD SERVICE MANAGER

Highlights of other experience:
SHIFT LEADER & NIGHT BAKER SHIFT LEADER. E-5 1992.
NIGHT SHIFT BAKER. E-5 1991.
COOK, BAKER & RATION SUPERVISOR. E-4 1991.
SHIFT LEADER & BAKER. E-3 1990.
SHIFT LEADER & SHORT-ORDER COOK. E-2 1989.
BAKER & COOK. E-1 1988.

EDUCATION
Cooper Valley High School, Mobile AL, 1988.

LICENSES
Military driver's license, Civilian driver's license, Operate both electronic and gas forklifts of varying sizes. Am licensed to operate: up to 15-passenger sedans, station wagons, and vans. 4X2 and 4X4 vehicles

OTHER
Am a Bodybuilder and Weight Lifter. Work daily with weights. Can bench press 350 lbs. Work out at McKellar's Fitness Center.

DRIVING AWARD
Certificate of Appreciation in recognition of "dedication to duties and constant care of his assigned vehicle, resulted in no accidents or breakdowns" as was given by the Commanding Officer in Nicaragua, 1995.

AWARDS
Meritorious Service Medal. Army Achievement Medal, Good Conduct Medal (six) National Defense Service Medal, NCO Professional Development Ribbon (two) Army Service Ribbon, Overseas Service Ribbon (five), Special Act Award Certificate of Merit.

TRAINING
Completed 75 hours of food preparation training, Huntsville Technical Institute, Huntsville, AL, 2000. On the job training as Cook and Baker, 1992-1998.
- Primary Leadership Course.
- Food Service Course
- Intro to Food Service Course

PERSONAL
U.S. citizen.

MILDRED R. BROOKHART
2344 E. 7ᵗʰ Street
Lake Charles, LA 77287
Home: (111) 111-1111; **Work:** (222) 222-2222, ext. 333
SSN: 000-00-0000

Position Title/Series/Grade: Housing Manager, GS-0000-00
Announcement Number: DN-00-000
Veteran's Preference:

EDUCATION & TRAINING	Completed extensive training and continuing education which has included: **Computers:** Microsoft Excel for Windows, MS Word 6.0, Microsoft Office 2000, PowerPoint and Systems Administration **Leadership and Professional Development:** programs emphasizing human relations, interacting and communicating with the public, Managing for the 21ˢᵗ Century, problems and trends in local government administration **Housing Management and Real Estate:** professional housing management seminars, fundamentals of real estate, (licensed real estate salesperson), fair housing workshops, and seminars on Evictions and Landlord/Tenant Law **Personnel Administration:** personnel actions, recognizing the legal problems of migrant workers, preventive techniques in employment, sexual harassment, management development and coaching supervision, diversity in the workplace
EXPERIENCE	**HOUSING MANAGER.** Department of Housing and Urban Development, 2638 McCormick Blvd, Lake Charles, LA 77210 (2001-present). Starting salary: $17,860, ending salary: $38,900. Supervisor: Malcolm Bloomfield, (333) 333-3333, ext. 444. Provide referral services, housing information, and assistance to low income family members who are authorized to live in the supplemental housing community; assist with management of special projects.

- Receive, investigate, mediate, and resolve landlord/tenant complaints; represent the Department of Housing at Community Development meetings; communicate on a daily basis with realtors and landlords; gather data and prepare documentation for discrimination complaints; inspect property for adequacy.
- Communicate with legal professionals such as magistrates, the State Attorney General's Office, the Staff Judge Advocate (SJA), and with clients of various governmental agencies including state and federal agencies.
- Receive and investigate tenant complaints and coordinate actions with the appropriate housing staff and /or installation officials to include preparing eviction letters; conducting sanitation inspections and clearing of abandoned quarters.
- Process applicants and manage Section 8 waiting lists; maintain a wide range of records/ reports; prepare letters, and memoranda.
- Develop and present awareness and informational briefings to Public Housing Organizations nationwide.
- Maintain working knowledge of Section 8 and other related regulations, policies, and procedures pertaining to maintenance/repairs, inspections, eligibility, assignments, occupancy, and terminations.
- Work closely with Housing Authority of Lake Charles on renovation projects, maintenance and repairs, and related issues.
- Operate a data access terminal online in order to enter, retrieve, and modify data in the Public and Supplemental Housing Programs (PSHP).
- From Jun 01-Oct 03, handled additional duties as the monitor for mobile home park inspections; provided clerical support using MS Excel to maintain statistics, attended the Housing and Urban Development Control Board Meeting.
- From Jun 02-Feb 03, administered the Utility Deposit Waiver Program to include

establishing and administering records and weekly reports, processing applications and coordinating with the Lake Charles Public Works and five other utility companies, acting as liaison for bad debt collections, and identifying trends and making recommendations.

- From Jul 01-Mar 02, was detailed as Customer Service Representative with a focus on receiving, investigating, and resolving complaints on personnel housed in government quarters referred by staff, department directors, and customers. Represented Louisiana State Housing Division meetings and socials which included City Council Meetings and staff meetings. Researched, set up, and monitored employee customer care and image training. Initiated improvements to customer service and employee morale and comfort. Processed exceptions to policy, prepared eviction letters, conducted sanitation inspections, and responded to client inquiries, coordinating actions with appropriate with government and state officials. Was Project Officer/Editor for a bimonthly housing occupant bulletin which included preparing monthly reports. Evaluated customer feedback and recommended changes/solutions. Developed public awareness information articles, bulletins, and news releases for publication and presentation, coordinating with the Public Affairs Office when appropriate. Responded to Community Mayors and sponsoring unit representatives. Accompanied the Director of Public Housing and Advisor of the Urban Development on community inspection tours and prepared correspondence for the Director's signature mandating corrections of deficiencies noted. Attended Family Symposiums and prepared follow-up responses.
- Serve as Housing Representative on Housing and Urban Development Control Board.
- Member, Professional Urban Development Association (PUDA); served as Vice-President, Treasurer, Secretary and Committee Chairs.

DIRECTOR, JEFFERSON-DAVIS COUNTY HUMAN RELATIONS DEPARTMENT. Jefferson-Davis County, Lake Charles, LA 77212 (1997-01). Salary: $16,000. Supervisor: Eugene Paige, the present County Manager. Position with the county was equivalent to a GS-9/10 in the federal grade structure. Served as an advisor to county officials and local businesses on equal opportunity, human relations, and community issues, reducing conflict and tension among citizens and promoting equal rights; reported directly to the County Manager.

- Managed two employees and worked closely with a 14-person Advisory Commission and the Board of County Commissioners as the liaison for resolving problems.
- Applied analytical skills while mediating and sitting in on meetings to discuss disciplinary actions to be taken against county and local business employees.
- Evaluated and counseled employees; maintained time sheets/ personnel records.
- Prepared/administered the departmental budget; developed department objectives.

- Interviewed and counseled individuals and groups with complaints and investigated each situation to find solutions to problems relating to housing, employment, and credit (workmen's compensation, employee-employer disputes, discrimination), maintenance/repair, contaminated water supply, poor drainage, road repair problems and domestic disputes).
- Prepared and delivered presentations at schools, churches, civic clubs, seminars and on radio and TV talk shows; prepared news releases and articles on human relations issues and programs and publicized noteworthy endeavors.
- Represented the County Manager at statewide and local meetings and served as liaison with other state, county, and federal agencies as well as with the local businesses and the general population to include the Governor's Office, Department of Social Services, Jefferson-Davis Metropolitan Housing Authority, the Lake Charles Health Department, and other organizations involved in human relations/equal opportunity matters.
- Conducted surveys and compiled and analyzed statistics on human relations issues.
- Developed a personnel polices handbook for one local manufacturing company which was having serious personnel problems with disgruntled employees; management adopted benefit enhancements and less stringent requirements and was rewarded with higher production and lowered turnover and complaints.
- Developed and implemented community awareness workshops and training for local businesses and the local population; member of state and national Human Relations Associations, Lake Charles-Jefferson-Davis County Housing Task Force, Jefferson-Davis County Youth Needs, Legal Aid, and Law Enforcement Relations Committees.
- Developed contests held in county schools to include judging/awards criteria.

EDUCATION & HONORS

Associate of Arts degree in Business Management, McNeese State University, Lake Charles, LA, 1999.
Received numerous certificates of appreciation and achievement including:
Jefferson-Davis County Public Service Award, for work "above and beyond," 2002
Professional Customer Service Award, for exceptional customer service, 2002
Vice President's Certificate of Achievement for "commendable service," 2001
PUDA William P. Fenton Award, 2001
Plaque from Department of Housing and Urban Development for "unselfish and dedicated services," 1999-01
Exceptional Performance Appraisals, 1997-1998, and 1998-99, with monetary awards
Certificate from Governor Carlton E. McDaniels for "outstanding citizen involvement," 1997
Profiled in the March 1997 issue of the Louisiana Human Relations Council newsletter
Certificate, St. Peters Baptist Church for "meritorious human relations service," 1999.

PERSONAL

Offer a keen eye for detail and excellent organizational and interpersonal skills.

INFORMATION SYSTEMS ANALYST

WAYNE S. BALDWIN
E-mail: waynebaldwin@bellsouth.net

Current: 13745 Easterling Avenue, Los Angeles, CA 90744
(999) 999-9999

Permanent: 87 Volturno Road, Los Angeles, CA 90740
(888) 888-8888

OBJECTIVE To contribute to an organization that can benefit from my technical expertise and extensive training as well as my background of experience in network management.

EDUCATION TRAINING & CERTIFICATIONS Pursuing **Bachelor of Science** degree in **Management Information Systems (MIS)** in my spare time; have completed approximately two years of course work at California State University, Los Angeles, CA.
Excelled in training including computer technology courses as well as technical training in the following areas:
Introduction to LAN "Network Essentials"
Microsoft TCP/IP
Hands-on Windows NT 4.0
Windows NT Server 4.0
Microsoft PowerPoint 4.0
Harvard Graphics for Windows
Through training and experience, have become familiar with and knowledgeable of **network management** from bulletin board systems, to peer-to-peer networks, to a 250-user network.
Am skilled in client and server hardware/software system configuration and troubleshooting:
Operating systems: Windows 95, Windows NT Server 4.0, Windows NT Workstation 4.0, and TCP/IP
Administration: Windows NT 4.0 Server, Exchange Server 5.0 and 5.0 Enterprise, TCP/IP, and Internet Information Server 3.0
Applications: Microsoft Office 2000, FrontPage, Outlook, Internet Explorer 4.0, and FTP Explorer 3.0
Currently preparing to take the battery of tests leading to **Certification as a Microsoft Certified Systems Engineer.**

EXPERIENCE *Have earned a reputation as a technically proficient young professional in a "track record" of promotions with Tech Data:*
2004-present: INFORMATION SYSTEMS ANALYST. 7848 Andover Street, Los Angeles, CA 90244. Patricia Sullivan, Supervisor (777) 777-7777. Administer both local and wide-area networks valued in excess of $325,000 while supervising twelve people and managing the operations of secure e-mail and web server systems as an Information Systems Analyst.

- Have served as the **Senior Network Administrator** for an NT network which services approximately 250 users.
- Load and configure user systems for a LAN using Windows 95, Windows NT Workstation 4.0, TCP/IP, Internet Explorer 4.0, and Microsoft Outlook 98.
- Determine equipment and software needs; supervise user system configurations.

- Was a key contributor during the conversion to Windows NT 4.0 from a peer-to-peer system.
- Received an Outstanding Customer Service Award for my performance in supervising the operation of the Automation Help Desk during an international project.
- Was praised in writing for my strong customer service skills in diagnosing and resolving problems as the only mid-level manager assigned to the Tech Data Information Support Center.
- As a junior manager selected for a job usually reserved for a senior manager, was praised for "performing flawlessly" and for "accepting any challenge placed before her."

1996-04: INFORMATION SYSTEMS ANALYST and **TEAM LEADER.** 3283 Peachtree Blvd, Atlanta, GA 37553. Crystal Donnelly, Supervisor (888) 888-8888. Provided leadership for six people while applying my technical knowledge upgrading, maintaining, repairing, and installing new hardware and peripherals including hard drives, sound cards, video cards, memory, and modems.

- Converted a 375-system network from Windows 3.11 to Windows 95 and then to Windows NT while also assisting with 1,500 systems with their upgrades.
- Installed a variety of software applications as well as troubleshooting and resolving conflicts with hardware and software.
- Supervised help desks both locally and national through network systems to ensure customer satisfaction.
- Earned recognition for my professionalism in ensuring uninterrupted LAN service support for 75 users during a 1998 training exercise.
- Received an Outstanding Performance Award for my support in installing and operating a 375-system network for a numerous million dollar accounts with local and national organizations.

PERSONAL   Entrusted with a Secret security clearance with Top Secret pending.

LAW ENFORCEMENT TRAINING COORDINATOR

FRANK P. IVEY

P.O. Box 5555

Miami, FL 11111-1111

Day: (555) 555-5555

Evening: (111) 111-1111

SSN: 000-00-0000

Announcement No: 123456-1234

Position: Highway Safety Specialist GS-0000-00

LAW ENFORCEMENT TRAINING COORDINATOR

This civilian law enforcement officer seeks an executive position in the federal government.

OBJECTIVE

To serve the National Highway Traffic Safety Administration as a Highway Safety Specialist through my demonstrated knowledge of criminal justice systems and traffic law enforcement as well as through my vast experience in developing, evaluating, and administering highway safety programs, vehicle safety systems, and other safety programs.

PUBLICATIONS

Currently responsible for the development, evaluation, revision, and marketing of the following publications:

The Specialized Driver Training Instructors' Manual

RADAR Operator Manual

Time-Distance Operator Manual

Law Enforcement Driver Training Curriculum for Basic Law Enforcement Training (1997 and 1999 draft)

SUMMARY OF EXPERIENCE

In the following track record of career advancement, have earned a reputation as one of the leading experts in Florida in program administration work concerned with highway, traffic, motor vehicle safety, accident/injury prevention, and public safety programs related to both the criminal justice system and the traffic law enforcement system; on a daily basis am utilizing my written and oral communication skills as well as my ability to plan, budget for, implement, and administer criminal justice or traffic enforcement operational programs. At national levels, am widely regarded as an expert in the development and administration of community highway or related safety programs, especially as pertaining to the licensing and training of motor vehicle operators.

EXPERIENCE

LAW ENFORCEMENT TRAINING COORDINATOR. Florida Department of Justice, Attorney General's Office, 8322 Palau Street, Miami, FL, 33344, John Griffin, Supervisor, phone: (111) 111-1111. (2002-present). Am responsible for program development and implementation of programs related to the criminal justice system and traffic law enforcement and handle key responsibilities in these and other areas:

Technical Assistance: Ensure that technical assistance is accurate and conforms to currently accepted practices; keep the Florida Justice Academy, Criminal Justice Training Standards and Sheriffs' Standards

Divisions and their staff informed on issues which have impact on the speed enforcement and driver training.

Course Coordination: Ensure that training environment is appropriately organized and that students' training needs are appropriately facilitated while coordinating the following courses:

    Specialized Driver Training Instructor Course

    RADAR Instructor Training Course

    Criminal Justice TD/SMI Instructor Training Course

    Re-Certification Training for RADAR Instructors

    Re-Certification Training for TD/SMI Instructors

    Driver Training Modules

Development: Ensure that curricula are job-related and applicable, reflect current information and practices, employ appropriate training methodology, and accurately measure student achievement while developing or redeveloping courses including: RADAR Instructor Training, Criminal Justice TD/SMI Instructor Training Course, and In-Service Driver Training Course; assess additional RADAR TD/SMI and law enforcement driver training needs and resources.

Teaching: Ensure that materials are applicable and job-related while instructing in: Specialized Driver Training Instructor Course, RADAR Instructor Training Course, Criminal Justice TD/SMI Instructor Training Course, Re-Certification for RADAR Instructors, Re-Certification Training for TD/SMI Instructors, and Driver Training Modules.

- Develop, evaluate, coordinate, and deliver training programs to law enforcement officers throughout FL seeking certification to instruct in driver training programs conducted within the state.
- Prepare program materials and translate enforcement issues into cohesive programs which are understood, accepted, and utilized by the law enforcement community.
- Provide guidance to develop, promote, and market program concepts and materials for use by law enforcement leaders, national associations, and state and local governments.
- Gather the results of program findings and evaluations and incorporate these findings into materials which can be used in functional areas of police traffic services.
- As School Director for the Florida Justice Academy's Specialized Driver Instructor Training Course, have trained more than 350 officers currently certified as Specialized Driver Instructors.
- Have developed and implemented a revised driver training curriculum for the Basic Law Enforcement Training Program which increased the training of basic recruits from 16 hours to 44 hours while also mandating training in emergency response and pursuit driving.
- Am School Director for the Academy's RADAR and Time-Distance Instructor Training Courses, and am responsible for development, revision, coordination, and delivery of training for law enforcement officers seeking certification to instruct in RADAR and Time-Distance Operator Training courses in the state (have personally trained all of the approximately 150 current instructors).
- Am staffed to the Florida Criminal Justice Education and Training Standards Commission, and am responsible for monitoring RADAR and Time-Distance Instructor and Operator Training curriculums.
- Since 2004, have planned and budgeted for more than 40 separate programs; during a normal year, am simultaneously budgeting for and administering more than 10 separate programs, which are mandated by the Criminal Justice Commission.
- Am proud of the contributions I have made to highway safety in FL; am indirectly responsible for every speeding ticket written in the state since 2003 because of my leadership in the RADAR program. Am also proud of the reduction in collisions projected to occur because of the revised and improved Driver Training Program which I am largely responsible for.

PRESIDENT. Dunlap Independent, Florida Department of Justice, Attorney General's Office, 945 Sycamore Lane, Tallahassee, FL, 33344, Maxwell Tookes, Supervisor, phone: (222) 222-2222. (1998-02). Served as an independent traffic accident/collision reconstruction consultant and training coordinator.

INSTRUCTOR/COORDINATOR. Florida Department of Justice, Florida Justice Academy, 2299 Breezewood Hwy, Tallahassee, FL 32585, Jason Greenburg, Supervisor, phone: (333) 333-3333. (1995-1998). Was responsible for coordination and instruction of training programs to law enforcement officers throughout Florida.

- Submitted training budgets for approval, and became known for my resourcefulness in stretching training dollars to their maximum effectiveness.
- Selected instructors to assist in training courses; formulated and revised lesson plans.
- Served on advisory committees for training programs such as the Basic Law Enforcement Training Course mandated by the Training and Standards Division of the Florida Department of Justice.
- Served as President for the Florida Law Enforcement Training Officers Association, responsible for providing training programs to law enforcement trainers throughout the state.
- Acted as a consultant to law enforcement agencies concerning administration and training.

TROOPER. Florida Department of Crime Control and Public Safety, Division of State Highway Patrol, 1561 Eastern Blvd, Tallahassee, FL 32445, Michael Brisbane, Supervisor, (444) 444-4444. (1988-1995). Excelled in these varied assignments:

- **April-September 1995** assigned to Jefferson County. Patrolled state highways within assigned area to monitor traffic, to arrest or warn persons guilty of violating motor vehicle law, criminal law, or safe driving practices; provided road information and assistance to motorists; directed traffic in accident or disaster areas and at special events, such as races and ball games; rendered emergency medical treatment to injured; investigated conditions and causes of accidents and prepared written reports; performed general police work by keeping order and apprehending criminals; appeared in court as witness in traffic violation and criminal cases; maintained records and reports of activities; spoke to civic organizations and school groups concerning programs supported by the highway patrol; broadcast taped and live radio safety announcements for the Governor's Highway Safety Program.
- **February-March 1995** assigned to Leon County: Performed the same duties as those mentioned above.
- **August-January 1994** assigned as **PHYSICAL TRAINING INSTRUCTOR**, Highway Patrol Training Center, Tallahassee, FL: Instructed newly employed cadets in accordance with training schedules and orders; oriented cadets in fundamentals of physical fitness, discipline, pride, and loyalty to patrol; trained cadets in close order drills and in care and use of equipment and uniforms;

instructed cadets in physical training and provided guidance in areas of dietary needs and weight training; secondary instructor in areas of defensive tactics, accident investigations, firearms, riot control, and vehicle operations; made daily inspections of cadets' personal appearance and living quarters; evaluated test results and performances of cadets and prepared performance evaluation reports.

- **March 1992-June 1994** assigned to **GOVERNOR'S SECURITY.** Governor's Mansion, Tallahassee, FL: Provided personal security and transportation for governor and first family; screened visitors and phone calls received at mansion; provided inter- and intrastate security and coordinated travel arrangements including transportation, lodging, and social functions; supervised housekeeping and grounds maintenance staff; maintained surveillance of mansion grounds; provided security of national and international VIPs.
- **August 1988-February 1992** assigned Wakulla County. Performed the same duties as those mentioned above.
- **April-May 1988**. Cadet. 82nd Basic Patrol, Highway Patrol Training Center, Tallahassee, FL.

PATROLMAN. Town of Shadeville, Shadeville Police Department, 2784 Mountain Drive, Shadeville, FL 30745, Daniel Carter, Supervisor, (555) 555-5555. (1987-88). Patrolled streets of city assisting motorists, investigating accidents and violations of criminal law. Enforced Federal, State and Local Laws. General and crime prevention duties.

TELECOMMUNICATOR. County of Wakulla, Wakulla County Sheriff's Department, 3895 Heyward Blvd, Crawfordville, FL 30568, Albert Lincoln, Supervisor phone: (666) 666-6666 (1985-87). Received and dispatched calls for Sheriff's Department, local police departments, county fire and rescue squads while also operating the Police Information Network Terminal. Worked with Dade County Ambulance Service in off-duty hours.

Other experience: NAPA Auto Parts, 3782 Goldboro Street, Crawfordville, FL 30854, Anthony Taylor, Supervisor, (777) 777-7777. (1982-1985).
- From 1984-85 as **Parts Manager**, maintained sales records, verified cash receipts, confirmed customer's credit references, and hired, trained, and supervised employees.
- From 1983-84 as **Sales Representative**, contacted prospective customers to promote sale of company equipment and services.
- In 1983 as **Internal Sales Representative**, sold or rented equipment to walk-in customers, arranged financing, and resolved complaints.
- From 1982-83 as **Parts Clerk**, sold auto parts and equipment from behind the counter.
- In 1982 as **Shipping and Receiving Clerk**, unloaded incoming merchandise from trucks and directed outgoing shipments via various carriers to their destinations.

EDUCATION

B.A. degree, **cum laude**, in Justice and Public Policy, Florida State University, Tallahassee, FL, 2000.
A.A.S. degree in Criminal Justice, Tallahassee Community College, Tallahassee, FL, 1996.

TRAINING

Have completed approximately 2500 hours of law enforcement related training (certifications available upon request); since there are too many training programs to list them all, following are *highlights* of significant training programs in various locations which have greatly refined my knowledge, skills, and abilities related to highway traffic safety:
- Standardized Field Sobriety Testing Instructor Training, Georgia State Justice Academy, (March 15-19, 2002), 40 hours.
- Traffic Accident Investigation Reconstruction II, Law Enforcement School, University of Florida (12-5-98), 40 hours.
- Traffic Accident Investigation Reconstruction II, Law Enforcement School, University

of Florida (11-30-98), 80 hours.

- Vehicle Dynamics, Law Enforcement School, University of Florida (7-20-98), 40 hours.
- Technical Accident Investigation, Law Enforcement School, University of Florida (7-14-98), 80 hours.
- At-Scene Accident Investigation, Law Enforcement School, University of Florida (6-25-98), 80 hours.
- Traffic Accident Reporting, Florida Governor's Highway Safety Program (5-16-90) 7 hours.
- Tallahassee 82nd Basic Patrol, Highway Patrol Training Center (July 1989) 711 hours.
- Basic Law Enforcement Training, Ian V. Burgess Technical Institute (March 1988) 160 hours.

**LAW ENFORCEMENT
TRAINING COORDINATOR**

**AFFILIATIONS
&
CERTIFICATIONS** Certified as a law enforcement officer with the Florida Criminal Justice Education and Training Standards Commission; currently sworn with the FL State Capitol Police as an auxiliary officer. Certified by the Florida Criminal Justice Education and Standards Commission as a:

Criminal Justice School Director
General Instructor
Specialized Driver Instructor
Specialized Firearms Instructor
Specialized Defensive Tactics Instructor
Specialized Physical Activities Instructor
Specialized Hazardous Materials Instructor
Specialized Emergency Medical Instructor
Specialized Electronic Speed-Measuring Instrument Instructor
Certified as an Emergency Medical Technician by the Office of Emergency Medical Services.
Certified as a Traffic Accident Investigation and Reconstruction Consultant by the Law Enforcement School, University of Florida, Gainesville, FL.

- Am accepted as an expert for the purpose of rendering opinions in the area of traffic accident investigations and reconstruction by the Courts of Florida.

MEMBERSHIPS Member since 2000, International Association of Law Enforcement Professionals.

- Served as Chair of a committee reviewing the association's bylaws.

Member since 1996, Florida Law Enforcement Officers Association.

- Served as Director for District I representing law enforcement officers from 25 eastern FL counties; served on Legislative Committee and Bylaws Committee.

Member since 1995, Southern Florida Association of Law Enforcement Officers.

- Served as President 2000-02 and, during my term, membership more than doubled from 200 to 500 members; established new standing committees and revised bylaws.

Consultant, National Highway Traffic Safety Administration's Highway Traffic Safety Division.

- Have played a key role in the revision of the speed measuring instrument instructor and operator training program; Served as member and subject matter expert on numerous task forces of the National Highway Traffic Safety Administration.

- Member of the task force responsible for developing a nationally recommended training curriculum for the RADAR Speed Measuring Instrument Instructor Training; served as subject matter expert in the development and production of this model training curriculum.
- Member of the task force that developed the nationally recommended RADAR Speed Measuring Instrument Operator Training curriculum.
- Member of the task force that developed a nationally recommended training curriculum for the Time-Distance Speed Measuring Instrument Operator Training.
- Member of the task force that developed a nationally recommended training curriculum for the SMIOT (laser) Speed Measuring Instrument Operator Training; served as subject matter expert in the development and production of this model training curriculum and recertification process.
- Member, *Florida Department of Transportation, Division of Motor Vehicles' Collision Report Form (DMV349) Committee;* was subject matter expert in providing the Division of Motor Vehicles' Administration with advice and experience for determining the structure and format of the form used to collect data from law enforcement officers investigating motor vehicle traffic accidents.

PERSONAL   Am a citizen of the U.S. Can provide numerous letters of recommendation which will attest to my excellence in every facet of professional responsibility as well as my meticulous regard to detail. Take great pride in the contributions I have made to highway safety in FL and our nation, and wish to contribute to the state of Florida at even higher levels of responsibility. Am known for absolute integrity.

LEAD SHIPMENT CLERK

LUCY BALLARD
5541 Vardaman Lane, Lawton, OK 87415
(111) 111-1111
SSN: 000-00-0000
E-mail: luceyballard@cs.com

Position, Title, Series, Grade:
Announcement Number:
Veteran's Preference:

LEAD SHIPMENT CLERK

TRAINING   Pursuing a **Bachelor of Arts degree** in **Business Administration,** Cameron University, Lawton, OK.
Receive continuous and ongoing training in the areas of Principles of Management and Customer Service.
Attended a Human Relations Course, Tulsa Community College, 1999, which emphasized methods for improving customer service.
Attended the Joint Personal Property Course given sponsored by Global Van Lines Training Center, 2001.

COMPUTERS   Fully knowledgeable and proficient with Microsoft Word, Excel, PowerPoint, and PageMaker.

EXPERIENCE   **LEAD SHIPMENT CLERK.** Global Van Lines, 9477 Adrian Hwy, Lawton, OK 87415 (2002-present). Supervisor: Simon D. Baker, (222) 222-2222. Counsel customers who include military and civilians while providing guidance, information, and assistance related to shipping entitlements; solve problems pertaining to scheduling, missent shipments, or lost shipments in a job which requires strong customer relations and communication skills.

- Coordinate arrangements for outbound shipments to anywhere in the U.S. and well as to foreign countries worldwide.
- Remain aware of all applicable regulations for shipping and storing household goods as well as privately owned vehicles, pets, mobile homes, weapons, unaccompanied baggage, and hazardous items.
- Review documentation to ensure authorization is valid and then assist the customer in filling out inventory forms while also informing them of weight restrictions, schedules, and of their responsibilities for preparing for services.
- Prepare paperwork for shipments of personal property which are at other installations and forward documents to the proper facility.
- Respond to mail applications; prepare correspondence, gather information, and determine how to process the application or forward it to another facility.
- Assist customers returning from oversees and in processing the release of their stored household goods and their delivery.
- Handle the difficult briefings for owners of mobile homes which require extensive preparation before shipping and often result in problems due to overloading or utility hook ups.
- Advise customers concerning various moving procedures and counsel them on equipment requirements and other entitlements once the move is completed.
- Interview customers with damage claims against the government and inform them of their rights for reimbursement.

- Operate automated systems while preparing paperwork required to complete all phases of my duties including correspondence and applications.

LEAD SHIPMENT CLERK. AAA Storage Co. Inc., 52153 Chateau Drive, Lawton, OK 87408 (1998-02). Supervisor: Joseph Wooten, (444) 444-4444. Originally hired as a storage manager for AAA Storage Co, Inc., an Interstate Agent for Global Van Lines. Advanced to supervise five counselors and train all new personnel on policies and procedures; was sought out for my guidance as well as my knowledge of transportation and customer service.

- Was evaluated as being skilled in assessing the skills of personnel and in fairly and equally dividing the work load so that the office ran smoothly and provided fast and efficient customer service.
- Reviewed orders and shipment files while utilizing and interpreting Federal Travel Regulations.
- Responded to problems by analyzing applicable directives and then counseled customers on any exceptions to policy on such areas as excess weight, extension of shipping entitlements, shipment or replacement of POV (personally owned vehicle), and nontemporary storage.
- Counseled customers and ensured they understood their responsibilities in cases of excess weight or unauthorized items and how to provide proper rebuttal if excess weight costs were requested.
- Maintained records and reports using the ORACLE database system to maintain and prepare logs, files, and statistics; prepared the monthly statistical report for the management review.
- Acted as the Territory Manager which called for me to make monthly visits to other AAA Storage facilities and provide brief and concise guidance on shipping household goods and POVs at retirement and separation briefings.
- Made reports to the supervisor regarding performance progress, training needs, and any instances of unsatisfactory performance or actions requiring disciplinary action; also advised supervisory personnel on issues related to employee promotions, and reassignments and of personnel worthy of recognition for outstanding performance.

Highlights of earlier experience:

Accounting Technician. Geico, Colorado Springs, CO (1997-98). Operated a visual display terminal (VDT) while performing a variety of functions related to maintaining and processing accounting documents and reports. Verified and reconciled cash reports, reconciled discrepancies; prepared insurance claim documents; made bank deposits; initiated adjustment reviews; ensured security for cash, and fixed assets.

Sales Associate. Walmart, Colorado Springs, CO (1995-1997). Provided customer service; operated a cash registers, stocked and displayed incoming merchandise.

Customer Service Clerk. Mountain Valley Goods, Inc, Colorado Springs, CO (1994-1995). Processed mail orders for men's clothing and accessories to include keeping records, selecting items, and preparing documentation of each order.

HONORS
Received numerous Customer Service Awards for Exceptional Performance each year from Global Van Lines, 2004.
Honored with a Certificate of Customer Service Excellence from Mountain Valley Goods (October 1995).

LANGUAGES
Speak Spanish fluently.

PERSONAL
Outstanding personal and professional references upon request. Strong work ethic.

LICENSED PRACTICAL NURSE

CECILIA N. STEINBERG
9546 Nathatch Road
Bloomfield, MI 53524
(999) 999-9999
E-mail: cnsteinberg@msn.com

SSN: 000-00-0000
Date of Birth: March 28, 1969
Country of Citizenship: United States
Highest Federal Civilian grade held, job series, and dates of employment in grade:
Vacancy Announcement Number: BC-000-00-0000
Position Title and Grade: Nurse, GS-00-000-000

LICENSED PRACTICAL
NURSE

EXPERIENCE

2002-present. **LICENSED PRACTICAL NURSE.** Craig-Hutton OB/GYN Medical Clinic, 8744 Arabello Road, Bloomfield, MI 53525. Salary: $12.50 per hour. Supervisor: Carla Mitchell, 888-888-8888. Currently employed with this private practice as a **Medical Assistant** in 2002, and was asked to continue my employment even after I became a Licensed Practical Nurse in 2003. Provide assistance to physicians during examinations while providing patient care, counseling, and support. Carry out a therapeutic plan of care in cooperation with general supervision of a Registered Nurse based on the national Nursing Standards of Care to include evaluation, monitoring, and intervention (physical, emotional, and social aspects). Am continuously involved in patient education activities which included collection of data. Oversee patient safety while maintaining, supporting, and preserving a safe environment. Provide for patient comfort and mental well-being. Am knowledgeable of patient rights and assure that patients' rights were preserved and protected. Promote effective customer service and customer relations and adhere to advanced medical directives per hospital protocols. Document nursing process, patient status, care, and services. Assist with invasive and non-invasive procedures. Clean work areas, instruments, and equipment after use. Perform/assist with the collection of laboratory specimens and other samples as required. Label specimens appropriately and dispatch specimens to lab. Obtain blood specimens by venipuncture. Test specimens and urine for sugar and acetone; test blood for glucose monitoring; and test specimens for occult blood. Start IVs; monitor maintenance intravenous infusion. Initiate cardiopulmonary resuscitation in emergency situations. Administer prescribed medications based upon a practical knowledge of the effects upon the physiological process of the patient's condition. Triage patients. Take vital signs. Supervise chart completion. Phone in prescriptions. Maintain sterile conditions, and drape and position patients. Set up and maintain special medical equipment and apparatus.

Accomplishments:
* Became respected for my medical knowledge as well as my strong communication skills, and answered a large volume of calls relating to patient problems.
* Excelled in working with other nurses on a team in order to provide high quality patient care and to develop a consensus about the best decisions related to patient care. Became skilled in applying textbook knowledge in clinical environments.

- Gained vast knowledge of obstetrical and gynecological issues and procedures.

Clinical rotations:

2001-02 (six months): **NURSING HOME NURSE.** Addison Nursing Home, 5436 Meadowview Lane, Bloomfield, MI 53526. Salary: N/A. Supervisor/Instructor: Angela Lambert, Phone (777) 777-7777. While completing my nursing degree, completed two clinical rotations which immersed me in geriatric nursing.

2001: (three months): **HOSPITAL NURSE.** Bloomfield Medical Hospital, 1747 Kenniston Road, Bloomfield, MI 53527. Salary: N/A. Supervisor/Instructor: Dana Medford, Phone: (666) 666-6666. Completed a three-month clinical rotation in this hospital, and gained experience related to Med-Surg, Obstetrics, and the Infant Nursery.

2000: (six weeks): **HOSPITAL NURSE.** Xavier Hospital, 3625 Fargo Road, Bloomfield, MI 53528. Salary: N/A. Supervisor/Instructor: Brian Patten, Phone: (555) 555-5555. Completed a six-week clinical rotation in this hospital, and gained experience related to Med-Surg.

1999: (two week): **DIALYSIS NURSE.** Northeastern Dialysis, 2632 Wedge View Avenue, Bloomfield, MI 53529. Salary: N/A. Supervisor/Instructor: William Gordon, Phone: (444) 444-4444. Completed a two week observation and gained insight into the specific nursing practices and procedures required in a dialysis center.

1996-1999: **TELLER II AND BACK-UP HEAD TELLER.** Bank of America, 4890 Hagen Boulevard, Bloomfield, MI 53530. Salary: $9.00 per hour. Supervisor: Heather Miller, (333) 333-3333. Received an award for my exceptional customer service skills, and was frequently commended for my nurturing attitude and cheerful disposition as I processed monetary transactions and expertly performed a variety of functions within the bank.

1995-1996: **SALES SUPERVISOR.** Added Dimensions, Hickory Ridge Mall, 3837 Drury Lane, Bloomfield, MI 53531. Salary: $8.00 per hour. Supervisor: Alfreda Davidson, (222) 222-2222. Hired, trained, and managed five employees while scheduling employees for work.

1993 and 1995: **CLERK.** Department of Housing and Urban Development, 3928 Leaflet Drive, Bloomfield, MI 53532. Salary: $6.00 per hour. Supervisor: David Taylor, (111) 111-1111. As a GS-03 Clerk, answered a heavy volume of phone calls while filing and handling confidential documents and making appointments for clients to reserve housing. Printed housing lists and acted as Assistant Secretary for the Housing Manager.
Accomplishments: Refined telephone and other communication skills as I handled customer enquiries and liaison with officials involved in providing housing for qualified families.

EDUCATION   Received Diploma in Practical Nursing, Oakland Community College, 7847 Anderson Street, Bloomfield, MI 53524; 2003.
Earned Associate Degree in Education, Oakland Community College, 7847 Anderson Street, Bloomfield, MI 53524; 2000.
Graduated from E.V. Thompson High School, 717 Coachway Road, Bloomfield, MI 53530, 1992.

LICENSE   Licensed as a Practical Nurse in Michigan, Certificate No. 1234567; Expiration June 30, 2005.

HONORS & AWARDS   Elected Class President, Licensed Practical Nurse Program, Oakland Community College, 2002-03.
Employee of the Month Award, Bank of America, Bloomfield, MI, 1998.

MEDICAL CLERK

SHANNON R. TROY
8521 Broughton Blvd
Grayslake, IL 41847
Home: (888) 888-8888
Work: (999) 999-9999

ANNOUNCEMENT NUMBER: 00-000-00
POSITION TITLE: Safety and Occupational Health Specialist
GRADE: GS-00
SOCIAL SECURITY NUMBER: 000-00-0000
CITIZENSHIP: U.S.

OBJECTIVE

I want to offer my knowledge of Safety and Occupational Health, knowledge of automation (software and operating systems), as well as my ability to communicate orally and in writing.

EDUCATION & TRAINING

Associate of Science degree in **General Studies.**
Associate of Science degree in **Laboratory and X-ray Technology.**
Basic Medical Specialist Course, eight weeks, 2004.
Race Relations/Equal Opportunity Course, four weeks, 2004.
Occupational Health and Safety Seminar, four weeks, 2003.

COMPUTERS

Knowledgeable of software including: Microsoft Word, Excel, and Access; Internet Explorer;
Outlook Express; numerous specialized software programs related to the medical field.

HONORS

Have been singled out for numerous honors and awards including the Good Conduct Medal, Meritorious Service Medal, three U.S. Army Commendation Medals; Peacetime Service Medal from duty in Panama; Humanitarian Service Medal, and eight Army Achievement Medals; National Defense Service Medal; US Army Training Ribbon; Noncommissioned Officer's Professional Development Ribbon; Army Service Ribbon; US Army Longevity Service Medal.

EXPERIENCE

MEDICAL CLERK. Lake County Medical Hospital, 6584 Southern Avenue, Grayslake, IL 41847 (2003-present). Hours per week: 40+. Supervisor: Katherine Swanson phone: 777-777-7777. Handle a variety of responsibilities in this administrative position which requires me to apply my extensive knowledge of safety and health program elements while continuously applying safety and occupational health standards, regulations, practices, and procedures to eliminate or control potential hazards.
Front desk duties: When patients arrive at the Emergency Room, am responsible for processing them and then direct them to appropriate personnel, usually the Triage Nurse or the fast-track process.
Monitoring public health and safety: Provide oversight of cleaning crews and alert them to the need to immediately clean and disinfect rooms after patients have been treated who have communicable diseases; most recently meningitis has been a problem.

Automation: Utilize a computer to inprocess patients; input patient data into a database and code medical information according to information provided by doctors and nurses.

SALES ASSOCIATE. Books-A-Million, Grayslake Mall, 2574 Habertown Road, Grayslake, IL 41836 (2002-03). Hours per week: 40+. Supervisor: Allison Kindred, phone: 666-666-6666. Assisted customers in selection and purchase of books. Audited inventory for reorders.

Other experience in the U. S. Army:
COMMUNICATIONS MANAGER. 437th Medical Group, Fort Stewart, GA (1999-2002). Hours per week: 40. Supervisor: Colonel Earl Borris, phone: 444-444-4444. For the Medical Group, was responsible for the procurement, storage, and security of automation, communications, and security equipment. Played a key role in the supervision of the brigade security force which protected sensitive signal sites. Was directly responsible for all communication equipment utilized all medical units on the southeast coast, including Hawaii, and by the Winn Army Hospital. Maintained constant liaison with all departments and clinics to ensure adequate signal support. Applied safety and occupational health standards and regulations in controlling potential hazards.

SECURITY MANAGER & COMMUNICATIONS NCO. U.S. Army, 83rd Med Comm, Fort Sam Houston, TX (1996-1999). Supervisor: Lt. Montrell C. Jordan, phone: 333-333-3333. Was Security Manager and Communications NCO for the 2,900-person battalion. Supervised installation and operation of all signal support systems to include local area networks (LANs), tactical radios, records management, an audiovisual system support and automation. Personally purchased $315,000 in computers and communications equipment.

Highlights of other U.S. Army experience:
Military Intelligence: During the Gulf War, served as an **Intelligence Analyst** and was responsible for the supervision of 75 personnel in installing and setting up all communications equipment wiring during Operation Desert Shield. Interfaced with foreign allied authorities in the setup and operation of equipment.
Military Police: Served in various security assignments including performing duty as monitor for joint intrusion detection systems for 30 high-security sites storing classified documents and weapons storage facilities at Fort Benning, GA. Also performed as Access Control Guard for high-level officer training courses; maintained accountability and security related to badges and access control devices. Maintained accountability of keys. Enforced physical security policies. Performed military police patrol duties and enforced military laws. Maintained statistical data for the Lieutenant Commander, and assisted in the crime prevention program.
Nursing and Occupational Health and Safety: Because of my strong management skills, was selected to take control of a disorganized medical facility at Ft. Rucker, AL which was experiencing a variety of control problems, including problems related to public safety and occupational health. Trained employees, rewrote Standard Operating Procedures (SOPs), and managed 25 people operating a medical outpatient facility serving a population of 1,250.

MILITARY TRAINING
Advanced Noncommissioned Officer Course, 19 weeks, 2002.
Battalion Training Management Course, 3 weeks, 2002.
Communications Security Course, two weeks, 2002
Health and Safety Course, two weeks, 2001.
Instructor Training, two weeks, 2001.
US Army Computer Science School, Local Area Network Training, 10 weeks, 1999.
Telecommunications Center Operator Course, 10 weeks, 1999.

CLEARANCE
Was entrusted with a **Top Secret security clearance.**

NURSE/LIAISON

RUBY U. DARLINGTON, BSN
8515 Windsor Avenue
Fairfield, CT 04455
888-888-8888 H
777-777-7777 W
SSN: 000-00-0000
Source: EXT

Highest Grade Held: N/A
Vacancy Announcement Number: 00000000
Position Title: Nurse (Various Specialties) (GS-0000)

EXPERIENCE

NURSE/LIAISON.
Start and End Dates: March 2004-present
Hours worked per week: 40+
Current Salary: $42,000 per year
Employer's Name and Address: Sacred Heart Medical, 2494 Walden Street, Fairfield, CT 04455
Supervisor's Name and Phone Number: Kevin Hopper, 888-888-8888

Manage a project which included completing clinical assessments of patents based on referrals in order to determine their placement into long-term, assist living, domiciliary, intermediate, or rest home-level care. Make determinations of financial feasibility. Determine the level of care needed and coordinate all phases of services required by each patient.

- Am credited with increasing community awareness of the assisted living option while educating patients and families.
- Work with discharge planners and case managers to form accurate assessments.
- Conduct outreach to local physicians and am in constant touch with 12 different offices.

HOSPICE COORDINATOR.
Start and End Dates: April 2001- March 2004
Hours worked per week: 40+
Salary: $36,500 per year
Employer's Name and Address: St. Joseph Hospice Care, 12900 Bullard Ave, Fairfield, CT
Supervisor's Name and Phone Number: Ryan Cullen, 777-777-7777.

Coordinated patient care services for the Hospice care portion of the hospital's programs. Supervised three registered nurses, three home health aides, and a chaplain. Made arrangements for and coordinated education and development activities for staff members and volunteer workers.

- Was credited with increasing referrals through networking.
- Provided marketing support services for the program.
- Developed a patient care guide distributed to patients and their family members; updated policy manuals.

- Participated in developing and ensuring compliance with the operating budget.

CASE MANAGER and **CLINICAL NURSE.**
Start and End Dates: September 1999-April 2001
Hours worked per week: 40+
Salary: $32,500 per year
Employer's Name and Address: Kindred Care-Connecticut, 8423 Cunningham Rd, Fairfield, CT
Supervisor's Name and Phone Number: Sharon Blackwell, 666-666-6666
Supervised nursing aides to ensure implementation of care plans while personally providing care to home health patients.
- Assisted in community health and education efforts including such activities as preschool physicals, Community Health Fair, and Kindred Clinic staffing.
- Was certified as a Home Health Nurse by the Connecticut Medical Administration (December 1999).

HOME IV NURSE.
Start and End Dates: October 1996-September 1999
Hours worked per week: 40+
Salary: $31,250 per year
Employer's Name and Address: Hartford Therapy, 302 Lake Avenue, Hartford, CT 01644
Supervisor's Name and Phone Number: Craig Wallace, 555-555-5555
Provided individualized, specialized IV infusion therapy while working in a variety of difficult patient care situations.
- Instructed and supervised nurse's aides and family members in therapy procedures.

COMMUNITY HEALTH NURSE.
Start and End Dates: July 1994- October 1996
Hours worked per week: 40+
Salary: $27,600 per year
Employer's Name and Address: Trident Regional Hospital, 37290 Ashley Avenue, Hartford, CT 01651
Supervisor's Name and Phone Number: Laura Hartwell, 444-444-4444
Implemented nursing care and provided educational services to individual and families who had been exposed to or were suffering from infectious diseases or illnesses.
- Applied communication and instructional skills while presenting a variety of formal lectures.
- Performed physical assessments and developed patient care plans for Hepatitis and Cancer patients.
- Performed the hospital's Hepatitis Hospital Admissions testing study.

CASE MANAGER.
Start and End Dates: September 1992- July 1994
Hours worked per week: 40+
Salary: $24,225 per year
Employer's Name and Address: Extended Care Services, 39095 Price Street, Columbia, SC 22846
Supervisor's Name and Phone Number: Michelle Wheeler, 333-333-3333
Excelled in meeting the special needs of the terminally ill and their families while providing quality nursing care and assisting in the training of hospice workers.

NURSE LIAISON

REGISTERED NURSE.
Start and End Dates: September 1990- September 1992
Hours worked per week: 40+
Salary: $22,300 per year
Employer's Name and Address: Kindred Care of South Carolina, 4903 Cedar Creek Drive, Columbia, SC 22865
Supervisor's Name and Phone Number: Jacqueline Greenwood, 222-222-2222
Performed a wide range of nursing duties for an outpatient clinic in Columbia, SC. Supervised training of department personnel and evaluated their medical skills.
- Implemented a grief support group.
- Taught health education classes.
- Acted as a community liaison.

HOSPICE NURSE.
Start and End Dates: January 1989- September 1990
Hours worked per week: 40+
Salary: $8.00 per hour
Employer's Name and Address: Roper Hospital, 2348 Rutledge Avenue, Charleston, SC 29401
Supervisor's Name and Phone Number: Shirley Thompson, 111-111-1111
Provided outpatient care for terminally ill patients.
- Helped train nursing students in patient care.
- Temporality filled the role of coordinator.

STAFF NURSE.
Start and End Dates: April 1988- January 1989
Hours worked per week: 40+
Salary: NA
Employer's Name and Address: Medical University of South Carolina (MUSC), 37290 Ashley Avenue, Charleston, SC 29401
Supervisor's Name and Phone Number: Belinda Carter, 999-999-9999
Provided total care for 22 patients on the internal medicine floor in a busy hospital; was recommended for promotion to Assistant Head Registered Nurse.

STUDENT/STAFF NURSE.
Start and End Dates: May 1986-April 1988
Hours worked per week: 40+
Salary: NA
Employer's Name and Address: Medical University of South Carolina (MUSC), 37290 Ashley Avenue, Charleston, SC 29401
Supervisor's Name and Phone Number: Patricia Triplett, RN, MSN; 888-888-8888
As a student nurse, was selected to fill roles of increasing responsibility in a busy high-risk labor and delivery center. Instructed medical students in delivery procedures. Managed staffing for 15 people.

EDUCATION	**Bachelor of Science in Nursing (B.S.N.) degree,** Medical University of South Carolina Charleston, SC 1988.
SPECIALIZED TRAINING	Have completed continuing education courses and training programs emphasizing pain control and chemotherapy as well as BCLS/CPR and infection control.
CERTIFICATIONS & LICENSES	Was certified as a Home Health Nurse by the Connecticut Medical Administration (December 1999).

OFFICE MANAGER

CARLA V. DALE
SSN: 000-00-0000
2462 Tradewinds Drive
Jonesboro, AR 40025
Home Phone: (111) 111-1111
Work Phone: (222) 222-2222

Highest Federal Civilian grade held, job series, and dates of employment in grade:
Vacancy Announcement Number: BC-000-00-0000
Position Title and Grade: Nurse, GS-00-000-000

SUMMARY OF SKILLS

Over ten years of experience in office management and personnel management, customer service and public relations, as well as computer operations and office equipment operation. Extensive knowledge of specialized terminology needed to type correspondence, reports, and memoranda along with knowledge of grammar, spelling, capitalization, and punctuation. Ability to type 55 words per minute.

EXPERIENCE

2003-present. 40 hours per week. **OFFICE MANAGER.** Merrimac Commercial Cleaning, 3524 Douglass Road, Jonesboro, AR 40025. Supervisor: Warren Simmons (333) 333-3333. Manage office operations, customer service, and the organization of accounting information for the company accountant. Type correspondence, memoranda, and reports in final form. Utilize my excellent knowledge of functions, procedures, and policies of the office.

- Have become known for my gracious manner when answering the phone. Utilize my communication skills while speaking with potential customers as well as existing clients by phone and in person to answer their technical questions about the company's cleaning services.

- Manage both commercial and residential accounts. Schedule appointments for company services and determine correct prices.

- Handle a wide range of bookkeeping functions; investigate and analyze previous invoices in order to attach them to current work orders.

- Have been commended for my ability to deal graciously with the public and have been credited with increasing company revenue through my public relations and customer service skills.

2001-03. 40 hours a week. **PERSONNEL ADMINISTRATIVE SPECIALIST.** Department of Veterans Affairs, 213 Third Street, Lexington, KY 39754. Supervisor: Camden Washington (444) 444-4444. Expertly performed a wide range of office duties. Coordinated benefit packets for discharged and retired veterans.

- Utilized a computer with Microsoft Office for word processing.

- Handled personnel administration activities which included processing hundreds of discharged and retired veterans in and out of our 325-person organization.

- Performed clerical support functions related to the preparation of personnel reports as well as documents pertaining to personnel assignments. Typed personnel evaluations including achievement awards as a part of our job placement assistance program.

- Proofread documents, reports, and communication.
- Arranged and scheduled appointments for personnel to obtain official documentation including IDs as well as financial information for veteran and personnel documents.

1999-01. 40 hours per week. **OFFICE MANAGER.** Baker-Reynolds & Associates, 8327 Barnard Avenue, Lawton, OK 65448 (555) 555-5555.
- Supervised one administrative assistant and up to five technicians involved in legal services. Handled accounts payable and receivable and performed bookkeeping functions.
- Prepared payroll for all company employees.
- Organized all accounting records for the company's accountant.
- Designed and coordinated marketing activities and advertising programs.
- Operated a computer, utilized a typewriter to type forms, and prepared correspondence.

Other experience in the US Army:
1995-99. 40 hours a week. **PERSONNEL ADMINISTRATION SPECIALIST & UNIT CLERK.** US Army, 3912 Armory Street, Fort Sill, OK 68741. SSG Alexander W. Graham, 888-888-8888. Utilized my skills in office procedures while excelling in a job as a Unit Clerk (1995-97) and then as a Personnel Administration Specialist (1997-99) within the same organization.
- Received a special award for my leadership as Unit Clerk in reducing a large backlog of personnel documents to zero – our unit was the first one to achieve that goal within a one year period in 1999. The citation for the Army Achievement Medal which I received praised my efforts in "reducing 295 critical data blanks using Microsoft Access, allowing Headquarters Company to become the first of 21 units to reach this target."

1993-95. 40 hours a week. **ADMINISTRATIVE SPECIALIST & PERSONNEL SPECIALIST.** US Army, 22nd Signal Battalion, Camp Casey, Korea APO AP 3039. Supervisor: MSG Frederick S. Keller 666-666-6666. Excelled in a job as a Clerk Typist and advanced to handle more complex office administration duties because of my cheerful attitude and ability to handle large volumes of work which had to be performed accurately and quickly.

TRAINING
Certificate, USAR Unit Administration Basic Course, 1999.
Certificate, Administrative Specialist Course, U.S. Army, 1999.
Certificate, Primary Leadership Course, U.S. Army, 1998.
Certificate of Training, Battalion Training Management Course, U.S. Army, 1998.
Certificate of Training, Maintenance Management Course, 1997.
Certificate of Completion, Clerk-Typist Course, U.S. Army, 1997.
Certificate, Unit Administration Basic Course, U.S. Army, three weeks, 1996
Certificate, Administrative Specialist Course, U.S. Army, 33 credit hours, 1996.
Certificate, Primary Leadership Development Course, U.S. Army, two weeks, 1995.
Certificate, Battalion Training Management Course, U.S. Army, two days, 1993.
Certificate of Training, Maintenance Management Course, two days, 1993.
Certificate of Completion, Clerk-Typist Course, U.S. Army, eight weeks, 1993.

EDUCATION
Graduate of E. K. Washington High School, Jonesboro AR, 1993.

CLEARANCE
While in military service, held a Secret clearance.

OFFICE SKILLS
Proficient with all office equipment: computers, typewriters, copiers, fax machines.

MEDALS & AWARDS
While in military service, received numerous awards and medals including the Army Service Ribbon, Army Reserve Components Overseas (Korea) Training Ribbon, Army Achievement Medal, NCO Professional Development Ribbon, Army Good Conduct Medal.

OPERATIONS MANAGER

STEPHEN H. PROCTOR
122 Elmwood Avenue
Killen, TX 77785
Home: (888) 888-8888
Work: (777) 777-7777, ext. 666

SSN: 000-00-0000
Position Title/Series/Grade: Operations Manager, GS-0000-00
Announcement Number: DN-00-000

OBJECTIVE

To benefit an organization that can use an educated and articulate natural leader with exceptional planning, organizational, and communication skills who offers a track record of success in operations management, supervision, and training.

EDUCATION

Master of Science degree in **Sociology**, with a concentration in **Political and Military History**, Central Michigan University, Fort Hood, TX 2004.

Maintained a **3.65 cumulative GPA** in this rigorous degree program.

- Distinguished Military Graduate, Georgia Southern University at Davis ROTC program, 2000, and Honor Graduate of ROTC Advanced Camp, 1999, Fort Stewart, GA.

Completed one year of graduate-level course work in **Sociology** and **Political and Military History** at Georgia Southern University prior to transferring to Central Michigan University; maintained a **3.8 cumulative GPA.**

Bachelor of Science in **Business** (Strategic Management), Georgia Southern University, Fort Stewart, GA.

Completed military training courses in leadership and personnel development, including: Officer Basic Course, ROTC (Reserve Officer Training Course), and others.

EXPERIENCE

OPERATIONS MANAGER. U.S. Army, 46th Fighter Squadron, Fort Hood, TX 77564 (2004-present). Supervisor: Lt. Marcus Howell, phone: 666-666-6666. Assist the General Manager, coordinating the operations of military branch units providing flight support to an organization with the mission of no-notice worldwide deployment within 24 hours of notification.

- Supervise and have trained three teams of nine personnel.
- Ensure operational readiness and accountability of equipment valued at $345,000.
- Assumed additional responsibilities as Information Security Officer, Automation Officer, Automation Security Officer, and Personnel Readiness Packages Officer.
- Described in an official evaluation as an "intelligent and dedicated officer...committed to improving the ability" of my personnel and as possessing "unlimited potential."
- "Masterfully" rewrote an organizational-level operations plan; was cited for my attention to detail in the "superb" fire support and operational graphics sections of the documents.
- Recognized for "flawlessly" planning and executing company-level support for an organizational field exercise.

- Trained a team which won a regimental-level Flight Support Team competition and advanced to division-level competition.
- Cited in a recent evaluation as one who "can never be overwhelmed by events," who is "ahead of the power curve," and "can anticipate things better than any of his peers"

MILITARY OFFICER and **STUDENT.** Flight Safety Officer's Basic Course, 2134 Commander Road, Fort McClellan, AL (2001-04). Supervisor: Lt. Philip J. McDaniels, phone: 555-555-5555. Further honed my exceptional supervisory skills and natural leadership ability while completing this rigorous training program.

ASSISTANT SUPERVISOR and **STUDENT.** Colorado National Guard, 494 Kensington Hills Road, Denver, CO 85463 (2000-01). Supervisor: SSG Harold A. Lamdin, phone: 444-444-4444. Selected on the basis of my leadership skills and previous experience to provide assistance to the supervisor in fulfilling leadership, training, and administrative duties.
- Provided support and assistance with fire damage restoration projects and relief efforts for victims of the Colorado wildfires in July 2001.

PUBLICATION ORDERS SPECIALIST. FORSCOM, HHC 16TH Field Artillery, Fort Stewart GA 31422 (1998-00). Supervisor: SGT Vera B. Payne, phone: 333-333-3333. Established, organized, and operated the fax publication orders system, processing orders for publications. Assisted book property officers in maintaining property accountability and technical advice.

TEAM LEADER. US Army, 48th Flight Support Brigade, Fort Polk, LA 74513 (1995-98). Supervisor: SGT Michael C. Kronenburg, phone: 222-222-2222. Rapidly promoted ahead of my peers and advanced to positions of increasing responsibility on the basis of my natural leadership ability, maturity, and dedication.
- Supervised and trained four personnel in two crews.

PERSONAL   Entrusted with a Secret security clearance. Known as an intelligent and dedicated leader with limitless potential. Excellent references are available upon request.

PERSONNEL ADMINISTRATOR

VICTOR G. UNDERWOOD
SSN: 000-00-0000
1783 Alford Place
New York, NY 10057
Home: (999) 999-9999
Work: (888) 888-8888

Vacancy Announcement Number:
Country of Citizenship: U.S.A.
Veterans' Preference:
Reinstatement Eligibility: N/A
Highest Federal Civilian Grade Held: N/A

SUMMARY

Offer well-developed planning and organizational abilities, strong leadership skills, and a reputation as a results-oriented professional and motivated trainer with exceptional technical knowledge and skills related to personnel management and staff development.

EXPERIENCE

PERSONNEL ADMINISTRATION SUPERVISOR. General Services Administration, Federal Protection Service Division, 3248 Desmond Drive, New York, NY 10005 (2003-present).
Supervisor: Timothy Pilcher, Director (777) 777-7777
Pay grade:
Hours worked per week: 40+
Duties: Was transferred to the corporate office after providing exemplary service at the Cincinnati branch. Provide managerial oversight as well as technical and training to as many as 10 personnel employees. Plan and coordinate the formulation of policies, procedures, and programs for highly sensitive personnel management actions for executives and managers, to include evaluation reports, requisitions, assignments, deferrals, promotions, retirements, and separations. Perform liaison between the personnel services department, finance department, and public affairs departments. Resolve problems stemming from contradictory and overlapping policy and regulatory requirements. Serve as a manpower management advisor for full-time personnel, using tables of distribution and allowances to perform strength accounting. Direct the timely and accurate completion of all personnel actions, including but not limited to: administration of travel expenses, finance, achievement awards and evaluation program, promotion boards and ceremonies, strength accounting transactions. Review, analyze, compile, and consolidate information from reports, statistics, and personnel actions.
Accomplishments:
* Received Employee of the Year awards for my exemplary performance in establishing successful awards and evaluations program as well as for providing expert training and assistance to personnel both in and outside of the General Services Administration organization.
* An employee that I trained and supervised was named to the Executive Director's List while completing the Managerial Development Course.
* Described in official evaluations as a "motivated trainer who sets

high standards and trains until personnel meet them."

- Continuously sought out by peers and superiors throughout the organization for technical advice on administrative issues.

PERSONNEL ADMINISTRATION SUPERVISOR. General Services Administration, Federal Protection Service Division, 1738 Spencer Street, Cincinnati, OH 30054 (2000-03).
Supervisor: Robyn W. Mitchell, Director (666) 666-6666
Pay grade:
Hours worked per week: 40+
Duties: Supervised and trained up to five employees. Wrote annual evaluation reports for junior managers under my supervision, as well as monthly evaluation statements for all employees. Provided advice and assistance to the Executive Director, peers, and employees from my extensive technical knowledge of personnel and administrative matters. Solely responsible for all personnel operations for a separate chemical organization. Accounted for $65,500 worth of computers and equipment with no loss.
Accomplishments:

- Operations of the office which I managed were credited as being instrumental in the unit's winning the Employee of the Month award for outstanding performance in 2001.
- Recognized in an official evaluation as being "the best Personnel Administration Department ever maintained in over three years of service."
- Made valuable contributions which allowed the organization to win the Excellent Performance award at the Division level.
- Supervised and trained a Public Relations Assistant who received a "commendable" rating on a major corporate inspection, as well as three personnel secretaries who were recommended for promotion into management.

ADMINISTRATIVE SUPERVISOR. Department of the Interior, 132 17th Street, New York, NY 10081 (1998-00).
Supervisor: Cecil James Hasse (555) 555-5555
Pay grade:
Hours worked per week: 40+
Duties: Assisted the Senior Executive, monitoring the management and preparation of all personnel actions for a three-service agency of the Department of State which oversees multiple operations located worldwide. Performed testing and instruction of personnel for the organization-level EPA Training Program. Provided training on the operation of new computer software to supervisors, peers, and employees, resulting in a savings in time and money for the organization. Wrote, interpreted, and reconciled reports for five unit processing codes generated with the KPAC system. Prepared and edited evaluation reports on officers and enlisted personnel throughout the organization. Performed liaison between the agency, the Finance, Human Resources, and Accounting Departments. Ensured that all evaluation reports, awards, and recommendations were completed and processed in a timely manner. Served as a Recorder, compiling data on the proceedings of both the Awards Board and the Board of Directors. Accepted additional responsibilities as administrator of the Personnel

Health and Financial Benefits Coordinator.

Accomplishments:

- Solely responsible for 100% accuracy of all reports generated in KPAC system for the entire agency over a 2 year period.
- Volunteered to assume full responsibility for the Awards and Achievements Program for the entire Agency.
- Aggressively assisted in the restructuring of the Department of the Interior awards and training program.
- Recognized as an expert in technical procedures, provided training in tri-service administrative procedures to agency personnel.

PERSONNEL ADMINISTRATOR

Other experience in the U.S. Army National Guard:

PERSONNEL STAFF SUPERVISOR. U.S. Army National Guard, 176th Wing, Anchorage, AK (1995-98).

Supervisor: SFC Arron P. Blanton (444) 444-4444

Pay grade: E-5

Hours worked per week: 40+

Duties: Oversee all aspects of the personnel and administrative operations for a 43-person communications organization in support of a joint service command to various U.S. Military Training Missions. Trained new employees quickly and effectively; assisted personnel deploying to South Korea. Planned and organized office operations, implementing new practices and procedures to increase efficiency. Prepared and supervised the preparation of all personnel actions to include in/outprocessing, evaluations, promotions, leaves, finance/pay, awards, and duty rosters. Maintained publications account.

- Displayed sound judgment and strong technical competence while serving as Squad Leader in preparation for group deployment to South Korea.

PERSONNEL ADMINISTRATION SPECIALIST. U.S. Army National Guard, 146th Airlift Wing, Channel Islands, CA (1993-1995).

Supervisor: SGT Louis Glenwood (333) 333-3333

Pay grade: E-5

Hours worked per week: 40+

Duties: Processed a high volume of Army Enlisted Evaluation Reports, ensuring all evaluations were performed on time and accurately. Demonstrated my technical competence, revising the Form Flow Series and developing a system of control and accountability to ensure that each office within the organization received all needed publications. Exercised skill in oral communications while providing briefings to senior NCOs. Made substantial contributions towards achieving the Army National Guard's goal of processing all personnel actions in a timely manner.

- Achieved a processing rate of 97.3% or better on all organizational personnel actions.
- Received the highest possible rating in all measured proficiencies on official performance evaluations.

EDUCATION & TRAINING

Have completed 21 semester hours of college-level course work towards a Bachelor of Science in Accounting, City College of CUNY, New York, NY. Completed training and development courses sponsored by the United States Army National Guard, including:

- Personnel Administration Specialist Course, eight weeks, 1998.
- Basic Non-Commissioned Officer Training Course, nine weeks, 1997.
- Primary Leadership Development Course, four weeks, 1997.
- Weaponeer Coach Training Course, one week, 1996.

COMPUTERS   Familiar with the operation of many popular computer operating systems and software, including: Windows 3.1, 95, and 98; Microsoft Word, Excel, and PowerPoint; WordPerfect; Forms Flow, Delrina Forms Pro, Microsoft Works, MS-DOS, Adobe Photo Deluxe 2.0, UNIX and KPAC Operating Systems.
Have also used proprietary software developed for the U.S. Army for Database Management, Data Processing, and Accounting Ledger Management.

HONORS   Received numerous awards and honors, including four Army National Guard Commendation Medals, five Army National Guard Achievement Medals, the National Defense Service Medal, Southwest Asia Service Medal, Overseas Service Medal, and NCO Professional Development Ribbon.

CLEARANCE   Was entrusted with a Top Secret security clearance with SBI.

PERSONAL   Outstanding personal and professional references are available upon request

PERSONNEL ADMINISTRATOR

MICHELLE A. HOFFMAN
9874 Ferrell Road
Washington, DC 20023
111-111-1111 **HOME**
222-222-2222 **CELL**
SSN: 000-00-0000
Source: EXTERNAL
Highest Grade Held: N/A
Vacancy Announcement Number:
Position Title:

PERSONNEL
ADMINISTRATOR

EXPERIENCE

2002-present. **PERSONNEL ADMINISTRATOR.** Office of Government Ethics, Human Resources Division, 43984 Mixson Hwy, Washington, DC 20023. Oscar E. Allen, 333-333-3333. Assigned to the Personnel Administration office with over 125 employees total. Handle administrative duties for all of the organization's personnel. Supervise 3 other administrative assistants and conduct seminars for human resources which was attended by 57 people annually, and maintain employee qualifications and training records for 125 individuals. Coordinate course registration with numerous outside organizations. Serve as an Training Instructor for new hires, and have earned a reputation as an articulate and enthusiastic communicator who genuinely cared for the well-being and success of all personnel. On my own initiative, developed and implemented filing system for the organization's records, and also developed a tracking system using ORACLE database used by qualified personnel. Played an active role in the development of eight course Training Programs of Instruction and seminar schedules. Evaluated as a "dedicated administrator willing to go out of her way for others."

2000-02. **ADMINISTRATIVE ASSISTANT.** Environmental Protection Agency, 488 Pinckney Blvd, Washington, DC 20561. Howard Millington, 555-555-5555. Managed personnel administration support which included processing financial transactions, coordinating personnel evaluations including human resource benefit packages, and preparing extensive paperwork. Trained and managed four employees, and incorporated risk assessment and safety awareness in all training sessions. On a formal performance evaluation of my work, was described as one who "instilled motivated in her department by her willingness to listen."

1999-00. **ADMINISTRATIVE ASSISTANT.** Berkshire Hathaway, 867 Tallaway Street Chicago, IL 45410. Simon Jackson, 444-444-4444. Performed office duties in support of a 30-person organization. Created filing systems. Developed and maintained recordkeeping systems. Was specially selected by the General Sales Manager to serve as his Administrative Assistant, and prepared correspondence for the signature of executives.

Other experience in the US Army:
1998-99. **NONCOMMISSIONED OFFICER IN CHARGE,** 24TH Mission Support Squadron, Fort Drum, NY. Supervisor: CSM Thomas Haigler, 999-999-9999. Was selected for a position as the Change of

Command coordinator for a 240-person Group. Ensured that employees' promotion board proceedings were accurately monitored and recorded in order to assure appropriate advancement to the next rank. Also supervised financial support provided to 395 soldiers in nine units, and assured that payroll processing was accurate and timely. Was commended for my meticulous attention to detail and outstanding management ability.

1995-98. **HEAVY WHEELED VEHICLE DRIVER**. US Army, 742nd Airlift Squadron, Fort Shafter, Hawaii. Supervisor: SFC Bryan K. Pete, 666-666-6666. In a medium truck company in Honolulu, was responsible for the delivery of U.S. mail, the air line of communication, and general cargo administration throughout Hawaii. Prepared all documentation and paperwork associated with operating one M915A1 14-ton tractor. Was selected over 26 other Sergeants as Motor Pool NCO, and on the citation for the Army Commendation Medal which I received, I was praised for "initiative and expertise which were instrumental in the development of the Motor Pool Standard Operating Procedures which the organization still uses today." Was Acting Squad Leader in charge of seven people during the recovery phase for a 30 day field exercise. On a written performance evaluation, was described as a supervisor who "inspired the confidence of subordinates."

1992-95. **SENIOR WHEEL VEHICLE OPERATOR AND ACTING SQUAD LEADER**. US Army, 85th Transportation Company 95th BN VHC, Fort Carson, CO 84456. Supervisor: Matthew S. Baker, 777-777-7777. Supervised five employees in an airborne light/medium truck company supporting the army airfield in Fort Carson. Received a respected Army Achievement Medal for my exceptional performance and "can do attitude." Transported more than 2,500 soldiers in support of the Special Forces Assessment and Selection Committee. On a formal evaluation was praised for "a safety first attitude which contributed to the platoon's achieving 75,000 accident-free miles in 6 months." On my own initiative, demonstrated a keen concern for maintenance, and took actions which greatly increased the availability of an aging vehicle fleet.

1989-92. **WHEEL VEHICLE OPERATOR**. US Army, 20th Regiment Battalion, Fort Benning, GA APO AP 1884. Supervisor: Terrell L. Donaldson, 888-888-8888. Conducted local and limited line haul operations of personnel and equipment in support of the Aviation Training facility (an M35A2). Gained a solid understanding of transportation policies and procedures. Was commended for making sound decisions during the performance of complex tasks.

EDUCATION   **A.A. degree in Business Technology** at Central Texas College, Fort Drum, NY 1999.

SPECIALIZED TRAINING LICENSES CERTIFICATES   1999, Convoy Operations and Winter Driving, Combat Maneuver Training Center. 1999, Bus Training Course, Fort Drum Support Battalion. 1998, Emergency Lifesaver, Army Education Center. 1998, Bus Driver Course, Training Integration Branch. 1997, Primary Leadership Development Course, NCO Academy. 1997, Equal Opportunity Representative Course, Fort Benning. 1996, Total Army Retention, Recruiting and Retention School. 1996, 88M Motor Transport Operator Course, Fort Shafter 1995, Parachute Rigger Course. Am licensed to operate military vehicles and light wheel vehicles.

AWARDS   Numerous medals including Army Achievement Medals (two), Army Service Ribbon, Army Lapel Button, National Defense Service Medal, Good Conduct Medals, and numerous letters of appreciation from supervisors and commanders praising my outstanding results.

COMPUTERS & EQUIPMENT   Operate PCs with software including Word and Excel; Operate all office equipment including copier, fax, switchboards, radios, and other equipment.

CLEARANCE   Secret security clearance

PERSONNEL SUPERVISOR

MAYRA C. GOODELL
1839 Wedgewood Avenue
Troy, MI 41124
Home: (111) 111-1111
Work: (222) 222-2222 ext. 3333

SSN: 000-00-0000
Source Code: External
Highest Federal Civilian Grade Held: N/A

PERSONNEL SUPERVISOR

SKILLS

Offer exceptional communication, organizational, and planning skills, as well as a "track record" of accomplishments in personnel supervision and training.

EXPERIENCE

PERSONNEL SUPERVISOR. Care-Regional Hospital, 2053 Sunset Road Suite 29, Troy, MI 40453 (2003-present).
Supervisor: Samantha Moriarty, (333) 333-3333
Pay grade:
Hours worked per month: 40+
Duties: Manage and train up to twelve employees responsible for processing personnel actions for a 175-person organization. Update and maintain personnel files on all individuals assigned to the organization. Edit, proofread, type, and prepare for submission a wide variety of correspondence, interoffice memos, and other written material, including patient medical evaluation reports for registered nurses, recommendations for performance awards, providing training schedules, etc. Conduct and supervise in-processing and department financial audits. Provide close supervision to all office employees to ensure that personnel actions are properly completed, for an office that is staffed primarily with medical administrative personnel.
Accomplishments:
Played a key role in facilitating an increase in department financial audit statistics, effecting a 22% increase, from 79% to 98%, within five months.

PERSONNEL SUPERVISOR and **TRAINING MANAGER.** Emergency Medical Services, 3811 Wyatt Avenue, Grand Rapids, MI 40978 (2000-03).
Supervisor: Tracey V. Morrill, (444) 444-4444
Pay grade: E-5
Hours worked per week: 40+
Duties: Supervised and trained as many as ten personnel members, oversaw the personnel records for a 120-man organization, ensuring that evaluation reports for physicians, nurses, and other personnel actions were managed properly and processed to higher headquarters. Updated and maintained training records for the unit as a whole as well as for individuals assigned to the unit. Ensured that all training required to maintain licenses and/or certifications was scheduled well in advance of expiration and was completed on time.
Accomplishments:
• Promoted ahead of my peers and selected for this position over three more senior personnel; cited for "effectively [blending] management skills with technical expertise."

- Consistently executed new training programs in order to enhance individual performance and improve procedure readiness; devised a cross training plan that ensured that the medical facility maintained a 85% readiness rate.
- Maintained a school allocation fill rate of better than 98%, ensuring that no position in desirable training schools or courses were lost through lack of enrollment.
- Described as "a quality performer" and "superb role model for new employees;" was selected to perform operation evaluations and received "noteworthy praise from higher headquarters" for my role in this matter.

Other experience in U. S. Army:
REASSIGNMENT SUPERVISOR IN CHARGE. U.S. Army, HHC 309th Corp Support Command, Reenlistment, Fort Hood, TX 70031 (1997-00)
Supervisor: Gloria Haswell, (555) 555-5555
Pay grade: E-6
Hours worked per week: 40+
Duties: Supervised and trained as many as 23 employees processing requests for transfer and reassignment orders. Authored annual evaluation reports for junior managers under my supervision and monthly counseling statements for all personnel. Performed additional duties as Retention Supervisor, advising personnel within the organization and providing information on the benefits of reenlistment to encourage them to extend their tour of duty in the military. Prepared reenlistment contracts as well as updating and maintaining the "reenlistment" roster, which tracks which personnel are approaching the end of service, which have already reenlisted, and which still have not decided whether or not to reenlist, on a monthly basis.
Accomplishments:
- Described in an official evaluation as a supervisor who "always seeks new and effective methods to enhance training and performance skills" and "skillfully [utilizes] available manpower to meet the demands of the section."
- Built a reputation for "consistently taking the initiative to implement new ideas and policies in the most effective and productive manner."
- Designed and implemented a more effective tracking system, which ensured 98% accountability of all Reassignment packages.
- Maintained a 99% Quality Assurance rating for accuracy of soldiers' assignment records.
- Exceeded all established retention quotas for reenlistment of personnel within the organization.

PERSONNEL READINESS SUPERVISOR. U. S. Army, 2nd BN 1/3rd Support Operations, Fort Sill, OK 74815 (1995-97).
Supervisor: Albert Lucas, (666) 666-6666
Pay grade: E-6
Hours worked per week: 40+
Duties: Processed and prepared personnel for overseas deployments. Coordinated readiness schedules, interacting with unit commanders and other supervisors to provide necessary information concerning the deployment readiness status of unit personnel. Ensured that all medical records, insurance information, and military identification cards were updated and accurate. Computed unit readiness statistics and prepared readiness reports. Verified that all personnel preparing for deployment had been issued all necessary equipment. Recorded and documented information related to the number of deploying personnel processed by the Readiness Center. Authored annual evaluation reports for junior managers under my supervision, and monthly counseling statements for all personnel, as well as recommendations for awards and other personnel actions.

ASSISTANT BENEFITS SUPERVISOR. U.S. Army, 158th Replacement Support Group, Fort Hood, TX 70455 (1992-95).
Supervisor: Henry C. Gabriel, (777) 777-7777
Pay grade: E-5
Hours worked per week: 40+
Duties: Supervised and trained up to nine personnel serving a high volume of customers in the installation ID card facility. Issued military identification cards to active duty military personnel, reservists, retirees, and their family members, providing exceptional customer service in a fast-paced environment. Oversaw the distribution and accountability of forms, publications, and military ID cards. Ensured that automated terminals were active, online, and functioning properly at all times. Contacted the regional office immediately to report any terminal service outages.

Accomplishments:

- Recognized in evaluation reports as "a true winner" who "accepts nothing less than the best from subordinates" and "consistently exhibits perfection in the technical aspects of her job."
- Described as a "superb motivator who promotes a winning attitude" and an "invaluable asset to customer service."
- Utilized unscheduled training time to enhance individual training.

Other experience:
ADMINISTRATIVE ASSISTANT. Monroe County Health Department, 1229 Eccles St., Monroe, MI 40056 (1989-92).
Supervisor: Frank Kennedy, (888) 888-8888
Pay grade: E-4
Hours worked per week: 40+
Duties: Composed and prepared a wide variety of office correspondence using word processing and other office automation software such as Microsoft Word, Excel, and Access. Tasked with typing, editing, proofreading, and processing of evaluation reports for registered and licensed nurses, recommendations for awards, and other personnel actions. Processed, updated, and maintained daily status reports, award records, and facility strength reports. Answered a multi-line phone system, directing calls to the appropriate person and taking messages when the party requested was not available. Assumed additional responsibility as Personnel Supervisor; ordered and maintained an adequate inventory of all supplies needed by the organization.

EDUCATION & TRAINING

Have completed nearly two years of graduate-level studies towards a **Master of Arts** in **Health Care Administration**, Wayne State University, Troy MI campus (degree expected May 2004).
Bachelor of Science in **Psychology**, University of Oklahoma, Tulsa, OK 1997.
Associate of Arts in **Liberal Arts**, Monroe County Community College, Monroe, MI 1989.

MILITARY EDUCATION

Completed extensive technical and management training, U.S. Army; Primary Leadership Development Course, Basic Non-Commissioned Officers Course, Personnel Actions Specialist Course, Army Medical Training Course, Nuclear, Biological, and Chemical Defense Course, USASSI Adjutant General School, Combat Lifesaving Course, Effective

USASSI Adjutant General School, Combat Lifesaving Course, Effective Writing Course, Basic Computer Course, Basic Spanish Course, and Basic Keyboarding Course.

COMPUTERS   Proficient in the operation of many of the most popular computer operating systems and software, including: Windows ME and XE; Microsoft Word, Excel, Access, PowerPoint, Publisher, Works, and Internet Explorer; Netscape Navigator; Harvard Graphics; and Corel Draw, as well as SARSS and other proprietary systems used by the U.S. Military.

HONORS &   Received numerous prestigious awards and honors, which included two Army Commendation
AWARDS   Medals, an Army Achievement Medal, two Good Conduct medals, the National Defense Service Medal, the Army Service Ribbon, two Overseas Service Ribbons, and the Expert Marksmanship Qualification Badge.

PERSONAL   Excellent personal and professional references are available upon request.

PERSONNEL SUPPLY SPECIALIST

GRAHAM F. KIESER
2809 Fifth Avenue
Bossier City, LA 77681
(999) 999-9999 **Home**

SSN: 000-00-0000
Country of Citizenship: US
Veteran's Preference:
Highest Civilian Grade Held: N/A

PETROLEUM SUPPLY SPECIALIST

Job Vacancy Announcement Number:
Job Title: Petroleum Supply Specialist
Grade for which applying:

OBJECTIVE

I wish to serve the federal government in some capacity in which I can apply my experience in aircraft refueling and aircraft servicing, warehouse operations and forklift operations, as well as materials expediting and fuel system distribution operations.

WORK EXPERIENCE

PETROLEUM SUPPLY SPECIALIST & FORWARD AREA REFUELING MANAGER. 2002-present. Lockheed Martin, 1649 Westcross Lane, Barksdale AFB, LA 77602. Hours per week: 40+. Salary: $1,250 month. Supervisor's name and phone number: Steven Powell, (777) 777-7777.

- As **Petroleum Supply Specialist,** refueled fixed and bomb-wing aircraft. Manage bulk and package petroleum storage, dispensing, and distribution activities at multiple facilities. Manage pipeline systems associated with those facilities. Oversee all aspects of petroleum movement and storage operations including forklift conveyor and crane operations. Direct the proper marking and classification of all products to ensure safe storage and proper disposition. Am extensively involved in quality control as I conducted safety inspections of storage facilities. Perform preventive maintenance on storage and handling equipment. Am responsible for refueling fixed and rotary wing aircraft. Ensured adequate and proper storage, handling, and delivery of petroleum products. Requisitioned and issued various types of aviation and ground petroleum products including jet fuel, diesel, gasoline, and a variety of packaged products. Operated 3,750-gallon semi-tractor trailer fuel tankers, 28-foot cargo and fuel trucks, fixed and temporary aviation hot fueling equipment, single-unit 3-ton capacity vehicles, and pumping equipment with a production capacity of 40-450 gallons per minute.
- As **Forward Area Refueling Manager**, established and directed refueling operations in support of Huey, Blackhawk, Apache, and Long-bow helicopter operations in support of the Kuwait deployment and during military exercises and Air Force Flight Test Center objectives. Performed fuel tanker, cargo, and utility vehicle scheduled preventive maintenance and service. Tested fuel supplies daily to ensure product quality.

Accomplishments:
- Received an Excellence Service Award in May 2003 and was praised in writing for "exceptionally meritorious service in support

of attaining and exceeding organizational objectives and goals." Was recognized for "outstanding technical and management skills in support of global operational requirements."

- While excelling in work performance with Lockheed Martin, developed and refined my leadership skills and was recognized for my leadership and supervisory abilities. Provided guidance to junior employees while mentoring and training numerous co-workers who responded to my motivation and encouragement with outstanding on-the-job results.
- I was commended verbally on numerous occasions because of my creativity in developing new methods of performing tasks and because of my cheerful disposition and positive attitude. Achieved a perfect safety record for 5 years of daily operations.

WAREHOUSE TECHNICIAN. 1999-02. Worzalla Publishing Company, 3535 Jefferson Blvd, Stevens Point, WI 55781. Hours per week: 40+. Salary: $12.50/hr. Supervisor's name and address: Michael Kimball, (666) 666-6666. For a major book publisher, was involved in performing a variety of jobs related to warehousing and controlling inventory. Stocked inventory and utilized a forklift. Replenished shelf stock. Operated a cardboard baler.
Accomplishments: After rapidly mastering the task of separating the most high priority orders from other orders, I played a key role in improving shipment time by 47%.

RAMP/FUEL AGENT & BAGGAGE HANDLER. 1996-99. Stevens Point International Airport, 1303 Marie Victor Hwy, Stevens Point, WI 55786. Hours per week: 40+. Salary: $10.50/hr. Supervisor's name and phone number: Cedric D. Hannigan, (555) 555-5555. Worked for a subcontractor which provided aircraft services at the Stevens Point International Airport. Managed aircraft loading and off loading baggage and commercial freight, including hazardous materials. Supervised refueling operations for Delta and American Airline aircrafts. Loaded and unloaded baggage, mail, and various other types of freight which needed to be loaded and unloaded from aircraft.
Accomplishments: Because of my outstanding technical skills and reliability, was rehired by this employer for which I had worked previously. Learned how to guide planes in and out of landing zones safely. Learned how to communicate with pilots using two-way radio equipment. On my own initiative, devised a new and unique method of loading passengers' personal baggage onto baggage carts and planes. This new method reduced loading time and created greater space efficiencies because it required minimal loading space. I was praised by my employer for my creativity in developing new methods of performing tasks and because of my strong work ethic and positive attitude. Possess an outstanding safety record.

LICENSES & CERTIFICATES
- Received Dangerous Goods Handlers Certification, Delta Airlines, 2001.
- Skilled in operating all types of aircraft refueling vehicles and equipment.
- Trained to drive wheel and track vehicles including single-unit wheel vehicles with 3-ton and below capacity in all types of weather and terrain conditions; semi-tractor fuel tankers; 28-foot cargo and fuel trucks; and 3,750-gallon semi-tractor trailer fuel tankers; fixed and temporary aviation hot refueling equipment.
- Highly skilled in aviation refueling of both rotary and fixed wing aircraft with specialized expertise in performing Crystalline and Grand Port test as well as in utilizing closed circuit refueling nozzles.

EDUCATION & SPECIALIZED TRAINING
Graduated from the Petroleum Supply Specialist Course, 2002. Extensive training related to the receipt, storage, inventory control, and issuing of aviation, ground petroleum, and cryogenic products. in hazardous materials storage and disposal including proper fuel handling procedures. Extensive training in safety and safety management as well as quality assurance. Advanced training in fire fighting techniques.

CLEARANCE
Held a Secret security clearance.

POSTAL FINANCE CLERK

JAMES D. CAMERON

5982 Riverside Drive, Charleston, SC 29405

111-111-1111

E-mail: JDCameron@aol.com

SSN: 000-00-0000

Country of Citizenship: United States

Veteran's Preference: _____ preference

Vacancy Announcement Number:

Position Title:

MILITARY EXPERIENCE

2003-present. **POSTAL FINANCE CLERK.** United States Air Force, 315th Communication Squadron, Postal Division (USAF), Charleston Air Force Base, South Carolina 29418. Salary: $38,500 Hours per week: 40+. Supervisor: Dillon McPherson, Phone: 222-222-2222. Perform postal financial services using the UNISYS III Integrated Retail Terminal, and sell postage stamps, postal validation imprinter labels, and money orders. Maintain a minimum $2,750 flexible-credit account and adequate postage stock to service postal patrons. Remit funds derived daily from selling postage stock and money orders to the Custodian of Postal Effects. Accept items for mailing and advise patrons of applicable postal and customs requirements. Compute charges for postage and special-service fees and affix appropriate endorsements for category mail and special services. Prepare receipts on items accepted as Express, Insured, and Certified mail. Safeguard all mail items. Worked overtime hours to complete all daily assignments.

Accomplishments:

* Qualified as a Postal Finance Clerk within 4 weeks instead of the usual 6 weeks.
* Processed over $42,500 in financial transactions monthly with flawless accuracy.
* During an operational surge, worked extra hours to reduce mail delivery time by 45%.
* Was nominated as the "Finance Clerk of the Year" because of my knowledge of the finance section and continued drive to understand new operations and train new finance clerks."
* Provided exceptional customer service while working the finance window; produced an 89% customer service satisfaction rating.

2001-03: **POSTAL CLERK.** United States Air Force, 315th Communication Squadron, Postal Division (USAF), Charleston Air Force Base, South Carolina 29418. Salary: $36,350. Hours per week: 40+. Supervisor: Thomas Guillard, Phone: 333-333-3333. Processed more than 2,750 pieces of incoming mail weekly. Unloaded incoming mail trucks and break down personal and official correspondence to include express, first, second, third, and fourth class mail. Processed express mail in a timely manner. Opened pouches and broke down letter trays and flats using sorting equipment. Distributed personal mail to individual U.S. Postal Service lock boxes. Wrote up accountable mail and large items using delivery notices of receipt and provided customer service at the parcel pickup window. Off-loaded and processed mail from Moore Drums containers. Assisted patrons in completion of mail disposition forms and standing delivery forms.

Accomplishments:

- Ensured the efficient processing of 98,000 pounds of mail to 4,325 patrons and their families monthly.
- Was commended for my initiative in aggressively researching and reviewing postal guidelines, which led to 95% compliance with all U.S. government and host country rules and regulations.
- Was evaluated as an outstanding supervisor; was praised in writing for strong communication skills, and was commended for my skill in briefing the entire postal branch on current initiatives, programs, and quality of life improvements.

1999-01: **PASSENGER SERVICE SPECIALIST.** United States Air Force, 52nd Transportation Squadron, Travel Division (USAF), Tyndall Air Force Base, Florida 33948. Salary: $34,000. Hours per week: 40+. Supervisor: Carl Stephenson, Phone: 444-444-4444. Obtained passenger travel reservations for military personnel, DoD civilians, and temporary duty personnel. Issued transportation requests, travel authorizations, and related documents. Maintained files and registers. Prepared military travel warrants via air, rail, and ferry. Made reservations for military professionals and civilians. Audited commercial reservations provided by the Scheduled Airline Travel Office (SATO). Operated the Global Air Transportation Execution System (GATES).

Accomplishments:

- Was evaluated as "an extremely skilled and reliable transporter with a high level of knowledge and expertise."
- Played a key role in the expedient processing of over 1,125 passengers monthly involved in transactions valued at over $965,000.
- Aggressively collected over $27,500 in excess costs from travelers exceeding their authorized travel entitlement and returned those monies to the government.
- Continuously utilized my strong communications and public relations skills: provided briefings to military and federal employees on travel entitlements.
- Was credited with making a significant contribution toward achieving a 90% customer satisfaction rate; noted for my commitment to teamwork and completing tasks above expectations.

1996-99: **QUALITY CONTROL PERSONAL PROPERTY SPECIALIST.** United States Air Force, Defense Courier Service (USAF), Vance Air Force Base, Oklahoma 77485. Salary: $32,700. Hours per week: 40+. Supervisor: Suzanne Ramsey, Phone: 555-555-5555. Maintained surveillance over transportation policies and procedures pertinent to the movement of personal property from the largest U.S. military community overseas. Maintained the courier performance files of over 125 stateside couriers. Evaluated and monitored courier performance scores, performed witness reweighs, and inspected agents' facilities and equipment. Prepared semiannual carrier performance reports and identified negative trends in the movement of personal property. Resolved disputes between agents' personnel and customers, and negotiated and managed contracts with local firms. Monitored the performance of 95 personal property couriers.

Accomplishments:

- Was cited as "instrumental in maintaining a 89 percent inspection rate, which minimized loss and damages while also reducing overall claims filed against the government." Ensured all shipments received top quality service.
- During routine quality control inspections over a nine-month period, accurately identified 185 out of 750 shipments as being out of tolerance, which permitted early resolution of the problem and saved over $34,500 in government funds. On another occasion, saved $13,500 in excess weight costs.

- As a Quality Assurance Evaluator, ensured the error-free expenditure and processing of over $96,500 of contractual services for the local Direct Procurement Method Packing and Crating Contract.
- Monitored 14.333 inspection documents and identified the substandard performance of 12 carriers while making recommendations for appropriate actions.
- Was commended in writing for "possessing the ability to handle many and varied problems associated with the movement of personal property" and for effectively resolving problems "with laudatory comments from customers."
- Updated the Transportation Operational Personal Property Standard System (TOPS) computer system, which enabled end users to access up-to-date information when performing inquiries in the TOPS system.

1992-96: OUTBOUND PERSONAL PROPERTY SPECIALIST. United States Air Force, Defense Courier Service (USAF) Vance Air Force Base, Oklahoma 77485. Salary: $30,350. Hours per week: 40+. Supervisor: Eric S. Linwood, Phone: 666-666-6666. Prepared and reviewed International Through Government Bills of Lading for commercial carriers for accuracy and completeness. Advised Personal Property Processing Offices in writing of carrier/agent selection and confirmation pickup dates. Prepared Government Bills of Lading and other shipping documents for International, Direct Procurement Method, Door-to-Door, and Local Moves. Maintained documents and files. Acted as a liaison between Personal Property Shipping Offices and carriers' local agents. Maintained surveillance over transportation policies and procedures pertinent to the performance files of over 135 stateside carriers. Evaluated and monitored carrier performance scores.
Accomplishments:
- Was described in writing as "an excellent performer who provided outstanding service to over 6,250 government personnel members relocating from other communities."
- Expertly prepared 1,950 Government Bills of Lading for household goods shipments worldwide.
- Was instrumental in collecting $10,500 on personal property shipments; ensured strict compliance with guidelines related to waste, fraud, and abuse.
- Earned a reputation as an outstanding communicator: A formal performance evaluation praised my "ability to articulate personal property issues during briefings for 2,750 inbound personnel." Also earned praise for my written communication skills: prepared and submitted articles on constantly changing personal property entitlements.
- On my own initiative, prepared a guide for administrative policies and procedures for the Outbound Section which eliminated redundancy, increased productivity, and resulted in a 95% customer satisfaction rate.
- On one occasion, streamlined the processing of over 450 Government Bill of Lading correction notices, which saved more than $4,500 in supplies and labor yearly.

EDUCATION	**Master of Public Administration degree**, Charleston Southern University, Charleston, SC, 2003. Excelled academically with a 4.0 GPA. **Bachelor of Arts degree in Management**, University of Oklahoma, Enid, OK, 1998.
AFFILIATIONS	Member of General Administration Society Affiliate of the Honorary Society of Public Administrators in South Carolina
CLEARANCE	Secret security clearance
COMPUTERS	Gained working knowledge of Microsoft Word, Excel, Access, and PowerPoint
HONORS & AWARDS	Recipient of Meritorious Service Medal and Air Force Commendation Medals Air Force Good Conduct Award 2001 and 2000 Air Force Achievement Award 1999 and 1997

REGISTERED NURSE

RHONDA GENENE GREER
9837 Dean Forest Road
Providence, RI 02894.
Home phone: (111) 111-1111
Work phone: (222) 222-2222

Veteran's Preference: _____ preference
Vacancy Announcement Number:
Position Title:

LICENSES & CERTIFICATIONS	Registered Nurse: license number 8888, issued by the State of Massachusetts, valid until October 31, 2005. BCLS Certificate: renewed October 1, 2004.

SKILLS

Nursing specialties: pediatric wards and clinics, medical and surgical wards.
Member of the Professional Nurses Association of America.
Programs: Training in medical assessment and administration skills.
Computers: knowledge of ICHCS, Windows NT, and PowerPoint.
Languages: Totally bilingual in French, Spanish and German.

WORK EXPERIENCE

Registered Nurse, Xavier Regional Hospital, 2123 Harden Street, Providence, RI 02894. Supervisor: Mellisa Nevins (333) 333-3333. Salary: $49,289 (RN). Hours per week: 40. From March 1999 to present. Provide professional nursing support for Xavier with primary emphasis on screening for potential surgical procedures and secondary emphasis on screening for enrollment in special needs treatment and counseling programs.

- Apply professional nursing and related medical knowledge while evaluating the medical, psychological, and social needs of the patient and their family members and assessing their ability to cope with caring for handicapping conditions.
- Act as a consultant for medical staff, community-based support and service groups, state and federal agencies, and other concerned individuals and groups: explain program goals and objectives and educate personnel in identifying potential candidates and needs.
- Establish and maintain files, records, and logs. Administer and interpret first-stage and second-stage development tests.
- Inform patients and their families of findings, the consequences of enrolling in the program, and of available resources for care and support in the nearby Providence community.
- Provide screening through local clinics including the Pediatric, Geriatric, and Family Practice Clinics, as well as outlying schools.

Clinical Nurse, Wentworth Medical Institute, 3278 Canebrake Road, Boston, MA 04535. $45,000. Supervisor Dillon Hancock (444) 444-4444. Salary: GS-9. Hours per week: 40. From March 1996 to March 1999. Supervised and trained as many as five people (LPNs, CNAs, and Student Nurses) while performing professional nursing duties caring for newborn and/or pediatric patients.

- Provided comprehensive care based on a combination of the needs of the patient, nursing care plan, and physician's medical plan.
- Evaluated nursing care based on patient response and revised the

nursing plan when needed.

- Administered oxygen as well as prescribed medications by oral, rectal, topical inhalation, intravenous, subcutaneous, and intramuscular routes; initiated intravenous infusions; administered blood and blood products; regulated rates and monitored infusions.
- Performed nasal-pharyngeal and gastric suction and managed a variety of other tubes as well as foley catheters.
- Set up, monitored, and operated a variety of equipment which included infant monitors, respiratory equipment, incubators, auto-infusion pumps, and traction.

Clinical Nurse, Boston Medical Center, 343 53rd Street, Boston, MA 04577, $37,000. Supervisor: Rick Hammill (555) 555-5555. Salary: GS-10. Hours per week: 40. From June 1993 to March 1996. Supervised and trained as many as five employees including LPNs, CNAs, and Student Nurses while performing Charge Nurse duties which included administrative functions duties in support of the Head Nurse with an emphasis on providing comprehensive nursing care to pediatric and adult medical and surgical patients.

- Made nursing care assignments for professional and paraprofessional staff members with various skill levels according to patient needs and staff expertise.
- Ensured staff members provided appropriate patient education, made nursing entries which were legible and correct, and dealt with emergencies appropriately.
- Verified and annotated physician's orders and advised the attending physician of any significant changes in a patient's condition.
- Monitored and provided oversight during orientation and preceptorship periods in order to verify personnel were receiving appropriate and thorough training.
- Provided care for pediatric and adult medical and surgical patients ranging from those who were ambulatory to those receiving complex new or nonstandard treatments.
- Cared for patients requiring intensive care such as postoperative and burn patients, accident victims, etc. Initiated emergency resuscitative measures and assisted physicians with further emergency responses.

Clinical Nurse, Dorchester Heights Medical Hospital, 5124 Habersham Road, Boston, MA 04513. Supervisor: Matthew Brushwood. (444) 444-4444. Salary: $32,800. Hours per week: 40. From February 1990 to June 1993. Provided comprehensive nursing care to patients on pediatric, general, medical, or surgical wards as well as patients in the post-anesthesia recovery unit while handling responsibilities for preparing and documenting patient health records.

- Taught patients, family members, and care providers the disease process and therapy.
- Provided on-the-job and in-service training for staff personnel and assisted with new-employee orientations.
- Prepared patients for surgical or diagnostics procedures; observed post-operative patients and those receiving medical therapy for adverse reactions; took immediate action in response to medical emergencies. Categorized patients according to acuity standards and entered data into an automated system.
- Administered medications by oral, subcutaneous, intramuscular, intradermal, intravenous, or inhalation routes to patients of all ages.
- Performed specialized procedures such as oxygen administration, inhalation therapy, nasal-pharyngeal and gastric suction, blood gases, gastric lavage, and others.
- Operated and monitored specialized equipment which included: cardiac monitor and defibrillator, oxygen analyzer, mist tent, IPPb, glucometer, and insulin pump.

EDUCATION   Diploma awarded upon completion of a three-year program from the School of Nursing, Tufts University, Boston, Massachusetts, February 1990.
Completed an additional 45 hours of additional training every two years, in order to update and maintain my nursing skills and certifications.

SAFETY & HEALTH OCCUPATIONAL MANAGER

LESTER V. KINARD
SSN: 000-00-0000
7451 Waldron Avenue
Columbus, GA 30648
(888) 888-8888
(777) 777-7777
Vacancy Announcement Number:

Country of Citizenship: U.S.A.
Veterans' Preference:
Reinstatement Eligibility: Yes
Highest Federal Civilian Grade Held:

SAFETY & HEALTH OCCUPATIONAL MANAGER

SUMMARY

Offer well-developed planning and organizational abilities, strong leadership skills, and a reputation as a results-oriented professional and skilled negotiator with specialized knowledge and skills in the areas of general and industrial safety, explosives, range safety, and staff operations.

EXPERIENCE

SAFETY AND HEALTH OCCUPATIONAL MANAGER. McDonald Douglass, 3868 Lubbock Drive, Columbus, GA 30648 (2004-present).
Supervisor: Edward Franklin (666) 666-6666
Pay grade: GS-12
Hours worked per week: 40+
Duties: Held multiple and varied responsibilities for the development and management of a comprehensive safety program for units geographically separated throughout the United States, Southeast Asia, and several European countries. Supervise one U.S. military, one U.S. civilian, and two local national employees.

- Analyze the operation of the long-haul highway fleet of 950 tractors and 3200 trailers which travel approximately 36 million miles annually while servicing 825 customer sites in Seoul Korea; Narita, Japan; and Palermo, Italy.
- Develop, scheduled, and carry out annual Standard Army Safety and Occupational Health Inspections (SASOHI) for all supported units.
- Coordinate with U.S. military and local authorities for the utilization of public roads for transporting heavy tanks and oversized loads.
- Conduct in-depth research on safety, occupational hazards, transportation, and driver requirements issues and integrated new material into existing policies and procedures.
- Conduct announced and unannounced inspections; investigate major accidents; compile and analyze accident data in order to identify trends and develop solutions.
- Supervised a driver training program which graduated more than 675 people a year.

MILITARY EXPERIENCE

GROUND SAFETY OFFICER. U.S. Army, Public Safety Administration Center, 98th BN 353rd Support Group, Fort Benning, GA 30677 (2001-04).
Supervisor: Richard Parkerson (555) 555-5555
Pay grade: E-7

Hours worked per week: 40+

Duties: As a Safety and Occupational Health Specialist, was responsible for OSHA, hazardous communication, accident reporting and investigation, and statistics. Exercised my early-out option due to extensive reductions in the workforce.

EXPLOSIVE SAFETY SPECIALIST. U.S. Army, HQ Panama/USAR Safety Unit 27658, APO AP 28487-5417 (1998-01).
Supervisor: Clarence Sharpton (444) 444-4444
Pay grade: E-7
Hours worked per week: 40+
Duties: Assigned to a command safety office in Panama City, Panama, was responsible for the explosive safety of U.S. stored and titled ammunition at more than 65 sites.
Accomplishments:
* Served as the staff's resident expert on explosive safety issues while reviewing storage license applications, waivers, and exemptions.
* Was assigned as the Range Safety Officer for approximately 53 U.S. and Panamanian ranges.
* Credited with successfully coordinating a pre-inspection prior to a biannual safety inspection which was described by the inspection team manager as "best prepared ever."

GROUND SAFETY MANAGER. US Army, 59th Ordinance Bn, Camp Humphries, Korea FPO AP 19658-8554 (1993-98).
Supervisor: Gerard C. Brown (333) 333-3333
Pay grade: E-7
Hours worked per week: 40+
Duties: Provided oversight for OSHA, hazardous communication, accident reporting and investigation, and statistics. Supervised three local national employees.
Accomplishments:
* Supervised the annual comprehensive safety inspection program for facilities, operations, explosive storage areas, firing range, training, and hazardous storage sites.
* Served as chairman of the Camp Humphries Safety Council, a member of the Safety/ Hazard Committee, and supervised the Vehicle Safety Education Program.
* Revised and thoroughly reorganized the Base Safety Inspection and Evaluation Program.
* Trained local Korean safety specialists in the concepts and practices of safety program evaluation.

SAFETY AND HEALTH OCCUPATIONAL SPECIALIST. Department of Defense, 1138 32nd Street, Washington, DC 20054-6709 (1993).
Supervisor: Allan Trudeau (222) 222-2222
Pay grade: E-6
Hours worked per week: 40+
Duties: For four months, provided administrative, investigative, and training support for the safety and occupational health programs of an organization with more than 40 units geographically dispersed throughout the U.S. and Europe. Carried out annual comprehensive safety inspections to include reviewing nuclear and chemical storage licenses, restricted area decrees, and surveys of storage areas.
Accomplishments:
* Reviewed and analyzed accident reports from subordinate units; reviewed, evaluated, and made recommendations of drawings, plans, and specifications for new construction or modifications to existing storage facilities.

COMMUNITY SAFETY MANAGER. US Army, Grounds Security Division, 197th Ordinance Brigade, Fort Campbell, KY APO AE 20359-8645 (1988-93).
Supervisor: Joseph Cooke (111) 111-1111
Pay grade: E-6
Hours worked per week: 40+
Duties: Managed the Community Safety Program for a 6,570-person community. Supervised a traffic safety program; conducted annual inspections of more than 230 facilities; provided technical assistance and guidance.
Accomplishments:
* Brought about a decrease in the number of hazards after analyzing conditions and initiating corrective actions in potentially hazardous areas.

SAFETY SPECIALIST. US Army, HHC 3/294th, HQ, 14th Area Support Group, Fort Benning, GA 30677 (1984-88).
Supervisor: Malcolm Bailey (999) 999-9999
Pay grade: E-5
Hours worked per week: 40+
Duties: Acted as Range Safety Specialist for an organization with 84 active firing ranges which included three laser ranges located in 22 geographically separated locations. Provided technical assistance to the explosives safety officer, as needed.
Accomplishments:
* Established a range safety program which was well received and earned a monetary award for my suggestions.
* Managed the OSHA Health and Safety Program for the corps: controlled $2.3 million in funds and prepared the annual budget while conducting annual surveys and evaluations for 22 communities with a total population of 82,500.

Other experience:
HIGH SCHOOL ROTC INSTRUCTOR. Wellington High School, Fort Benning, GA 30921 (1983-84).
Supervisor: Dane Ellison (888) 888-8888
Pay grade: E-5
Hours worked per week: 40+
Duties: Served as ROTC (Reserve Officer Training Corps) Leadership Education Instructor for 73 students. Researched, prepared, and presented classroom instruction for students at three levels. Administered the annual budget and ordered equipment and uniforms.

Highlights of earlier experience:
* As a Location Service Manager for U-Haul Truck Rental in Birmingham AL, supervised five employees and controlled 43 trucks and 40 long-haul trailers with accountability for $2.7 million worth of equipment.
* As a Foreman at a U-Haul Truck Rental District Shop in Huntsville, AL, supervised 11 employees in a heavy truck maintenance operation which operated 24 hours a day.
* As a Sales Representative for Smith's Nissan Dealership in Birmingham AL, was rated the #1 salesman of Nissan automobiles.

- As an Industrial Safety Superintendent for the Hunter Army Airfield, monitored Lockheed Martin Company and subcontractors working on a $75.8 million missile rehabilitation project; left this position to retire after 22 years of service.
- As a Airfield Traffic Safety Specialist at Davis-Monthan Air Base, Arizona, administered the traffic safety and vehicle inspection programs at eight bases in southwest region.
- As a Communications Operator with the US Army in various locations worldwide, served as Crypto Operator/Communications Operator.

EDUCATION & TRAINING

B.S., Safety Administration, Columbus State University, Columbus, GA, 2002.

A.A., Safety Technology, Central Michigan University, Fort Benning, GA, 1989.

Completed numerous training courses sponsored by the U.S. Army including:

- How to Thrive on Chaos and Achieve Total Quality Management, 2003
- Total Quality Management Teams and Tools, 2003
- Hazardous Communications (Training the Trainer), 2003
- Laser Systems Safety, 2002
- Driver Supervision and Training, 2002
- Tactical Safety Course, 2002
- Sexual Harassment Prevention, 2001
- Respiratory Protection Workshop, 1999
- Explosive Safety Course, 1997
- Safety Management for the Supervisor, 1997
- U.S. Army Accident Investigation Course, 1996
- Programming and Budgeting Course, 1995
- Aviation Shop and Flight Line Safety, 1993
- Safety Program Management Course, 1993
- Effective Army Writing, 1993
- Range Safety Course, 1992
- Equipment Custodian Training, 1990
- U.S. Army Senior NCO Course and Senior NCO Academy Program, 1990
- Human Communications Workshop, 1989
- U.S. Army Two- and Four-Wheel Vehicle Course, 1989
- Career Development Course for Safety Specialists, 1987
- Numerous earlier courses in Multi-Media Teaching Systems, Standard Base Supply System, NCO Leadership, Communications Specialist and Supervisory Training, and Records Maintenance and Disposition, 1986

HONORS

Received honors including the General Commander Achievement Award for traffic programs, three Good Conduct Medals, and numerous Letters of Appreciation for my professionalism and accomplishments.

PERSONAL

Am fluent in Spanish with good working knowledge of the Korean language. Held a Secret security clearance with Background Investigation. Relocatable worldwide on short notice.

SECRETARY

STUART B. INGRAM
1717 Revere Street
Plymouth, NH 00922-0456
999-999-9999 **Home**
888-888-8888 **Work**
Country of citizenship: U.S.A.

SSN: 000-00-0000
Source: EXT
Highest Grade Held: N/A
Vacancy Announcement Number:
Position Title:

EXPERIENCE

CHIEF SECRETARY. GS-00
Start and End Date: Apr 2003-present. **Hours worked per week:** 40+.
Starting Salary: $12.00 per hour; **Ending Salary:** $14.00 per hour.
Employer's Name and Address: Federal Reserve System/Board of Governors, 09894 Parsonage Street, Plymouth, NH, 00905-0460.
Supervisor's Name & Phone Number: Major Darren Coles, 777-777-7777. Review and reconcile bi-weekly payroll reports, and perform extensive problem solving related to pay and benefits. Respond to customer problems orally and in writing. Review and complete forms for input into a national database, and observe an extensive set of rules, regulations, and policies governing federal pay issues. Receive and direct telephone calls to appropriate officials. Interview callers and obtain information related to their background and problems. Implement supervisor's instructions, and advise colleagues on office procedures. **Simultaneous volunteer work: Counselor Intern (Part-time, 20 hours per week).** Jun 2003-Mar 2004. Continuing Education Center for Hesser College campus known as English Cove. Coordinate, analyze, and evaluate fee waivers for eligible senior-citizen students in order to determine eligibility for both part-time and full-time admittance utilizing payment plans including installment payments. Create health awareness seminars under the supervision of professional advisors. Create a career opportunity board listing all current jobs. Gain professional counseling skills while counseling students on social, psychological, and political issues presented by the global economy.

REGISTRATION TECHNICIAN. GS-11.
Start and End Dates: Sep 2001-Apr 2003. **Hours worked per week:** 40+.
Current Salary: $11.00 per hr. **Employer's Name and Address:** Department of Social Services, 4357 Seaford Drive, Suite 100, Manchester, NH, 00912. **Supervisor's Name & Phone Number:** Randall Howard, 666-666-6666. Manage the Registration function and represent the DSS on all Registration matters; serve as the primary point of contact with the public as well as various government agencies. Receive and review applications for Registration from low income clients, adoption agencies, and foster parents and homes. Examine referrals from state on licenses which have been revoked, investigated, or placed on probation by the state. Verify DSS Registration information pertaining to social services and state license inquiries. Work with DSS investigators.

Simultaneous volunteer work: Counselor's Aide (Part-time, 20 hours per week). Mar 2002-Feb 2003. St. Luke's Cathedral. Assisted in the coordination of the food distribution program. Conducted visits to local area rest homes in order to conduct seminar for seniors. Utilized special counseling techniques to assist seniors in dealing with their problems and in bringing closure to the counseling process. Managed a series of group discussions on matters pertaining to life after retirement.

ASSISTANT TRAINING COORDINATOR. GS–05.
Start and End Dates: Feb 1999-Sep 2001. **Hours worked per week:** 40+. **Salary:** $10.50 per hour. **Employer's Name & Address:** Merit Systems Protection Board, 4554 Manor Court, Manchester, NH 00902-8532. **Supervisor's Name & Phone Number:** Julian Capers, 555-555-5555. Managed a computer database which collected the training history of 12 personnel members in the Performance Enhancement Division. Maintained strict attention to detail as I observed the need for accuracy and timeliness of information. Became proficient in database sorting, indexing, and manipulation to provide selective criteria listings. Expertly operated a locally created computer application which contained information on training courses and personnel in those courses. Notified personnel accepted for classes. Maintained training files. Reserved classrooms for training. Maintained course schedules pertaining to 13 courses. Acted as division control point for correction action reports, and reviewed performance reports. Coordinated approvals for courses.

CLERK TYPIST. GS-03.
Start and End Dates: Apr 1996-Feb 1999. **Hours worked per week:** 40+. **Salary:** $9.75 per hour. **Employer's Name & Address:** Social Security Administration, 9045 Ridge Avenue, Durham, NH 00152-4301. **Supervisor's Name and Phone Number:** Graham Washington, 444-444-4444. Prepared correspondence including reports and charts, and maintained an extensive filing system. Operated word processors. Logged in incoming and outgoing messages.

CLERK TYPIST/OFFICE MANAGEMENT. GS-04.
Start and End Dates: Jan 1993-Apr 1996. **Hours per week:** 40+. **Salary:** $8.00 per hour. **Employer's Name & Address:** Montgomery County Court House, Immigration and Naturalization Division, 5330 Linden Road, Huntington Valley, PA 10312. Supervisor's Name & Phone Number: Arthur Cummings, 333-333-3333. Determined the suitability of noncitizens for admission to the U.S. while examining passports and visas. Examined applications and supporting documents for proof of citizenship. Identified instances of alteration, false identity, untruthful statements, and other fraud. Maintained liaison with passport officers to provide interpretation on cases.

CLAIMS DEVELOPMENT CLERK. GS-05.
Start and End Dates: Nov 1990-Jan 1993. **Hours per week:** 40+.
Salary: $7.56 per hour. **Employer's Name & Address:** New York Life, 1847 Adolphus Avenue, Huntington Valley, PA 10312.
Supervisor's Name and Phone Number: Charles Hannahan, 222-222-2222. Established a tally system for new accounts which improved the efficiency of claims handling. Assisted the Claims Representative in handling processing related to overpayment and underpayment.

EDUCATION
Master's Degree, Gerontology Option, Plymouth State College of the University System of New Hampshire, Plymouth, NH, 2004.
Bachelor of Liberal Arts, Hesser College, Manchester, NH, 2002.
Associate of Arts, Hesser College, Manchester, NH, 2000.

COMPUTERS
Extensive training related to computer operations including PageMaker, Microsoft Word, Windows, Microsoft Power Point, Microsoft Outlook, Excel, and Access.

SECURITY OFFICER

ANGUS G. JULIAN
APPLICANT ID #: 0000000
10953 Tyner Boulevard
Portland, OR 99628
Home: 888-888-8888
E-mail: angusjulian@earthlink.net
SSN: 000-00-0000

SECURITY OFFICER

Country of Citizenship: United States
Veteran's Preference:
Highest Federal civilian grade held: NA
Vacancy Announcement Number: ABC-000-000
Position Title: Security Officer: (000-00-0000)

LANGUAGES

Fully fluent in Spanish (reading, writing, and speaking). Limited knowledge of Spanish.

CLEARANCE

Top Secret security clearance

EXPERIENCE

MASTER NUCLEAR SECURITY OFFICER (promoted October 31, 2004). 2003-present. William Metcalfe Nuclear Plant, 353 Hollow Court, Portland, OR 99628. Supervisor: Robert Laughlin, (777) 777-7777 due to the fact that this is a nuclear site. Hours per week: 40. Salary: $16.75 per hour. Because of my outstanding performance, have been promoted to Master Nuclear Security Officer, and am involved in training and motivating other nuclear security personnel while handling a variety of duties.

Personnel Management: In my new capacity as Master Nuclear Security Officer, continuously demonstrate my skill in managing a staff working various shifts, and train junior employees in the theories, dynamics, and factors underlying the screening process. As a Shift Supervisor, manage up to 32 people and make safety presentations during platoon briefings. Train personnel to operate basic security equipment at screening checkpoints. Have demonstrated my ability to manage a diverse workforce and to lead others while carrying out job functions which include planning and assigning work; monitoring and evaluating performance; providing input into the selection process of employees; and promoting equal employment opportunities, human relations, and employee participation.

Security and screening management: As necessary, detain suspects. Prevent dangerous or deadly persons or objects from entering the nuclear site. Routinely act as Screening Manager and communicate training briefings by radio to nuclear site personnel.

Use of firearms and protective equipment: Am fully qualified to carry side arms, long rifles, ammunition, protective masks, and other equipment while patrolling. Am continuously involved in discovering, preventing, and dealing with threats to nuclear security.

Operation of X-Ray and scanning devices: In the course of carrying out my duties, utilize the E-Scan X-ray System. Monitor alarms from explosive and metal detectors. Search personnel, vehicles, and packages to deny the introduction of contraband including fire arms, explosives, incendiary devices, and controlled substances.

NUCLEAR SECURITY OFFICER. A. C. Strickland Security Services, William Metcalfe Nuclear Plant, 353 Hollow Court, Portland, OR 99628. 2000-2003. Supervisor: Juan E. Mendez (666) 666-6666. Hours per week: 40. Salary: $14.75 per hour. Controlled access to the nuclear site, conducted searches, monitored hand geometry, and processed visitors.

MILITARY EXPERIENCE

TACTICAL COMMUNICATIONS CHIEF. U.S. Army, 49th Special Operations Division, 18th Tactical Support Battalion, Fort Lewis, WA 98508 and other worldwide locations 1990-00. Supervisors: Lt. Todd Wheeler, (222) 222-2222. Hours per week: 40-plus. Salary: $1,950 monthly. Was promoted ahead of my peers in a track record of advancement to jobs which refined my skills in handling complex technical responsibilities as well as management duties. Constantly maintained vigilance over the security of information conveyed by radio as I planned, supervised, coordinated, and provided technical assistance in the installation, operation, management, and unit-level maintenance of radio, field wire, and telephone switchboard communications systems. Oversaw the management, safety, and accountability of military and civilian personnel.

EDUCATION

Earned an Associate of Science degree, Commercial Art Design, Lane Community College, Eugene, OR, 1996.
Graduated from Lane County High School, Eugene, OR 1991.

LICENSES & CERTIFICATES

Licensed to carry firearms of various sizes. Qualified as an expert with numerous small arms and long weapons; as a Master Nuclear Security Officer, am required to undergo refresher training periodically.
Extensively trained in Hazardous Material Handling.
Extensively trained in the procedures for screening for illegal and dangerous materials.

SPECIALIZED TRAINING

2004, Armed Guard Training, onsite at William Metcalfe Nuclear Facility.
2004, X-ray Machine Operator Training: was trained to operate an electronic scan, metal detector, and explosive detector.
2004, Nuclear Security Officer Training, William Metcalfe Nuclear Facility.
1996, Compact Disc/VCR Service & Repair, Lane Community College (LCC).
1996, Business Math, Lane Community College (LCC).
1996, Business Occupational English, Lane Community College (LCC).
1990, Basic Microcomputer Repair, Lane Community College (LCC).
1994, Single Channel Ground and Airborne Radio Systems Operator and NCS AI Course, Department of the Army.
1994, Headstart and Equal Opportunity, Department of the Army.
1994, Senior Leadership Course, Department of the Army.
1993, Alcohol/Drug Abuse Military Leaders Course, Department of the Army.
1993, Desert Warfare Training Course, Bosnia.
1993, Desert Warfare Training Course, Desert Operations Training Center, Bosnia.
1992, Headstart to Spanish Department of the Army.
1992, Tactical Communications Chief NCO Advanced Course, U.S. Army Field Artillery School.

HONORS

2004 Letters of Commendation and Letters of Recognition citing my "excellent performance" as a Master Nuclear Security Officer. 2004, was nominated for Nuclear Security Officer of the Quarter and received a cash bonus. 2000, was selected as Nuclear Officer of the Quarter for the First Quarter of 2001 and received a cash bonus of $200.00. 1994, Meritorious Service Medal for service as Assistant Communications Chief. 1993, Army Commendation Medal. 1993, Army Commendation Medal. 1992, Good Conduct Medal. 1992, Army Commendation Medal. 1991, Army Achievement Medal. 1991, Army Achievement Medal. 1991, Army Achievement Medal. 1990, Army Commendation Medal.

SLAUGHTER INSPECTOR

HARVEY T. BELLMAN

5107 Donnett Lane, Los Angeles, CA 90846

Home: (111) 111-1111

Work: (222) 222-2222

SSN: 000-00-0000

SLAUGHTER INSPECTOR

Announcement number: BC 6548-900

Commissary Management Positions:

Series/Grade: GS-0000-00-00

Country of Citizenship: U.S.A.

Veteran Preference: 30%

Highest Federal civilian grade held: GS-00 (_____job series & dates held)

EDUCATION

High School: Mulholland High School, Los Angeles, CA 90545, 1986.

College: University of California, Los Angeles CA, 90200, 2002.

Major: Culinary Arts.

Completed one year towards Associate degree. Total credit hours: 84.

WORK EXPERIENCE

SLAUGHTER INSPECTOR. (series, grade). Angus Beef Corporation (USDA), 8521 Reseda Boulevard, Los Angeles, CA 90784

Supervisor's name and phone number: Phillip Lusane, (333) 333-3333. (You may contact him.)

Starting and ending dates: 10/2004-present

Hours per week: 40

Salary: $42,000

In a red meat plant which employees 14 of employees, perform antemortem and postmortem inspections. While performing antemortem inspections, inspect live animals to determine that they are in a normal and healthy condition, and pass normal animals for slaughter. Reject animals with unwholesome conditions, and hold suspicious animals for examination and final determination by a Veterinary Medical Officer. While performing postmortem inspections, inspect slaughtered animals to ensure that no pathological or sanitary condition renders the product unfit for human consumption. Inspect entire carcass including all parts, organs, and body tissue to determine whether disease, parasitic infection, or other abnormal conditions exist. Make condemnation of whole carcasses. Perform all inspection processes during animal slaughter. Inspect the handling of products in coolers, freezers, storage areas, shipping docks, etc. to insure that Federal requirements are met. Inspect the plant for general sanitary conditions and potential sanitary hazards, and ensure that plant and equipment are kept clean and maintained in the condition appropriate for the purpose for which they are intended, including that equipment and utensils are properly cleaned and sanitary before and during the slaughter processing operations. Also inspect the packaging and labeling of whole or cutup parts. Deal with plant foremen and supervisors on matters which include potential sanitary problems, need for repairs on equipment, etc.

SLAUGHTER INSPECTOR. (series, grade). Angus Beef Corporation (USDA), 5801 Permastone Road, Portland, OR 91860.

Supervisor's name and phone number: Curtis Meyers, (444) 444-4444.

Starting and ending dates: 04/2001-10/2004
Hours per week: 40
Salary: $39,500
Performed the duties of a slaughter inspector as described in the previous job. Transferred to Los Angeles plant.

FOOD SERVICE MANAGER. (rank). Portland Veterans Hospital, 8151 Billingsworth Hwy, Portland, OR 91706
Supervisor's name and phone number: Robert Williams, (555) 555-5555.
Starting and ending dates: 11/1998-04/2001.
Hours per week: 40+.
Salary: $37,000
Supervised a staff of five consisting of cooks and food service workers. Developed a rotating menu consisting of five-day weeks, four-week months based on USDA meal guidelines appropriate to the needs of children ages six weeks to six years old. Managed food supplies in excess of $200,000 within strict budgetary guidelines. Managed accountability of government purchase card worldwide of up to $300,000.

* Developed an international logistics and procurement network which lowered food costs while boosting quality.
* Supervised food service operation for the annual Veterans Health Fair sponsored by Proctor & Gamble.
* Organized, planned, and directed a pancake breakfast for a 8-mile run in Seattle, WA.
* Developed a preventive maintenance schedule which improved productivity.
* On my own initiative, directed and implemented food service sanitation training; provided leadership in formulating new food menus based on product availability.

SHIPPING AND RECEIVING AGENT. Hargray Contractors, 5689 Maas Boulevard, Reedley, CA 90542
Supervisor's name and phone number: Carlton Foley, (666) 666-6666.
Starting and ending dates: 04/1996-11/1998
Hours per week: 40+.
Salary: $32,335
Managed a budget of $2.75 million utilized by 19 geographically separate recreation facilities. Supervised a staff of five individuals involved in conducting and maintaining monthly inventories while also distributing supplies to the 19 facilities. Developed an accounting spreadsheet which greatly improved financial control.

KITCHEN SUPERVISOR. Orleans Restaurant, 1039 Affinity Road, Reedley, CA 90542.
Supervisor's name and phone number: Jason Dennison, (777) 777-7777.
Starting and ending dates: 09/1994-04/1996.
Hours per week: 40+.
Salary: $30,787
Supervised a staff of 15 cooks and bakers involved in a large kitchen

operation which prepared 3 meals a day for at least 60 customers per week.

- Supervised monthly scheduled banquets for local businesses and organizations throughout the Reedley Community.

HOTEL MANAGER. The Courtyard, Marriot, 1937 Sardonyx Lane, Reedley, CA 90542.
Supervisor's name and phone number: John Forbis, (888) 888-8888.
Starting and ending dates: 08/1992-09/1994.
Hours per week: 40+.
Salary: $29,400
Managed a 42-room hotel and supervised the professional maintenance of accommodations for the surrounding Reedley area.

SHIPPING AGENT. U.S. Navy, Naval Station Pearl Harbor, 850 Ticonderoga Street, Ste 100, Pearl Harbor, HI 96860-5102
Supervisor's name and phone number: Captain Antonio Tyler, (999) 999-9999.
Starting and ending dates: 01/1989-08/1992.
Hours per week: 40+.
Salary: $25,870
Supervised a staff of 36 people involved in ordering base food store items valued at $1.9 million.

- Developed and organized logistics of food provisions to support Naval Station of 180,000 personnel sailors and officers in Pearl Harbor.

ACCOUNTANT. U.S. Navy, Navy Region North East, Box 100 Groton, CT 06349-5100.
Supervisor's name and phone number: Brian Devanney, (000) 000-0000.
Starting and ending dates: 03/1986-01/1989
Hours per week: 40+.
Salary: $21,000
Managed accounting records for a food service operation.

Highlights of other U.S. Navy experience:
CATERING CHIEF. Organized and catered special meals for military and civilian social functions including retirement ceremonies, promotion parties, weddings, funerals, employee get-togethers, and social gatherings of all types.

TRAINING CHIEF. Trained apprentice-level cooks in food preparation.

REMOTE FACILITIES MANAGER. Organized and supervised operation of field mess operations serving hundreds of soldiers three meals a day in remote locations.

TRAINING

Graduated from U.S. Navy training programs including the following:
Management Food Operations, 1987.
Advance Management Food Operations, 1987.

Advance Food Preparation, 1991.
Accounting for Food Service, 1991.
Health and Sanitation Instructor Course, 1991.
FDA certification, 1991.
Restaurant Cost Control Course, 1991.
Helo Crash Crew, 1990.
Firefighting, 1990.
Preventive Maintenance Coordinator Course, 1990.

CERTIFICATES   FSP qualified, 1990.
Certified Preventive Maintenance Coordinator, 1990.
Certified Health and Sanitation Instructor, 1990.
Certified in First Aid and CPR, 1990.

AWARDS   Received Unit Commendation in Pearl Harbor, HI
Honorable discharge from the U.S. Navy

CLEARANCE   Held Secret security clearance

LANGUAGE   Speak, read, and write Italian.

LEADERSHIP ACTIVITIES   Elected President of California Regional Bowling Association, Los Angeles, CA 2003.

OTHER SKILLS   **Organizational abilities:** Extensive experience in organizing and playing team sports; have coached junior varsity basketball girls and boys team. Have participated in team sports including flag football, softball, volleyball, and other sports.
- Offer exceptionally strong organizational skills, and have organized sports and morale-boosting activities for people of all ages, ranging from children to adults.
- Graduated from U.S. Navy training programs including the following:

Writing skills: Am experienced in the marketing and promotion of athletic and recreation activities through my ability to develop and produce brochures, pamphlets, and flyers which explain and market team sports and other programs.

Fundraising and marketing skills: On numerous occasions have successfully solicited funding from private industry, local communities, and individuals in order to set up recreation activities for youth and adults. Have also raised funds which were donated to the United Way of Los Angeles, CA other charities.

Teaching and public speaking skills: Have gained strong oral communication skills while teaching food service skills to small groups and giving speeches to large groups while serving as a volunteer leader of sports/recreation activities.

Computers: Skilled in utilizing computers with Microsoft Word. Have used spreadsheets for financial analysis. Have used automated systems for purchasing.

PERSONAL   Highly motivated individual with an outstanding personal and professional reputation. Can provide outstanding references.

SPECIAL AGENT

JESSE M. HAAS
APPLICANT ID #: 0000000
9848 Quailridge Road
Fort Lewis, WA 98784
999-999-9999 **H**
888-888-8888 **W**
E-mail: jessehaas@bellsouth.net
SSN: 000-00-0000
Country of Citizenship: United States
Veteran's Preference:
Highest Federal civilian grade held: NA

Vacancy Announcement Number: ABC-000-000
Position Title: Security Officer (000-00-0000)

OBJECTIVE	To obtain a position as a Special Agent with the Drug Enforcement Agency.
EDUCATION	**Master of Science** degree in **Sociology**, with a concentration in **Political and Military History**, University of Tennessee, Chattanooga, TN, June 2003.

- Maintained a **3.65 cumulative GPA** in this rigorous degree program.
- Distinguished Military Graduate, University of Tennessee at Martin-Rowe ROTC program, 2001, and Honor Graduate of ROTC Advanced Camp, 2001, Chattanooga, TN.

Completed one year of graduate-level course work in **Sociology** and **Political and Military History** at Turabo University in Puerto Rico prior to transferring to University of Tennessee; maintained a **3.8 cumulative GPA.**

Bachelor of Science in Business (Strategic Management), McNeese State University, Lake Charles, LA 1994.

Completed military training courses in leadership and personnel development, including: Officer Basic Course, ROTC (Reserve Officer Training Course), and others.

EXPERIENCE	**OPERATIONS MANAGER.** U.S. Air National Guard, 48th Airlift Wing, Fort Lewis, WA (2004 to present). Assist the General Manager, coordinating the operations of Army, Air Force, Marine, and Naval units providing artillery support to an organization with the mission of no-notice worldwide deployment within 18 hours of notification.

- Supervise and have trained three teams of nine personnel.
- Ensure operational readiness and accountability of equipment valued at $350,000.
- Assumed additional responsibilities as Information Security Officer, Automation Officer, Automation Security Officer, and Personnel Readiness Packages Officer.
- Described in an official evaluation as an "intelligent and dedicated officer...committed to improving the ability" of my personnel and as possessing "unlimited potential."

- "Masterfully" rewrote an organizational-level operations plan; was cited for my attention to detail in the "superb" fire support and operational graphics sections of the documents.
- Recognized for "flawlessly" planning and executing company-level support for an organizational field exercise.
- Trained a team which won a regimental-level Airlift Support Team (AST) competition and advanced to division-level competition.
- Cited in a recent evaluation as one who "can never be overwhelmed by events," who is "ahead of the power curve," and "can anticipate things better than any of his peers"

MILITARY OFFICER and **STUDENT.** U.S. Air National Guard, Flight Officer's Basic Course, 241st Engineering and Installation Squadron, Chattanooga, TN (2000-04). Further honed my exceptional supervisory skills and natural leadership ability while completing this rigorous training program.

ASSISTANT SUPERVISOR and **STUDENT.** U.S. Air National Guard, Muniz Air National Guard Base, Muniz, Puerto Rico (1997-00). Selected on the basis of my leadership skills and previous experience to provide assistance to the supervisor in fulfilling his leadership, training, and administrative duties.
- Provided support and assistance with flood damage restoration projects and relief efforts for victims of the Puerto Rico floods and hurricane damage.

PUBLICATION ORDERS SPECIALIST. U.S. Air National Guard, 193rd Special Operations Wing Command, Harrisburg IAP, Harrisburg PA (1994-97). Established, organized, and operated the fax publication orders system, processing orders for publications from Zenith customers.

TEAM LEADER. U.S. Army, 38/148th Flight Support, Fort Polk, LA (1992-94). Rapidly promoted ahead of my peers and advanced to positions of increasing responsibility on the basis of my natural leadership ability, maturity, and dedication.
- Supervised and trained four personnel in two air crews.

PERSONAL   Entrusted with a Secret security clearance. Known as an intelligent and dedicated officer with limitless potential. Earned numerous awards for my athletic abilities in high school and college. Excellent personal and professional references are available upon request.

STAFF INTELLIGENCE OFFICER

GENE C. ROSS
3753 Magnolia Road
Fort Greely, AK 999877
(111) 111-1111 **HM**
SSN: 000-00-0000

Series/Grade: GS-0000-00-00
Country of Citizenship: U.S.A.
Veteran Preference: 30%
Highest Federal civilian grade held: GS-00 (_____job series & dates held)

EXPERIENCE

STAFF INTELLIGENCE OFFICER.
Start and End Dates: 2003-present. **Hours worked per week:** 40+.
Current Salary: $48,900 per year. **Employer's Name and Address:**
US Army, 284th Military Intelligence BN, Fort Greely, AK 99874.
Supervisor's Name and Phone Number: Lieutenant Commander
Matthew Hunter, phone: (222) 222-2222. Develop intelligence products,
annexes, and estimates for the Commander and Seventh Army Staff.
Supervise intelligence surveillance, collection, analysis, processing, and
counterintelligence activities at group, division, corps, or comparable
and higher headquarters. Train soldiers on expertise strategies in
responding to fatal incidents. Review intelligence regulations, field
manuals, and policy papers while acting as the trusted advisor to the
Commander. Request, collect, manage, and disseminate intelligence
products, files, and references supporting 50 people employed in a
Headquarters organization as well as two training support
organizations and associated brigades. Managed Top Secret sensitive
compartmented information (TS/SCI) positions. Work daily with the
Tactical Air Operations Division. Develop information used to prepare
intelligence units for deployment to the Afghanistan.

DETACHMENT COMMANDER.
Start and End Dates: 2001-03. **Hours worked per week:** 40+.
Salary: $46,740.
Employer's Name and Address: US Army, 67th S3 TRNG, Military
Intelligence, Germany, APO AE 50021. **Supervisor's Name and
Phone Number:** Lieutenant Leo Gardner phone: (333) 333-3333. Took
over the leadership of a specialized intelligence organization and made
numerous changes which transformed it into an organization which
was described as "a high performance unit with solid systems." Applied
my strong planning and organizational skills in eliminating over 95
lines of excess equipment which tied up at least half a million dollars
in worthless assets. Created a company maintenance team that
maintained an operational readiness rate of 99.3% over a 12-month
period. Was evaluated in writing as "a splendid leader and highly
professional officer of high moral character" as Chief Commander for
a military intelligence battalion which conducted missions on three
continents. Trained and supervised 48 employees in 19 different
occupational fields who were involved in collecting, analyzing,
producing, and disseminating intelligence in support of the
Commanding General's Priority Intelligence Requirements. Managed
$18.6 million in assets which included a fleet of tactical vehicles,
trailers, power generators, as well as intelligence and communications

processors. Was praised in writing for strong team-building skills which created a highly cohesive organization. Was described as an innovative thinker for developing the concept of the unit's maintenance support group and for implementing a program that resulted in a 99.3% average maintenance readiness rate. Was credited with leading the organization to new levels of productivity because of my emphasis on excellence. Built a cohesive and effective team which excelled in conducting peace support operations supporting a national-level real world mission in Iraq.

BATTALION LOGISTICAL OFFICER S-4.
Start and End Dates: 1998-01. **Hours worked per week:** 40+. **Salary:** $43,453.
Employer's Name and Address: U.S. Army, 2/478th Logistics Division. Fort Dix, NJ.
Supervisor's Name and Phone Number: MSG Issac Ulrich, (444) 444-4444. Managed logistics for a 38-person military intelligence battalion in support of Task Force Operation in Iraq. Managed a property book valued at $43.5 million and accounted for the task force's Class I, II, IV and VII accounts while supporting 53 intelligence teams located on 15 base camps spread over an area the size of the state of New Jersey. Was involved in an ongoing national level priority one mission and was credited with "deftly providing logistical support to sensitive intelligence missions and coordinating transportation, maintenance, and supply issues with multiple organizations and agencies." Was praised for handling complex issues with ease, and was described in writing as "a meticulous planner who prepares for every mission."

OPERATIONS AND TRAINING OFFICER.
Start and End Dates: 1996-98. **Hours worked per week:** 40+. **Salary:** $41,450.
Employer's Name and Address: U.S. Army, HHC 49th Fort Hood, TX 78484. **Supervisor's Name and Phone Number:** MSG Howard Simms, (555) 555-5555. Planned, organized, and directed law enforcement training for an organization with 50 military police, 58 Department of Defense Security guards, and 32 support personnel, 28 Department of Defense Police Officers. Planned law enforcement activities to support a community of 73,050 people. Planned patrol operations for a 36,500-acre area with 320 structures. Devised a system described as "flawless" for managing DoD Police, DoD Security Guards, and administrative support personnel training files.

COUNTERINTELLIGENCE COUNTERTERRORISM WATCH OFFICER.
Start and End Dates: 1993-96. **Hours worked per week:** 40+. **Salary:** $39,000.
Employer's Name and Address: U.S. Army, 583rd Regiment, 4/49th MI Bn, Fort Greely AK **Supervisor's Name and Phone Number:** MSG Paul S. Riley /SFC Timothy Owens (666) 666-6666. Filled a critical position and gained vast knowledge of diverse terrorist groups.

Southeast Asia. Provided reasoned, predictive counterterrorism support to forces in the Phillipines, and Southern Korea. Wrote over 63 current intelligence articles praised as "superb" which related to potential threats to deployed forces. Produced finished force protection reports, and conducted database searches while collecting information from classified and unclassified multiple sources for all 83 countries. Supported operations joint endeavor, provide comfort, assured response, and able sentry as well as Japan forces.

STAFF INTELLIGENCE OFFICER

COMMANDER, SPECIAL SECURITY DETACHMENT (CSDS).
Start and End Dates: 1991-93. **Hours worked per week:** 40+. **Salary:** $36,930.
Employer's Name and Address: U.S. Army, 1st and 3rd MI Brigade, Fort Benning, GA 35568
Supervisor's Name and Phone Number: SFC David L. Courie, phone: (777) 777-7777.
Acted as operations manager for the Internal Controls Program. Excelled as Security Operations Officer of a 32-person strategic counterintelligence (CI) detachment. Managed all source intelligence elements of major command, corps, Army, or higher headquarters engaged in combat intelligence, strategic intelligence, training, or combat. Serve as a enlisted assistant to commanders and heads of staff elements, and as staff NCO for major commands and fixed and tactical units engaged in EW /SIGINT operations, combat development, or training. Coordinated threat briefings tailored to customer needs. Conducted liaison with DoD, military and civilian intelligence, security, and law enforcement agencies. Routinely worked with indexed database and technical references to identify known intercepted signals. Directed and evaluated a highly effective battalion level strategic program for over 375 soldiers while preparing and delivering numerous Commanding Officer level briefings which were praised for their insight and clarity. Advised the commander on all communication matters. Trained more than 375 people in this intelligence unit. Learned the process of contractor support related to Department of the Army agreements, and became knowledgeable about the relationship between ECB contractors and the Strategy Support Officers (SSOs). Commanded a Special Security Detachment which provided Sensitive Compartmented Information (SCI) security advice and oversight to 65 Department of the Army contractors with 132 contracts in 25 southeastern/central states. Supervised all personnel, physical information, and technical security support to corporations providing SSO contractual work. Trained SSOs and Army contracting personnel in all security measures.

PATROLMAN & DETECTIVE.
Start and End Dates: March 1986-91. **Hours worked per week:** 40+. **Salary:** $32,500 _____. **Employer's Name and Address:** Senatobia County Police Department, 9234 Hillsboro Road, Senatobia, MS 46674
Supervisor's Name and Phone Number: Lieutenant Louis B. Roseboro phone: 888-888-8888. Enforced traffic and criminal laws of the State of Mississippi, and was a member of the Patrolman Team providing intelligence and surveillance of targeted business areas. As

a member of the Investigation Team, recovered evidence leading to a murder conviction, armed robberies, and grand theft larceny.

EDUCATION   **B.S., Administration of Justice and Pre-Law**, Northwest Mississippi Community College, Senatobia, MS 1988.

CLEARANCE   Top Secret Security Clearance/SBI

SPECIALIZED TRAINING   Awarded Special Agent Counterintelligence Badge and credentials in July 1996.
Extensive training related to counterterrorism, Security Access Programs, special operations, and operations security (SSF). Proficient with SPACO1 intelligence software. Completed training related to All Source Tactical Intelligence Staff Operations. Graduated from the Counterintelligence Officer Course, from vehicular and foot surveillance courses, from courses related to Special Access Programs, and from the Strategy Support Fundamentals (SSF) course. Extensive experience in preparation for threat briefings.

HONORS & AWARDS   Recipient of Meritorious Service Medal and Army Commendation Medals.

STAFF OPERATIONS & TRAINING SPECIALIST

ARTHUR S. FAIRLEY
4358 Holly Street
Lakewood, NJ 10078
Home Number: (111) 111-1111
SSN: 000-00-0000
E-mail: arthursfairley@aol.com
Position, Title, Series, Grade: Special Agent/Narcotics Division
Announcement Number: DN-00-000

STAFF OPERATIONS & TRAINING SPECIALIST

OBJECTIVE

To offer extensive managerial and supervisory experience with an emphasis on personnel, administrative, finance, and operations management along with a reputation as an intelligent, versatile, and adaptable self-starter with high degrees of initiative and creativity.

EDUCATION & TRAINING

Earned an A.A. degree in Technology, Georgian Court College, Lakewood, NJ 2003.

Excelled in extensive training which included an emphasis on developing training, managerial, and supervisory skills for specialists in personnel and administrative services.

EXPERIENCE

Am displaying my versatility while excelling in dual status positions with the Department of State and the U.S. Army Reserves:
STAFF OPERATIONS AND TRAINING SPECIALIST. Department of State, 443 Jayce Avenue, Lakewood, NJ 10064; Supervisor: Tom Densmore (222) 222-2222; 10/01-present. Provide technical plans and programs guidance to all staff in the computer operations division, provide training for eleven state personnel members the serve approximately 250 clients per week.

- Manage the Information Resource and Requirements System in order to coordinate training requirements for more than 1,500 people in a New Jersey State region.
- Oversee a $2.5 million budget used to fund travel and training.
- Earned a Employee of the Year in recognition of my expertise in managing a remote training site which is now in its third successful year of operations: this task is made more difficult by the fact that our branch is located in Lakewood, NJ.
- Consistently exceeded performance standards and earned commendable ratings in all functional areas of operations inspected and am frequently cited for my analytical and problem-solving skills as well as for my positive attitude.

PERSONNEL ACTIONS OFFICER. U.S. Army Reserves, 48th/84th Field Artillery Division, Fort Dix, NJ 10055; Supervisor LTC Reginald Middleton (333) 333-3333; 12/99-present. Simultaneously with the above, hold a reserve position as a CW2 (Chief Warrant Officer) in charge of supervising, training, and evaluating 34 personnel specialists supporting personnel at the Fort Dix Army Reserve facility.

- Handpicked to direct an inspection and administrative assistance team, ensure that the team is sent to respond when subordinate units are having problems and that the decisions are made which will alleviate the problems.
- Revised, modified and published Standard Operating Procedures as well as Policy Guidelines for headquarters and supported units.

- Guided the unit's Equal Opportunity program to commendable ratings in a major inspection as its advisor; receive and resolve complaints and grievances.

ADMINISTRATIVE TECHNICIAN. Department of Commerce, 438 Gaddy's Hill Road, Columbia, SC 29656; Supervisor: Sheryl Cooke-Walker (444) 444-4444; 6/98-10/01. Held multiple responsibilities in functional areas which included employee supervision and training, personnel administration program management, finance and accounting support, and inventory control management.
- Received outstanding evaluations which cited my success based on my commitment to helping others and my ability to achieve results with limited resources.
- Refined my knowledge of finance, budgeting, inventory control, and compliance with regulations.
- Reviewed pay records and ensured personnel actions were properly prepared and processed.

PERSONNEL ADMINISTRATOR. U.S. Army Reserves, 132nd USAR School, Fort Jackson, SC 29661; Supervisor: SSG Peter Patterson (555) 555-5555; 6/98-10/01. Simultaneously supervised the operation of a School Administrative Section which ensured the smooth and efficient operation of support for personnel and administrative services.
- Was credited with actions which allowed a functional reorganization to proceed smoothly: planned, organized, and transferred 65% of personnel to new units; completed the reclassification of 23 instructors; and served as a representative on transfer and transition meetings in order to ensure the project was completed on time.
- Earned the respect of my superiors for my efforts in listening to personnel who were confused and even hostile about the changes taking place and reassured them while resolving problems.

Other civilian experience:
ADMINISTRATIVE ASSISTANT. Benedict College, 3894 Price Road, Columbia, SC 29644; Supervisor: Anita Haynes (666) 666-6666; 01/96-6/98. Transformed several operational areas as the supervisor and point-of-contact for administrative functions for a 80-person organization.
- Took the initiative to revamp a physical exam program which had become outdated and quickly ensured personnel took their required exams and that records were updated.
- Made substantial improvements in the finance management area after inheriting a "very poorly managed set of records and numerous pay problems" and was credited with bringing this area into excellent shape.
- Stepped into a position which had been vacant for eight months and turned what had been described as an impossible situation around; brought the program up to exceed standards despite working with no assistance and having to do the job alone.

Highlights of earlier military experience: Advanced to the rank of Staff Sergeant (E-6) in the U.S. Army Reserves while achieving excellent results in administrative and personnel management roles in locations including Fort Dix, NJ, and Fort Jackson, SC.

COMPUTERS   Offer knowledge of automated systems operations, the Windows operating systems, and software including Access, Excel, PowerPoint, and ARGON-RTS.

CLEARANCE   Was entrusted with a Secret security clearance.

PERSONAL   Outstanding personal and professional references available on request. Offer exceptional skills in customer service support. Excel in training, mentoring, guiding, and advising others.

SUPERVISING INTERROGATOR

DANA M. JACKSON
7835 Huntsfield Road
Lexington, KY 40049
Home: (111) 111-1111
Work: (222) 222-2222, ext. 333

SSN: 000-00-0000
Position Title/Series/Grade: Supervising Interrogator GS-0000-00
Announcement Number: DN-00-000

OBJECTIVE   To obtain a position as a Supervising Interrogator with the CIA.

EDUCATION   Bachelor of Science in Liberal Arts, University of Kentucky, Lexington, KY 2003.

CLEARANCE   **Top Secret/SBI** security clearance.

TRAINING   **Intelligence Basic Noncommissioned Officer Course**, Fort Campbell, KY 2003.
Counterintelligence Force Protection Source Operations (CFSO) Course, Fort Campbell, KY, 2002.
Basic **German Course,** Stuttgart, Germany, 2002.
Basic **Korean Course,** Foreign Communication Institute, Fort Greely, AK, 2001-02.
German Language Course, Foreign Communication Institute, Fort Greely, AK, 2001.
Primary Leadership Development Course, Fort Greely Education Center, Fort Greely, AK, 2001.
Basic **Interrogator Course,** Fort Campbell Education Center, Fort Campbell, KY, 2000.

LANGUAGES   Highly proficient in listening, reading, and writing German (scored 3/3 on **German** Defense Language Institute Proficiency Test).
Certified as a Basic Linguist in the Modern Standard **Korean** Language.

EXPERIENCE   **GRADUATE STUDENT.** University of Kentucky, 834 Ferguson Street, Lexington, KY 40856 (2004-present). Am taking these graduate courses which are part of the curriculum leading to a Master of Arts in Political Science: World Politics & War and International Organization & Law.

LANGUAGE INSTRUCTOR. US Army, Fort Campbell Education Center, 7898 Tally Lane, Fort Campbell, KY 40165 Supervisor: Lt. Mario Barnes, (333) 333-3333 (2001-04). Was specially selected for this position teaching German to officers and enlisted personnel from the all branches of the armed forces. Developed and revised instructional materials and tests.

- **Honors:** Received the Army Achievement Medal for my excellent performance in this job. Was selected as **Assistant Coordinator** of the Teaching Team.
- **Initiative and dedication:** Played a key role in the 25%

improvement of the student success rate in the German department as the success rate increased from 65% to 85%. Was praised for spending many volunteer hours tutoring 22 at-risk students; their eventual success contributed significantly to the institute's improved success scores.

- **Special projects:** Was chosen to conduct a German language-training course for 13 Louisville Police Department officials in June 2003. The aim was to improve high-intensity drug trafficking. Was chosen as Language Coordinator for the International Language Curriculum German contribution to the 2002 National Language Competition, 2002. Deployed to Stuttgart, Germany for six months for extensive language training and development.
- **Program development:** Developed and implemented a safety program recognized as "the best on the installation" in 2001.

SUPERVISING INTERROGATOR. U.S. Army, 79th Military Intelligence Brigade, Fort Greely, AK 00456 Supervisor: Williams Canton, (444) 444-4444 (1999-01). Trained and supervised three personnel on an Intelligence Investigation team which was selected as a skilled and highly-trained Interrogator. Received numerous Army Achievement Medals for exceptional performance.

- **Leadership:** Took the lead in cross-training counterintelligence soldiers in interrogation tactics, techniques, and procedures.
- **Knowledge of counterintelligence investigative and operational concepts:** Demonstrated outstanding human intelligence collection abilities, and on my own initiative created an intelligence collection plan which provided the Detachment the ability to process interviews at a much higher efficiency. Cross-trained counterintelligence soldiers in interrogation procedures; was evaluated as "a superb instructor." Completed many Asian interrogation courses.
- **Special projects:** In preparation for an assignment in Korea, scored highest on the Korean language final exam. Competed in the National Language Competition.

OPERATIONAL CONTROL MANAGER. US Army, 4-198TH Military Intelligence Brigade, Fort Lewis, WA 40028 Supervisor: Paul Singleton, (555) 555-5555. (1996-99). Trained and supervised two soldiers while organizing Human Intelligence collection efforts. Successfully led numerous missions which provided valuable Human Intelligence information.

- **Program development:** Developed and organized a language maintenance program which increased proficiency among all linguists officers assigned to the organization. Was praised in writing for "providing definitive, thorough instruction" which aided Human Intelligence activities.

OPERATIONS NCO. U.S. Army, Camp Donald, South Korea APO AP 9439. Supervisor: Steve Langley, (011) 666-666-6666 (1993-96). Trained and supervised other individuals while supporting missions throughout Asia.

- **Honors:** Was selected from among 20 other linguists to work with the Fire Arms Division. Excelled while performing as a transcriber in support of infantry operations which resulted in the apprehension of high-profile suspects in Seoul.
- **Automated reporting proficiency:** Quickly learned the new computerized report format, and became the organization's in-house expert on the new report which was designed to improve reporting. Trained staff and subordinate organizations on new computer capabilities.

Counterintelligence activities: Conducted liaison with military police at other Korean law enforcement officials as a Counterintelligence/Interrogation team member. Was publicly praised for producing 22 reports which significantly enhanced the 1994 murder investigation of a U.S. soldier.

- **Administration:** Improved reporting accuracy of the Unit Status Report to above 90% through my persistent attention to detail. Was commended for my strong leadership qualities.

SPECIAL SKILLS   Offer strong skills in the following areas:

ANALYSIS: Proven ability to apply inductive and deductive principles to resolve a problem, question, or issue. As a **Military Language Instructor** and Teaching Team Assistant Coordinator, analyzed student performance and identified student deficiencies. Developed training strategies which helped students succeed. As **NCO in charge of the Operational Control Element for Intelligence**, analyzed intelligence priorities and planned intelligence collection efforts to meet those needs. As a **Supervising Interrogator,** analyzed Human Intelligence collections needs.

SUPERVISING INTERROGATOR

WEAPONS: Skilled and qualified in the use of .40 caliber semiautomatic pistol, Heckler & Koch MP5/Colt AR15/Olympic Arms .45 caliber rifle, and 12-gauge shotgun.

RESEARCH: As NCO in charge of the Operational Control Element for Intelligence, created and managed an intelligence database, and was responsible for researching political, military, social, and cultural situations. As **Operations NCO,** analyzed problems and identified key ingredients for assuring that the Unit Status Report was completed accurately. Developed and implemented a plan which resulted in the first error-free report in the organization's history.

WRITTEN COMMUNICATION: Displayed exceptional written communication skills while reports, employee evaluations, and operating updates. As **Operations NCO,** produced reports for the Army Intelligence Investigations. During the Counterintelligence Force Information Management Course, was described as having "excellent written skills."

ORAL COMMUNICATION: Adept at using communication skills to draw information vital to the investigation from the interview subject. Trained in the psychology of the criminal mind and in detecting leads during the interview and interrogation process. Have performed with distinction as a **Language Instructor** in the prestigious Foreign Communication Institute. As **Operations NCO**, developed the briefing given to visiting VIPs.

ORGANIZING/PLANNING/PRIORITIZING: Frequently selected to handle multiple responsibilities because of my ability to multi-task. As **NCO in charge of the Operational Control Element for Intelligence,** planning and prioritized collections needs. As **Language Instructor** at The Fort Campbell Education Center, organized the efforts of the German Language Instructors at the 2002 National Language Competition. Personally prioritized the essential elements of each competition and developed a schedule for each individual competing—the result was that our school at the Foreign Communication Institute was the only one to meet all deadlines.

COMPUTERS   Familiar with popular computer operating systems and software, including Windows XP and ME, Microsoft Word, Excel, Access, and PageMaker.

HONORS   Received 12 medals and awards including the Joint Service Achievement Award.

SUPERVISORY SOCIAL WORKER

ANITA M. WALLACE
6523 Austin Street
Glendale, AZ 84132
999 999-9999 H
888 888-8888 W

SSN: 000-00-0000
Source: EXT
Highest Grade Held: N/A
Vacancy Announcement Number: DNM00000
Position Title: Supervisory Interdisciplinary (GS-11),
Supervisory Social Worker (GS-0000)

EXPERIENCE

CLINICAL SYSTEMS MANAGER, YOUTH BEHAVIOR AND DEVELOPMENT SERVICES.
Start and End Dates: November 2003-present
Hours worked per week: 40+   **Current Salary:** $65,000 per year
Employer's Name and Address: Department of Health and Human Services (DHHS), 3872 Cole Avenue, Glendale, AZ 84166
Supervisor's Name and Phone Number: Tanya Norman, 777-777-7777. Provide clinical consultation and clinical supervision and training to component supervisors in the Outpatient, In-Home, Geriatric, and Arizona Home Health Care, as well as to consultative and administrative personnel in Psychological Services. Oversee the operations of the Senior Citizens Homes, Adoption Agencies, and Youth Behavior and Development Services, directing the work of all supervisors in these areas and indirectly supervising 142 personnel members.

Contribute clinical input to single portal/treatment team meetings and coordinate all "mandated" services for "E. U. Baxter" class members. Conduct consultation and treatment of individuals, families, and groups, as deemed appropriate. Supervise clerical staff providing support for "E. U. Baxter" Services; interview, hire, and train personnel for various employment positions throughout the Department of Health and Human Services.

- Developed and implemented several residential treatment programs, opening group homes for children and adolescents.
- Work within assigned budgetary limits, providing valuable input during budget development sessions for allocating an operational budget in excess of $2.4 million.
- Have developed a strong rapport with the Health and Human Services staff, as well as with officials from various local and state mental health organizations.
- Played a key role in developing an employee training video for the E. U. Baxter Program which was distributed to area programs throughout Arizona for staff training.

PROGRAM DIRECTOR, DEPENDENT AND INDEPENDENT LIVING SERVICES.
Start and End Dates: February 2000-November 2003
Hours worked per week: 40+   **Salary:** $58,000-61,000
Employer's Name and Address: Department of Health and Human Services (DHHS), 1388 Whitfield Drive, Phoenix, AZ 84102.

Supervisor's Name and Phone Number: Darnell Greene, 666-666-6666. Was responsible for developing and managing a $1.8 million budget. Supervised six supervisors, including the case manager supervisor, while serving as Director of the Court Mandated "E.U. Baxter" Services program for certified E.U. Baxter class members. Oversaw Outpatient, Case Management Services and Residential and Life Care Services (Group Homes and Therapeutic Homes). Supervised independent living, dependent living, Disability Assistance Programs, and Day Treatment Services. Indirectly responsible for the management of as many as 110 employees. Planned, developed, and implemented a wide array of services appropriate for the needs of "E.U. Baxter" class members.

CASE MANAGEMENT/RESIDENTIAL SERVICES SUPERVISOR.
Start and End Dates: June 1998-February 2000
Hours worked per week: 40+   **Salary:** $55,000 per year
Employer's Name and Address: Department of Health and Human Services (DHHS), Residential Services Division, 3872 Landings Hwy, Mesa, AZ 84119.
Supervisor's Name and Phone Number: Wesley Madden, 555-555-5555. Oversaw both the Case Management and Residential Services Programs, managing the Residential Services Managers and directly supervising the Case Managers. Assisted in the planning, development, and implementation of services appropriate to serving the identified treatment needs of the class members. Consulted with officials from the State Office of the "E.U. Baxter." program on a regular basis, reporting on program needs and requesting funds for needed programs.

RESIDENTIAL SERVICES SUPERVISOR and CLINICIAN.
Start and End Dates: September 1994-June 1998
Hours worked per week: 40+   **Salary:** $46,500 to $49,000 per year
Employer's Name and Address: Maricopa County Mental Health Clinic, 1413 Tradewinds Drive, Maricopa, AZ 84007
Supervisor's Name and Phone Number: Mellissa Jones, 444-444-4444. Provided individual, family, and group therapy to clients and their families. Supervised Residential Services staff as well as planning, developing, and implementing programs and services for clients.

CHILD PROTECTION REPRESENTATIVE.
Start and End Dates: February 1991-September 1994
Hours worked per week: 40+   **Salary:** $27,000 per year
Employer's Name and Address: Pinal County Hospital, Youth Protection Services, 2175 Middleground Road, Chandler, AZ 84012.
Supervisor's Name and Phone Number: Rhonda E. Parker, 333-333-3333. Act as a liaison for the Department of Social Services and Pinal County. Provided investigative and case management service to Protective Service clients and their families.

EDUCATION   **Master of Arts in Social Work**, with a concentration in Medical Social Work, Grand Canyon University, Phoenix, AZ, 2003.
Bachelor of Arts in **Sociology**, with a minor in **Psychology**, Weber State University, Ogden, UT, 1991. Graduated *summa cum laude*.

LICENSES   • Certification in Social Work, Arizona Department Certification
CERTIFICATES   Board for Social Work; renewal from 2001-2004.
& OTHER   • Recipient of numerous honors including being honored with a
INFORMATION   Certificate of appreciation from Governor Parham on behalf of the State of Arizona.

SPECIALIZED   Training related to social work ethics, child abuse and neglect, working with aggressive
TRAINING   youth, physical intervention techniques (PIC), hazardous communication, psychotherapy.

SUPPLY MANAGER

RUSSELL N. HERMANN
3837 Evanston Parkway
St. Louis, MO 56778
999 999-9999 (Work)
888 888-8888 (Home)
E-MAIL: russellhermann@aol.com
SSN: 000-00-0000
VACANCY POSITION:
VACANCY ANNOUNCEMENT NUMBER:

SUPPLY MANAGER

EXPERIENCE

SUPPLY MANAGER.
Start and End Dates: Aug 2003-present. **Hours worked per week:** 40+. **Current Salary:** $27,000 **Employer's Name and Address:** Lowe's, 4933 Haynes Avenue, St. Louis, MO 56778. **Supervisor's Name and Phone Number:** Phillip Gaston, 777-777-7777. Manage $15 million in home repair equipment and supplies while prudently utilizing an Lowe's company credit card for purchases. Utilize the automated system known as to monitor spending. Manage a financial database using the ORACLE system to record purchasing transactions. Advise the General Manager on all matters related to supply while supervising, training, and counseling four junior employees. Was praised in writing for "providing critical budgeting support for 2003 fiscal year"

SUPPLY & WAREHOUSE SUPERVISOR.
Start and End Dates: Sep 2001-Aug 2003. **Hours worked per week:** 40+. **Salary:** $24,600. **Employer's Name and Address:** Home Depot, Warehouse Division, 63 17th Street, Parkville, MO 54335. **Supervisor's Name and Phone Number:** Andrew Malone, 666-666-6666. Was promoted to this position after working as a bookkeeper during my first year with Home Depot. Managed over $12.5 million in equipment distributed to numerous chains throughout the U.S. Trained, motivated, and supervised four employees while advising the Warehouse General Manager on all supply operations matters. On my own initiative, developed a program that reduced fraud, waste, and abuse. Resourcefully integrated the use of illustrations, exhibits, and charts into the training process which I used for junior employees.

Other military experience:
SUPPLY MANAGER (SUPPLY SERGEANT).
Start and End Dates: Dec 1999-Sep 2001. **Hours worked per week:** 40+. **Salary:** SSG. **Employer's Name and Address:** US Army, 7/89th Supply and Services Brigade, Fort Leonard Wood, MO 58556. **Supervisor's Name and Phone Number:** Matthew Clemmons, 555-555-5555. Accounted for $18 million in equipment, installation property, and furnishings while managing, training, and motivating two employees. Purchased and managed the receiving and distribution of class I, II, III, and V supplies which included hazardous materials, perishable items, office equipment and computers, and other materials. Was the resident expert on all logistical matters and advised the organization's CEO. Was commended in writing for providing flawless logistical support during the company's field training exercises, and was praised as "a key player who promotes harmony and team work."

On my own initiative, improved the organization's efficiency by cross training numerous individual in supply functions. Was praised for "maintaining one of the best arms rooms in the Army."

SUPPLY & TRANSPORTATION MANAGER (SUPPLY & TRANSPORTATION NCO).
Start and End Dates: Oct 1996-Dec 1999. **Hours worked per week:** 40+. **Salary:** SSG. **Employer's Name and Address:** US Army, 17th Support Battalion, Fort Hood, TX. **Supervisor's Name and Phone Number:** Jonathan Baker, 444-444-4444. Was handpicked to serve as the Supply and Transportation Manager for the Maintenance and Operations Coordination Center located at the Vandenberg Air Force Base in California. Managed over $650,000 in equipment while providing rigorous oversight for maintenance and inventory control in three different organizations. Became knowledgeable of both the Materials and Manufacturing Directorate and routinely utilized both information sources. On a formal evaluation, was evaluated as "an exemplary soldier who presents a professional image and standard for all to follow." Managed transportation and logistics of both Army and Air Force equipment valued at $850,000 during detrimental military operations. Demonstrated my resourcefulness by acquiring gymnasium equipment which resulted in a savings of $11,900. Was praised in writing for "providing critical logistical support for the European Peace Order which assured that all of their training was a complete success." Was commended for "extraordinary instructional capabilities" which resulted in 93% of all soldiers passing DSC map reading training. Strictly controlled a $162,000 budget for supplies and equipment, and ensured that funds were spent only for essential items.

SUPPLY & TRANSPORTATION NCO.
Start and End Dates: Mar 1992-Oct 1996. **Hours worked per week:** 40+. **Salary:** SGT. **Employer's Name and Address:** US Army, Combat Training Center, Fort Buchanan, Puerto Rico, APO AP 04586-1894. **Supervisor's Name and Phone Number:** Samuel Rhodes, 333-333-3333. Excelled in managing the supply and transportation function for a dual service/ multinational computer-assisted exercise training center. Thoroughly trained more than 180 armed forces and civilian contractors on military supply accountability procedures. Was described in writing as "totally focused on customer satisfaction" and earned praise for my ability to take charge of daily situations and analyze customer needs. Received special praise for my "exceptional control of expendable and nonexpendable supplies" and was praised for my ability to "maximize the tax dollar while conserving valuable resources." Became skilled in purchasing, receiving, storing, and distributing inventory of all types. A formal performance evaluation cited my "mission focus" as a key to the success of combat training exercises.

ARMORER.
Start and End Dates: Mar 1989-Mar 1992. **Hours worked per week:** 40+. **Salary:** SPC. **Employer's Name and Address:** US Army, 74th Supply and Services Brigade, Fort Gordon, GA 32448. **Supervisor's Name and Phone Number:** Jason Hilliard, 222-222-2222. Flawlessly controlled 137 weapons for the most forward deployed signal organization from Fort Hood, TX to numerous remote combat areas. Maintained ledgers accounting for $154,000 in funds. Conducted small arms training for more than 96 soldiers.

UNIT SUPPLY SPECIALIST.
Start and End Dates: Jul 1985-Mar 1989. **Hours worked per week:** 40+. **Salary:** SPC. **Employer's Name and Address:** US Army, 17th Support Battalion, Fort Hood, TX 77851. **Supervisor's Name and Phone Number:** Ellis Jackson, 111-111-1111. Performed maintenance adjustments and diagnostic certification and verification testing of assemblies and sub assemblies of LANCE, SHILLELAGH, TOW AND DRAGON weapon systems. Worked within a Supply Management Section and was commended for my attention to detail

in flawlessly processing more than 745 requisitions. Was singled out for rapid promotion ahead of my peers into supervisory roles because of my strong personal initiative and leadership.

SUPPLY MANAGER

EDUCATION & TRAINING	Received an **Associate in Arts,** Columbia College, Columbia, MO, June 2000.

SPECIALIZED TRAINING

Received Certificates of Training from numerous courses including these:
- MS PowerPoint 97 Course, 2001.
- Standard Property Book System Course, 2001.
- AIT Supply Services Training, 2001.
- Defense Hazardous Materials Handling. 2000.
- Justice and Pre-Law, Columbia College, 2000
- Introduction DBASE IV, 2000.
- Introduction to Harvard Graphics, 2000.
- Physical Security Officer Training Program, 2000 and 1999.
- Maintenance and Operations Coordination Training, 1999.
- Unit Alcohol Drug Coordinator and Breathalyzer Operator Certification, 1998
- Logistics Team Training Course, 1996
- Unit Armorer Course, 1989
- Base Supply Equipment Management Custodian Training Course, 1989
- Airborne Course, 1989
- Primary Leadership Development Course, 1986
- Operator Training for LANCE, SHILLELAGH, TOW and DRAGON weapon systems, 1986

CLEARANCE

Secret Security Clearance and Physical Security Officer Training, May 2000.

LANGUAGE

Proficiently read, write, and speak Spanish and studied Latin.

COMPUTERS

Strong working knowledge of software including Word, Excel, PowerPoint.

HONORS & AWARDS

Recipient of numerous medals and awards, including the Air Force Organizational Excellence Award and the Army Superior Unit Award. Was named **NCO OF THE QUARTER**, 2000 Medals received included an Armed Forces Expeditionary Award, the National Defense Medal, and two Good Conduct Medals.

SUMMARY OF KNOWLEDGE & SKILLS

Proven ability to gather, analyze, and present data. Highly skilled in applying evaluative techniques to identify and resolve problems. Vast logistics knowledge along with an ability to communicate clearly.

SHIRLEY HENDREN
SSN: 000-00-0000
213 Malloy Street
Fort Sill, OK
Home: (111) 111-1111 or (222) 222-2222
Work: (333) 333-3333
E-mail: vreynolds@yahoo.com

Vacancy Announcement #: DN-00-000
Source Code: External
Country of Citizenship: U.S.A.
Veteran's Preference: N/A
Reinstatement Eligibility: Yes
Highest Federal Grade Held: GS-0000-00

SUMMARY

Skilled in performing various communications, office automation, administrative, and accounting functions; known for my attention to detail and ability to perform complex tasks in a timely and accurate manner; possess exceptional communication and organizational skills.

EXPERIENCE

TELEPHONE OPERATOR/CLERK. US Army, Head Quarters, 31st Bn Information Services, Fort Sill, OK 77777-7777 (2004-present).
Supervisor: SFC Aaron Maddox, (444) 444-4444
Pay Grade: GS-0000-00
Hours worked per week: 40
Duties: Process a large volume of incoming calls, operating two separate communications, consoles for receiving and routing both secure and non-secure calls. Handle high priority local, calls occurring in a Top Secret environment. These included complex and extremely sensitive calls for general officers assigned to the Chief of Staff, the Inspector General, and the Division Signal Office, as well as other major military commands.

Highly skilled in the application of specialized procedures required for operating various circuits or networks. Provide service over a variety of secure and nonsecure communications networks and switches without compromising system security. Complete numerous difficult calls, such as connecting one or both parties to facilitate complicated conference calls, as well as making difficult overseas connections to third world countries, which require alternate calls and routing through other countries and operators.

Coordinate with the appropriate organization or contractor in the event of a communications outage, receiving and documenting the initial report of a system or circuit outage and communicating this information when placing the service or repair call. Monitor progress of repairs and perform any necessary follow-up actions to ensure that the communications system is fully functional with the least possible loss of service. Operate the command alerting system, which is comprised of two different paging networks. Update and maintain the pager listing and recall roster on a daily basis, using an automated data system to enter changes into the database.

Entrusted with responsibility for the issue and receipt of cellular phones, dial-up pagers, and other communications equipment worth thousands of dollars. Perform operational checks on communications equipment prior to issue and instruct user in the proper use of the cellular phones and dial-up pagers. Maintain issue and turn-in documentation to preserve accountability for all equipment. Hold additional responsibility for the vehicle assigned to the Chief of Staff. Maintain control logs, issue keys, and keep maintenance logs for the vehicle up-to-date. Open, sort, log and route incoming correspondence. Sign for certified and registered mail. Prepare, receive, file, dispatch, and safeguard classified documents.

Accomplishments:

- Demonstrated the maturity, stability, and self-confidence required to overcome the stress and anxiety of working in a high pressure, Top Secret environment.

VOUCHER EXAMINER. US Army, 34th Protocol Office, Fort Meade, MD 66666-6666 (2001-04).
Supervisor: SFC Katherine Brandon, (555) 555-5555
Pay Grade: GS-00
Hours worked per week: 40
Duties: Audited travel vouchers and other documentation related to travel, transportation, and relocation expenses for the operation and control of personnel and cargo movement by air, rail, motor transport and water. Supervised subordinates performing duties of the motor operator, traffic management coordinator, and terminal operations coordinator. Provided assistance to the Operations sections of the transportation battalion and higher level headquarters. Verified travel and transportation expense claims matched up with official orders and dates. Processed all categories of travel and transportation vouchers, including family member travel, delayed travel, invitational travel, and shipment/storage of personal effects. Verified information related to requests for allowances or entitlements, such as claimant status, individual or group travel, and purpose of travel. Interviewed individuals in person, by telephone, and through correspondence to obtain additional information or clarify information previously provided. Reviewed all supporting documents for accuracy and validity, performing mathematical computations of time and distance as well as converting expense amounts from foreign currencies.

Processed travel vouchers, operating an automated data system that used a proprietary software system designed by the Executive Officer of Finance and Accounting. Once a voucher was fully researched and documented, posted advance payments, collections, and outstanding amounts to the claimant's travel record cards. Composed letters to individuals who owed money to the government to collect overpayment of travel and transportation expenses. Referred any cases that appeared to be fraudulent to my supervisor.

VOUCHER EXAMINER. US Army, 52nd COMSEC Branch, Finance and Accounting Division, Fort Shafter, HI 55555-5555 (1998-01).
Supervisor: SSG Edward Vaughn, (666) 666-6666
Pay Grade: GS-000-00
Hours worked per week: 40
Duties: Processed and reviewed travel and transportation vouchers and supporting documentation to determine the claimant's eligibility for reimbursement of official travel expenses. Verified that the claimant had completed all required paperwork and checked the accuracy of the claim expense, correcting or modifying vouchers based on any changes or amendments to orders. Determined appropriate procedures for

TELEPHONE OPERATOR/ CLERK

completing vouchers requiring claims, advance payments and settlements, and a variety of other authorized travel claims. Calculated the amount of authorized allowance according to type of expense and itemized funds, balances, and totals. Compared expenses claimed to those authorized in order to determine the validity of a claim and turned down any inappropriate vouchers, noting the statutory or procedural cause for rejecting the claim. Took appropriate action on delinquent advances by annotating chargeable data. Performed customer service by telephone and in person, serving the local community and servicing organizations as well as personnel throughout the military community, in locations worldwide. Prepared and updated travel records, making modifications as transactions were processed and posting travel date, travel order number, voucher number, dollar amount, and other pertinent information to the system. Composed, typed, and prepared correspondence related to the processing of claimants travel vouchers and orders and maintained the office filing system in accordance with established procedures.

Accomplishments:
- Processed 1,247 travel records and vouchers ensuring that all travel advances were settled within 10 days of completion of travel.

QUALITY INSPECTION ASSISTANT. US Army, Lockheed Martin, 321st Aviation Battalion, Korea APO AP 44444-4444 (1995-98).
Supervisor: SSG Geraldine Walsh, (777) 777-7777
Pay Grade: $1,355 DM per month
Hours worked per week: 30
Duties: Conducted physical inspections of schools, day care centers, and office buildings to monitor performance of cleaning crews assigned to these locations and ensuring that all facilities under company contract are cleaned properly. Verified quality and quantity of cleaning materials to assure that merchandise delivered matches what was ordered and all materials are used on the job for which they were ordered. Composed and prepared correspondence for the Lockheed Martin Quality Assurance Specialist to report any incidences or discrepancies which require corrective action. Reviewed Quality Assurance provisions of procurement documents for accuracy and compliance with regulations. Operated an automated data system to maintain and update files related to condition codes as well as to file reports of any discrepancies according to established policies, practices, regulations or procedures.

Other experience:
MEDICAL FILES CLERK. Department of Veterans Affairs, 2898 McArthur Road, Easton, PA 33333-3333 (1991-95).
Supervisor: Mr. Eric Stokes, (888) 888-8888
Pay Grade: N/A (Volunteer)
Hours worked per week: 25
Duties: Used an automated data system to retrieve records needed for admissions, as well as for scheduling clinic appointments and laboratory testing. Located printed copies of records that had been removed to perpetual storage or retired to the Data Storage Center. Before returning printed records to the file room, screened all documents to ensure that they were updated and ready for filing, returning any records containing incomplete information to the appropriate area for updating prior to returning them to the files. Returned completed, up-to-date records to their appropriate location according to the terminal digit filing system.

Ensured that all laboratory reports, consultations, and other medical documentation forwarded from other civilian and military organizations affiliated with Veterans Affairs. Reports were filed in proper sequence, utilizing my knowledge of VA content, arrangement, and filing system procedures for medical and administrative records. Maintained the filing system in an accurate and orderly manner. Strictly adhered to and was highly knowledgeable of VA regulations concerning the confidentiality of patients' medical records. Resigned from this position to enter active duty service with the US Army.

NURSE'S AIDE. Cedar Valley Nursing Care, 2387 Archdale Rd, Easton, PA 22222-2222 (1988-91).
Supervisor: Ralph Bivens, (999) 999-9999
Pay Grade: $980.00 per month
Hours worked per week: 40
Duties: Measured and recorded patient's vital signs (blood pressure, pulse, temperature, and respiration), using a stethoscope and sphygmomometer when assigned to designated areas of the facility. Administered medication as ordered by the attending physician or nurse and recorded on the patient's medical chart. Immediately reported any unusual circumstances or sudden changes in the patient's condition to my supervisor, usually resulting in performance of a follow-up examination; noted the results of this examination on the patient's records. Assisted patients at meal times, feeding patients who were unable to feed themselves; recorded patient's intake and output on their medical chart. Scheduled and transported patients to and from doctor's appointments.

TELEPHONE OPERATOR/ CLERK

EDUCATION & TRAINING

Completed two years of college-level course work towards **Associate of Science** in **Medical Technology** at Lafayette College.
Excelled in a variety of medical training courses offered through Harrisburg Area Community College, including:

Gentle Teaching Course	Protective Intervention Course
Crisis Management	Person Centered Planning
OCD Symptomology	Assessment Treatment
Medication Administration	CPR Resuscitation
Development of Treatment Plans	Behavior Management

Recently finished four weeks of college-level training in computer operation, focusing on Windows XP and ME, Microsoft Word, and Microsoft Excel.

CERTIFICATIONS

Certified in Community CPR (adult, child, and infant) from Easton Medical Center expires 12/05.

HONORS

Was awarded several cash incentives for exemplary performance in civilian service from the Department of Veterans Affairs, as well as a cash award from Cedar Valley Nursing Care.

CLEARANCE

Hold a current **Top Secret** security clearance.

PERSONAL

Excellent personal and professional references are available upon request.

TRANSITION SERVICES MANAGER (CAREER CHANGE)

IRENE P. FOYE
782 Stoney Point Road
Ft. Monmouth, NJ 11111-11
Home: (111) 111-1111

E-mail: irenepfoye@earthlink.net
SSN: 000-00-0000
Position, Title, Series, Grade: Transition Services Manager, GS-0000
Announcement Number: DN-000-0000

EDUCATION Earned a **B.S in Zoology**, University of Louisville, Louisville, KY 1995.

- Financed my college education through full-time jobs — often worked in simultaneous jobs while refining time management and organizational skills as well as the ability to work with others as a contributor to team efforts in jobs as a Security Guard and Lifeguard.

Graduated from G. P. Hyatt High School, Baltimore, MD, 1988.

- Displayed leadership skills and the ability to manage my time while participating in a wide range of activities from captain of the advanced band, to captain of the varsity cheerleaders, to membership in Drama Club and JR ROTC.
- Maintained a 3.8 GPA, was selected for membership in the Honors Club in recognition of my academic achievements, and excelled in advanced placement classes in English, calculus, physics, and chemistry.

EXPERIENCE *Am building a reputation as a results-oriented young professional who excels in solving problems, dealing effectively with people, and applying an energetic and enthusiastic leadership style to everything I attempt, while excelling in a wide range of military, educational, and leadership environments:*

FLIGHT SCHOOL STUDENT. U.S. Army, 28th Aviation 4th BN, Ft. Monmouth, NJ 11111-1111 (2004-present). Supervisor: James Falcone, (222) 222-2222. Salary: $45,000. Maintained a 98 average in the demanding and technically oriented program for rotary-wing aviators with class averages around 85.

- Completed in excess of 120 hours of accident-free rotary wing aircraft flight hours.
- Named as the Safety Officer for my class, refined research, technical writing, and oral presentation skills while carrying out inspections and presenting safety briefings to the company's Safety Officer.

WARRANT OFFICER. US Army, Aviation Training Center, Ft. Eustis, VA 11122-2222 (2001-04). Supervisor: Leonard Allbrooks, (333) 333-3333. Annual salary: $41,000. Held multiple leadership roles in a 175-student program as a candidate for a presidential appointment as a military warrant officer being groomed to hold managerial roles in highly technical environments.

- As Administrative Officer, contributed numerous personal hours to oversee the in-processing of new soldiers and flow of documentation on administrative and personnel activities for 18 people.
- Consistently exceeded standards in all areas being evaluated while learning to take responsibility for seeing that my peers completed paperwork accurately and on time.
- Elected as the Executive Officer or "second in command" of my 175-person student company; expertly handled leadership activities to include planning and carrying out a class project working with the local Boys and Girls Club at Fort Eustis.
- Counseled other soldiers with personal or professional concerns.
- Earned the rare honor of being invited by the commandant of the school to remain as an instructor upon completion of the program.

CADET EXECUTIVE OFFICER. US Army, Combined Support Center, Eatontown, NJ 11133-3333 (1998-01). Hours per month: 36. Supervisor: Edwin Cox, (444) 444-4444. Salary: $36,000. Gained a strong base of experience in team building in a managerial role with a 150-person company, and learned to guide a combined work force of military and civilian personnel to work together to meet Army standards of readiness and skill levels.

- Became known for my maturity and problem-solving skills while counseling and supervising many people who were older and more experienced.
- Organized and implemented a training program for combat defense training.
- Received the opportunity to accompany members of an antidrug force on tours to scout for drug activity.
- Represented the military at various community activities where static displays were set up and allowed the public to ask questions about the helicopters and equipment.

MAINTENANCE FIRST-LINE SUPERVISOR. US Army, 237th Military Police Company, Fort Drum, NY 11144-4444 (1995-98). Supervisor: Warren Evans, DSN 555-5555. Salary: $30,000. In a summer program of active duty service, refined leadership skills as a Maintenance Supervisor ensuring reliability of maintenance support for a $24.5 million inventory of Black Hawk helicopters.

- Represented the section in weekly staff meetings by preparing and presenting briefings on maintenance status.
- Applied a keen eye for detail while planning and organizing social events such as "Hail and Farewells" to honor incoming and departing personnel.

SQUAD LEADER. US Army, Headquarters, 23rd Battalion, Fort Knox, KY 11155-5555. (1991-95). Hours per week: 25. Supervisor: SSG Daniel Cummings, (666) 666-6666. Salary: $27,000. Advanced in leadership roles including First Sergeant, Platoon Secretary, and Platoon Leader to hold the senior student management assignment while simultaneously working for Louisville Security Services, working two jobs to finance my education, and attending college full-time at the University of Louisville.

- Worked closely with Military Science professors while planning, coordinating, and organizing fund raising activities, tactical field exercises, and day-to-day activities.
- Organized and led the physical training and conditioning program.
- Competed in the VIPOR physical training program as the leader of the portion of preparations for a mentally and physically demanding program.

CLASS LEADER. U.S. Army, Company C, 1/248th Motor Pool, Fort Dix, NJ 11166-6666 (1988-91). Supervisor: Richard Blough, (777) 777-7777. Salary: $22,000. Was the Distinguished Honor Graduate of my 80-person class and set the standard which allowed the class to achieve the highest average scores (98) of any class in a Vehicle Maintenance Program.

- Utilized refined communication and interpersonal skills as the liaison between the drill sergeants and the academic instructors; counseled and tutored students.
- Led the class to an average PT score of 225 on a 300 scale.
- Earlier in Mission Strategy Training (Aug 88-Nov 88), was honored two Army Achievement Medals while motivating my team to exceed standards in all evaluated areas of performance.

TRAINING

Received U.S. Army training which has included:
Advanced Individual Training, Ft. Eustis, VA 1988.
Basic Combat Training, Ft. Eustis, VA, 1988.
Cadet Troop Leadership Training, Fort Hood, TX, 1998.
Rotary Wing Flight School, Fort Hood, TX, 1997.
ROTC Advanced Camp, Fort Hood, TX 2000.
Warrant Officer Candidate School, Fort Hood, TX, 2001.

SUMMARY OF SKILLS

Offer more than seven years of leadership experience in military environments and have carried out a wide range of personnel and administrative actions:
coordinating preparation of performance appraisals
monitoring programs for evaluations, promotions, grievances, and incentive awards
advising supervisors on personnel actions
identifying problem areas and recommending solutions
developing the organizational structure for daily operations
researching, analyzing, and preparing data and presenting briefings

COMPUTERS

Word, Excel, WordPerfect

PERSONAL

Am in excellent physical condition: have scored 325 points on a 300-scale for annual physical fitness testing and am training for marathons and triathlons. Secret clearance.

TRANSPORTATION MANAGER

ROGER C. JACOBS
3789 Cambridge Avenue
Washington, DC 11111-1111
999-999-9999 **Home**
E-MAIL: rogerjacobs@aol.com

SSN: 000-00-0000
Country of Citizenship: United States
Veteran's Preference:
Contact current supervisor: Yes
Vacancy Announcement Number: AR 0000-000
Job Title: Transportation Manager, GS-00

EXPERIENCE

SENIOR TRANSPORTATION TERMINAL MANAGER.
Start and End Dates: 2004-present. **Hours worked per week:** 40+.
Current Salary: $42,000 per year. **Employer's Name and Address:** Department of Defense, 3876 7th Street, Washington, DC 11111-1111 **Supervisor's Name and Phone Number:** Walter Smalls, 888-888-8888. Because of my vast transportation knowledge and distinguished career, was handpicked as Senior Transportation Terminal Manager of the most diversified ocean terminal ordered to transship ammunitions, explosives, and sensitive cargo worldwide. Supervise the safety of 15 military, 195 civilian employees, and 120 contractor/longshoremen. Revitalize a stagnant training program and develop a training brief which became a model worldwide.

OPERATIONS SERGEANT MAJOR.
Start and End Dates: 2001-04. **Hours worked per week:** 40+.
Salary: $38,500. **Employer's Name and Address:** Department of Defense, 5127 Timber Lane, Miami, FL 33355. **Supervisor's Name and Phone Number:** Dennis Strickland, 777-777-7777. Commended for the success of the Armed Forces Identification and Evaluation organization methods and testing regiments by the Chief of Military Intelligence, Major General Frank D. Hoffman.
- Oversee the individual and group training for personnel in 18 different job specialties.
- Ensure the company is ready to respond with no notice and carry out support missions.
- Accountable for the readiness of 48 vehicles, ensure the quality of training, welfare, and readiness of imagery specialists operating and maintaining vehicles.
- Directly oversee the administrative and logistics support for 25 people operating and maintaining $12.5 million worth of imagery and intelligence equipment.

VEHICLE PROCESSING CENTER & OPERATIONS MANAGER.
Start and End Dates: 1997-01. **Hours worked per week:** 40+.
Salary: $35,000. **Employer's Name and Address:** Department of Transportation, 35347 Bishamon Avenue, Chicago, IL 45018. **Supervisor's Name and Phone Number:** Heather Wright, 666-666-6666. Operated two vehicle processing centers, a documentation section, and an administration section with 4 military bases and including, Fort Knox and Fort Campbell, KY; Fort Riley, KS and Fort Leonard Wood, MO. Accounted for $1.9 million in assets.

BATTALION SERGEANT MAJOR & VEHICLE MAINTENANCE MANAGER.
Start and End Dates: 1995-97. **Hours worked per week:** 40+. **Salary:** $32,000.
Employer's Name and Address: Department of Transportation, 2436 Haywood Boulevard, Detroit, MI 45833. **Supervisor's Name and Phone Number:** Jermaine Yarborough, 555-555-5555. Assured the rigorous training of 75 enlisted employees and 32 officers working in eleven different organizations. Was the organization's subject matter expert on all matters pertaining to the maintenance and management of vehicles as well as on coordinating and arranging transportation support. Provided aggressive leadership and training management which boosted soldier readiness from an unacceptable 58% to 88%. Played a key role in planning and executing transportation support for special operation in Central American and Israel.

Other military experience:
MOTOR TRANSPORTATION COMPANY MANAGER & FIRST SERGEANT.
Start and End Dates: June 1993-95. **Hours worked per week:** 40+. **Salary:** $28,900.
Employer's Name and Address: US Army, 34th Motor Pool Division, Fort Drum, NY 10054
Supervisor's Name and Phone Number: SFC Mark Harris, 444-444-4444. Served as mentor and trainer for 62 employees while managing equipment valued at $8 million. Directed administrative and logistical support for a trucking company with a fleet of 115 wheeled and tracked vehicles. Developed new Vehicle Safety procedures which instilled in employees a new respect for safety and quality assurance and which resulted in more than 180,000 accident-free miles in an arctic environment.

TRUCKING OPERATIONS COMMANDER.
Start and End Dates: 1990-93. **Hours worked per week:** 40+. **Salary:** $25,000.
Employer's Name and Address: US Army, 23rd ATC Maintenance Group, Fort Bliss, TX 73215-5940. **Supervisor's Name and Phone Number:** SFC Derrick Iverson, 333-333-3333. Managed operations of a medium truck company with a fleet of 85 vehicles, and directed long-haul transportation and distribution of cargo throughout Korea for an organization which accumulated 2 million driving miles annually. Managed 180 employees. Supervised operations of a driver's training academy, four trailer transfer points, and a trailer maintenance center. Developed new Vehicle Operation procedures which expedited the Department of Transportation cargo throughout Southwest Region. Solved complex problems during several combat mission exercises. Set up and managed a dining facility in a remote location which earned us a Specialized Unit Award in 1992. Developed a driver's education course evaluated as "superb."

Highlights of other military experience: Began serving my country in 1983 as a Truck Driver; was promoted ahead of my peers and subsequently served in roles as a Chief Dispatcher, Light and Heavy Vehicle Operator, Transportation Company Squad Leader, Vehicle Operators Instructor, Vehicle Maintenance Manager, Truck Platoon Supervisor, and Senior Drill Sergeant.
- 1989. Was **Instructor** in the Vehicle Operating Course; trained and tested 36 students daily on coupling and decouping, backing into a simulated loading dock, and operations over open roads.
- 1988-89. As **Senior Drill Sergeant** in a training organization, oversaw the training of 1250 soldiers annually.
- 1984-85. Senior Supervisor of a utility truck platoon. Managed 36 people and supervised operations/maintenance of 25 vehicles ranging from ¼ ton to 5 tons annually. Also supervised the training of 190 individuals.

TRANSPORTATION MANAGER

EDUCATION

Completing **Master of Science degree in Management**, University of the District of Columbia, Washington, DC.

Bachelor of Science (B.S.) in Management, St. Thomas University, Miami, FL 2001.

Bachelor of Science (B.S.) in Liberal Arts, Northeastern Illinois University, Chicago, IL, 1998.

Associate in Arts, Marygrove College, Detroit, MI, 1997.

Associate's degree in Management, Marygrove College, Detroit, MI, 1997.

Associate in General Studies, Watertown Community College, Watertown, NY, 1995.

CLEARANCE

Secret Security Clearance

HIGHLIGHTS OF MANAGEMENT & TECHNICAL TRAINING

Completed extensive executive-level training including the Leadership and Development Training Course, March 1995 and the Loadmasters Operation Course 1995; the Non-Commissioned Officer Training, 1995; Manager Development Course, 1994; the Defense Reutilization & Marketing System Course, 1994.

Emergency Management Institute: At this institute affiliated with the Health and Safety Management Course 1994, National Emergency Training Center, completed the Emergency Program Manager Course, 1994; the Hazardous Materials Course, 1993; and the Radiological Emergency Management Course, 1993; Guide to Disaster Assistance, 1993; Emergency Preparedness, 1993.

Logistics Management College: At the U.S. Army Logistics Management College, received diplomas for completing the Army Maintenance Management Course, 1994, and the SMPT-5 Hazardous Materials Handling Course, 1993.

Army Institute for Professional Development: At his famed institute which refines leadership skills and technical knowledge, completed the Weapons Specialist Course, 1992; Defense Financial Management Course, 1992; Supervisor Development Course, 1992; Defense Hazardous Materials/Waste Handling Course, 1991; Manager Development Course, 1991; Intelligence/Operation Sergeant's Course, 1991; the Chemical Senior NCO Course, 1990; the NCO Logistics Program, 1990.

Other training: Lifesavers Course; the Arabic Language and Culture Course; computer operations; light and heavy expanded mobility tactical trucks; drug and alcohol abuse prevention; Vehicle Operation Course.

HONORS & AWARDS

Received 34 medals and awards during 25 years of military service.

COMPUTERS

Proficient with software including Microsoft Word, PowerPoint, Access, and Excel; have utilized supply, inventory control, purchasing, and logistics software.

SUMMARY OF EXPERTISE

Extensive expertise related to special-purpose and specially equipment vehicles. Outstanding track record in safeguarding government assets from waste and abuse through applying my strong planning skills and resourcefulness. Have developed preventive maintenance programs, driver education programs, and accident reduction programs. Extensive experience in cost analysis and budget management for budgets ranging from thousands of dollars to many millions of dollars. Am considered an expert on the legal, technical, and policy matters related to motor-vehicle related matters.

UNITED STATES MARSHAL

NORMAN E. MCDANIELS
SSN: 000-00-0000
276 East Surrey Cove
Chicago, IL 44444-4444
Home: (999) 999-9999
Work: (888) 888-8888
Vacancy Announcement Number: 00-000-00

Country of Citizenship: U.S.A.
Veterans' Preference: 10 point
Reinstatement Eligibility: NA
Highest Federal Civilian Grade Held: 15

SUMMARY

Offer well-developed planning and organizational abilities, strong leadership skills, and a reputation as a results-oriented professional and skilled negotiator capable of building effective interagency coalitions to achieve common goals.

EXPERIENCE

CHIEF DEPUTY UNITED STATES MARSHAL. United States Marshals Service, 1789 Locklear Avenue, Eastern District of Pennsylvania, Philadelphia, PA 11166 (March 2003-present).
Supervisor: Warren Hunt, United States Marshal
Pay grade: 15
Hours worked per week: 40+
Duties: Assists the U.S. Marshal, directing the daily operations of the District. Provide managerial oversight and training to as many as 80 deputies, including other deputies who served in supervisory positions. Serve as liaison between the U.S. Marshals Service and various local, state, and federal law enforcement organizations; develop effective coalitions and build strong working relationships across agency lines. Supervise and participate in the serving of all types of civil and criminal writs, including criminal warrants that necessitated the apprehension and arrest of potentially dangerous offenders who were evading arrest. Coordinate with Federal Judges, Magistrates, and other court personnel, providing security for prisoners awaiting trial during detainment and transportation and trial security for court proceedings. Plan and direct activities related to the Federal Witness Protection Program. Oversee administration and negotiations of jail contracts with federal, state, and local officials.
Accomplishments:
• Selected to serve as acting U.S. Marshal for the Eastern District of Pennsylvania from April 2003-January 2004.

UNITED STATES MARSHAL (Acting). United States Marshal Service, 14884 McLeod Drive, Las Vegas, NV 87451 (June 2001-March 2003).
Supervisor: Director Patrick Wayans
Pay grade: 15
Hours worked per week: 40+
Background of Appointment: Selected by the Director to assume leadership of this district after the resignation of the appointed marshal.
Duties: Oversaw the operation of the U.S. Marshals Office for this district until the new Presidential appointee was selected. Directed

the activities of 48 employees, to include administration and supervision of an extensive training program providing instruction to Marshals Service staff as well as outside agencies. Established lines of communication and forged alliances between various law enforcement organizations, brokering a number of interagency agreements that resulted in joint operations which achieved common goals.

UNITED STATES MARSHAL. United States Marshal Service, 8372 Shaw Boulevard, Dallas, TX 69974 (August 1999-June 2001).
Supervisor: Director Keith Oliver
Pay grade: 15
Hours worked per week: 40+
Duties: Directed the service of civil and criminal actions averaging 1,150 writs and warrants as well as approximately 125 seizures per month; property seized totaled more than $135 million annually. Oversaw the operation of the U.S. Marshals Office for the largest federal judicial district in the country, comprised of seven counties and serving a population of 12 million people. Directed the activities of 115 employees, to include administration and supervision of an extensive training program providing instruction to Marshals Service staff as well as outside agencies. Established lines of communication and forged alliances between various law enforcement organizations, brokering a number of interagency agreements that resulted in the accomplishment of common goals.
Accomplishments:
* Provided trial security and oversaw Task Force operations on several high profile cases, a joint operation which required my unique ability to create interagency coalitions and involved CIA, FBI, Marshals Service, Postal Inspectors, and IRS personnel in Atlanta, Las Vegas, and Detroit. This operation resulted in the seizure of more than $175 million in currency and precious gems
* Developed a training program to instruct U.S. Air Force personnel at Tyndall AFB, FL in vehicle ambush survival tactics for use in transporting the space shuttle.
* Created and implemented a system for seizing captured oil rigs while minimizing damage to personnel and property; this technique was used to recover rigs off the coast of Texas which were taken over illegally by union workers during a labor dispute.

CHIEF DEPUTY UNITED STATES MARSHAL. United States Marshal Service, 6452 Argyll Road, Boston, MA 16574 (July 1995-August 1999).
Supervisor: Harold Summit, U.S. Marshal
Pay grade: 13
Hours worked per week: 40+
Duties: Supervised and participated in the serving of all types of civil and criminal writs. Coordinated with Federal Judges, Magistrates, and other court personnel, providing security for prisoners during detainment and transportation and trial security for court proceedings. Planned and directed activities related to the Federal Witness Protection Program. Assisted the U.S. Marshal in directing Marshal Service operations for one of the largest federal judicial districts in the country. Provided managerial oversight and training to as many as 115 deputies, including others who held supervisory positions. Acted as liaison between the U.S. Marshals Service and various local, state, and federal law enforcement organizations; developed effective coalitions and built strong working relationships across agency lines. Selected by the Director to serve as U.S. Marshal for the Northern District of Massachusetts after the unexpected medical retirement of the Clinton appointee.

SUPERVISORY DEPUTY UNITED STATES MARSHAL. United States Marshal Service, 5276 Allenville Road, Denver, CO 68454 (May 1990-July 1995).
Supervisor: Eugene Cooper, U.S. Marshal
Pay grade: 13

Hours worked per week: 40+
Duties: Supervised 24 deputies in Marshal Service operations and seizures. Oversaw prisoner transportation for an average of 1125 prisoners per month. Coordinated and directed special assignments for the Western District of Colorado; assisted the Drug Task Force in joint operations with the FBI and U.S. Army National Guard throughout Western Colorado.

UNITED STATES MARSHAL

SUPERVISORY DEPUTY UNITED STATES MARSHAL. United States Marshal Service, 12544 Pinecrest Drive, Atlanta GA (September 1987-May 1990).
Supervisor: James E. Blair, Supervisory Deputy
Pay grade: 12
Hours worked per week: 40+
Duties: Supervised all seizures, prisoner movements, court operations, and special assignments for the district. Drug crimes in this region account for only 35% of all offenses in this region; activities were more heavily focused on bank robberies, fraud, interstate transportation of stolen goods, and counterfeiting.

DEPUTY UNITED STATES MARSHAL. United States Marshals Service, 3785 Russelldale Hwy, Portland, OR 92871 (December 1984-September 1987).
Supervisor: Clifford Mabry, U.S. Marshal
Pay grade:
Hours worked per week: 40+
Duties: Provided security and protection for key witnesses and their families, as well as for officers of the court. Tracked, located, and apprehended prisoners; seized vessels under admiralty; and executed criminal warrants issued by the federal courts. In 1986, served as Deputy-In-Charge of the Warrant Squad for Salem, OR. Participated in Anti-Piracy details in 1984 & 1985; made numerous arrests for illegal possession of drugs or weapons.

MILITARY EXPERIENCE

Volunteered to return to active duty; served as a Commanding Officer at the US Army installation in Fort Irwin, CA from 1990-1996. Served in several combat tours in the Middle East. Received numerous honors, including the Purple Heart, Army Achievement Medals, a Certificate of Appreciation, a Joint Meritorious Unit Award, two Good Conduct Medals, and a Combat Action Ribbon with 2 Gold Stars.

2004-present: Master Gunnery Sergeant, United States Army Reserves. Serve as Intelligence Operator while stationed at Fort Dix, NJ.
2001-2003: Gunnery Sergeant, United States Army Reserves, Las Vegas, NV.
1999-2001: Gunnery Sergeant, United States Army Reserves, Dallas, TX.
1992-1996: Various active duty assignments worldwide, including Platoon Sergeant, Fort Greely, AK; Recruiter, Pensacola, FL; Instructor, Fort Eustis, VA; and Supervisor-in-Charge of Corrective Custody, Fort Leavenworth, KS.

EDUCATION & TRAINING	Earned an Associate in Science degree in Police Science, Mountain View College, Dallas, TX, 2001.

Completed numerous training and development courses sponsored by the United States Army and United States Marshal Service, including the following:

US Marshal

- Federal Managers Financial Integrity Act Training, U.S. Marshals Training Academy, 2002.
- Deputy U.S. Marshal Training, Miami, FL, 2002.
- U.S. Marshals Training #801, U.S. Marshal Enforcement Institute, Los Angeles, CA 1999.
- Chief Deputy Management Training, New York, NY, 1999.
- Supervisory Training, U.S. Marshal Enforcement Institute, Glynco, GA, 1997-1998.

US Army

- US Army LDCRC – Leadership Development and Conflict Resolution Center, 1996.
- Certifying Officers Training, Albuquerque, NM, 1996.
- Joint Psychological Operations Staff Planning, U.S. Army JFK Special Warfare Center and School, 1996.
- Counter-Terrorism Course, U.S. Army Reserves Training School, Fort Jackson, SC, 1995.
- US Army Ground Combat Intelligence, Phases I & II, Fort Jackson, SC, 1995-1996.
- Communications Security Course, United States Army Reserves, 1995.
- Basic Combat Intelligence Phase, United States Army Reserves, 1995.
- Officer Survival School, United States Army Reserves, Louisiana, 1992.
- Specialized Anti-Aircraft Air Piracy School, Atlanta, GA, 1992.
- Corrective Custody Training, U.S. Army Reserves, Fort Leavenworth, KS, 1992.

HONORS

Received numerous prestigious awards an honors, including:

- Outstanding Performance Awards, U.S. Marshals, Service, 1994, 1996, 1999, 2001, 2003.
- Distinguished Achievement Award, Federal Bar Association, 1994.
- Letters of Appreciation from U.S. President, Attorney General Earnest H. Connelly, and Governor Carl R. Mendelsohn, 1993.
- Numerous Certificates of Appreciation and Commendation Plaques from Law Enforcement Agencies as well as local and state officials nationwide.

AFFILIATIONS

Former Vice-president, Pennsylvania State Lodge for Law Enforcement Officials. Member, American Society for Industrial Security, American Legion, National Association of American Veterans, US Army Intelligence Association, National Sportsmanship Association and Pennsylvania Warrant Squad Association.

PERSONAL

Excellent physical condition. Married, three children. Outstanding references are available.

Many agencies, such as the Central Intelligence Agency (CIA) and Federal Bureau of Investigation (FBI), accept a resume and cover letter as your first approach in seeking employment. We advise finding out from those specific agencies what they require, but this section is designed to show you samples of resumes and cover letters which have been used successfully in the past in obtaining employment with specialized government agencies.

In the preceding section which contains samples of the resumix, you probably noticed that cover letters were not shown. That is because cover letters are not usually requested by the job vacancy announcement. Therefore, it is not advised that you send a cover letter when a vacancy announcement does not request it.

The following resumes are introduced by cover letters, so you will gain some insight into how to prepare those specialized cover letters.

INTELLIGENCE AGENT & EXECUTIVE OFFICER

Date

Exact Name of Person
Exact Title
Exact Name of Company
Address
City, State, Zip

Dear Exact Name of Person: (or Dear Sir or Madam if answering a blind ad):

With the enclosed resume, I would like to make you aware of my background as an accomplished young professional with natural leadership abilities who offers exceptional organizational and training skills as well as a track record of excellence as a U.S. Army officer. It is my desire to embark upon a career with the Central Intelligence Agency, and the clandestine service field especially interests me.

As you will see from my resume, I am a captain stationed at Ft. Hood, TX, where I am excelling as an Intelligence Agent in the 345th Military Intelligence battalion. From May 1999 until early June 2004, I excelled in high-intensity operations in Germany, Korea, and Japan where I coordinated and planned numerous training exercises and real-world missions in close cooperation with personnel from other countries. During this period I managed a hurricane relief operations center, exchange programs with numerous foreign countries, and support for VIP visits.

Throughout my military career, I have been placed in highly visible roles in organizations with dynamic, constantly changing, and multiple simultaneous operations. I have consistently been described as an aggressive self-starter and have consistently earned evaluations as someone who can be counted on to work at a higher level than expected based on my age and actual years of experience. Able to handle the stresses of high operations tempos, I offer a keen analytical mind and ability to handle multiple simultaneous tasks and complete each one above expected standards. While attending college full-time, I was an ROTC student at the University of Arizona in Tucson, AZ.

Although I am earning top-notch evaluations and on the "fast track" for promotion with the military, I am at a point where I feel my analytical, organizational, and leadership skills would be best used in other environments within the U.S. Government. With a degree in Criminal Justice and a background in international settings, I believe I could make valuable contributions to any agency in need of physically and mentally tough leaders. I hope you will contact me to suggest a time when I might meet with you personally to discuss your goals and how my background might serve your needs. I can provide outstanding references.

Sincerely,

Mark Dyre

Name: Mark Dyre

Citizenship: U.S.

Social Security Number: 000-00-0000

PO Box 4444

Ft. Huachuca, AZ 00000-0000

Home telephone number: (222) 222-2222

Work telephone number: (333) 333-3333

E-mail: Mark.Dyre@aol.com

EDUCATION	**B.S., Criminal Justice,** University of Arizona, Tucson, AZ, 2002.

- Financed my college education through ROTC.

Graduated from **Bennetton High School,** Los Angeles, CA, 1991.

Skill Summary: Analyzing and planning operations within tight time constraints; exceptional written and verbal communication skills; mentally and physically tough; well-organized and focused; highly proficient both technically and tactically; detail oriented.

Foreign Language: Working knowledge of French and Spanish.

Foreign Area Knowledge: Very well versed in world events and an avid reader of international publications covering world news. As a military officer, have served on task forces and held military assignments in several foreign countries.

Foreign Travel: Australia, Germany, Korea, and Japan

EXPERIENCE   June 2004 to present. Full time. **Intelligence Agent and Executive Officer,** $52,000 per year, C Company, 345th Military Intelligence Battalion, Ft. Hood, TX, Lt. Graham Saideo, Supervisor, (111) 111-1111. Perform essentially the same functions as I did in the job below.

March 2001 to July 2004. Full time. **Battalion S-5 Air,** $47,000 per year, A Company, 54th Support Brigade, Ft. Huachuca, AZ, MAJ Ernest M. Hamm, (222) 222-2222. Planned, coordinated, and supervised all air requirements for deployments throughout Stuttgart, Germany in a light infantry battalion and heavy combat engineering company.

- Planned and coordinated exchanges with the military services in Australia, Korea, Italy and other countries operating in the area.
- Developed plans and provided support for a distinguished visitor program.
- Performed duties as the Battle Captain in the battalion's main command post.
- Selected to manage a humanitarian relief operations center established following the devastation of Hurricane Floyd, coordinated the airlift of in excess of 120 tons of food, clothing, and medical supplies.
- Cited for my ability to excel in a "challenging environment of multiple simultaneous operations," during one period deployed two companies by air and sea to Mexico while also arranging to send and return personnel and equipment to and from San Juan.
- Scored a perfect 300 during annual fitness testing.
- Was described on performance reports as "invaluable in the success of the battalion" in a complex and volatile environment with "planning and execution skills far surpassing his rank and experience."

May 1999 to October 2001. Full time. **Assistant S-3 Air,** $41,000 per year, Special Operations Division, DA VII Corp, APO AP 45444, MAJ Mackenzie Dayton, phone unknown. Coordinated and resourced fixed and rotary wing assets for a 554-person light infantry battalion and 120-person combat heavy engineering company defending Puerto Rico and carrying out contingency missions.

- Singled out for my ability to achieve exceptional results within tight time constraints, was evaluated as "an extremely tough leader able to operate under the most demanding situations" and to motivate others through a positive attitude and energetic manner.
- Applied my diplomatic and communication skills as manager of seven high-visibility

VIP visits for countries including Australia, Germany, and Japan.

- Managed a five-week multinational training exercise in Japan which included coordinating air movements for personnel from 24 countries and the relocation of helicopters each day.
- Increased my expertise and level of knowledge of civil disturbance operations, peacekeeping operations, and light infantry operations in jungle environments.

July 1997 to May 1999. Full time. **Executive Officer**, $39,000, I Company, 27th Land Combat Support, Camp Haggon, Japan, SFC Samuel Thomas, phone unknown. Was "second-in-command" of a 114-person light infantry company with the mission of defense of Korea as well as for training and contingency response throughout Asia.

- Coordinated administrative and logistical support as the headquarters platoon manager.
- Controlled maintenance and utilization of equipment valued in excess of $2 million.
- Consistently scored a perfect 300 during annual PT testing and was frequently recognized for my emphasis on physical conditioning.
- Was one of only two lieutenants in the battalion to earn the Expert Combatman Badge (ECB).
- Official performance evaluations described me as "tenacious… a selfless leader…the epitome of the professional officer who consistently exceeds the standard."

May 1995 to July 1997. Full time, $35,000 per year, **Rifle Platoon Leader**, B Company, E-123rd Demolition Support, Stuttgart Germany, PSG Alan J. Shumate, phone unknown. Oversaw training, performance, and support services for 31 soldiers and three German personnel; provided maintenance for four Bradley Fighting Vehicles and equipment valued in excess of $10 million.

- Emphasized tough and realistic training which resulted in highly skilled leaders with initiative and the drive to accomplish their assigned missions.

November 1992 to May 1995. Full time, $25,600 per year, **Automation Clerk**, HQ, Office of the General Commander, Ft. Campbell, KY, SGM Darryl Harborough, phone unknown. Edited correspondence to ensure compliance with applicable government regulations, responded to information requests, and accounted for supplies.

- Earned the respect of my superiors for my attention to detail, honest and candid manner, and ability to find ways of getting the work done more efficiently and productively.
- Certified as a Small Purchasing Agent in a prior job as a Procurement Clerk, wrote contracts up to $5,000.

Honors and Awards:
Recognized for my exemplary performance with honors including two Army Commendation Medals, a Good Conduct Medal, Joint Meritorious Service Ribbon, National Defense Service Medal, and a Humanitarian Service Medal.

Military Training:

Command and Staff Services School

Air Assault Course

Bradley Fighting Vehicle Commander Course

Infantry Mortar Platoon Officer Course

The Total Army Instructors Training Course

Infantry Officer Advanced Course

Ranger School

Infantry Officer Basic Course

The Airborne School

Firearms Skills:

An Expert Marksman, am proficient with most U.S. small arms.

Other Information:

Hold a **Secret security clearance**.

Familiar with many popular **computer operating systems and software.**

INTELLIGENCE ANALYST

Date

Exact Name of Person
Exact Title
Exact Name of Company
Address
City, State, Zip

INTELLIGENCE ANALYST

Dear Exact Name of Person: (or Dear Sir or Madam if answering a blind ad):

With the enclosed resume, I would like to make you aware of my background as an accomplished young professional with natural leadership abilities who offers exceptional organizational and training skills as well as a track record of excellence as an intelligence analyst, trainer, and supervisor.

In my current position as an Intelligence Analyst for the Central Intelligence Agency located in VA, I manage personnel and physical information, as well as automation security and security education programs; classes on Operations Security which I conducted resulted in no compromises of security during a major project. My strong technical knowledge of security issues and exceptional written communication skills are applied while authoring additions to the organization's standard operating procedures.

With an Associate's degree in Supervisory Leadership from Southwest Missouri State University in Springfield, MO, I have also excelled in numerous advanced military leadership and technical training courses. As an articulate communicator, I am frequently called upon to make presentations before tens of thousands of spectators at nationwide events. My strong emphasis on "safety first" has resulted in more than 35,850 free fall parachute jumps with no accidents.

Throughout my military career, I have demonstrated maturity, intelligence, and strong leadership traits which have resulted in my selection for promotion ahead of my peers and advancement to positions of increasing responsibility. My exemplary performance has been recognized with numerous awards

If you can use a highly-skilled leader with a strong background in information gathering and analysis, I hope you will welcome my call soon when I try to arrange a brief meeting to discuss your goals and how my background might serve your needs. I can provide outstanding references.

Sincerely,

Nelson B. Lujan

Alternate Last Paragraph:
I hope you will write or call me soon to suggest a time when we might meet to discuss your needs and goals and how my background might serve them. I can provide outstanding references.

Name: **Mr. Nelson B. Lujan**
Citizenship: U.S.
6565 Phillips Blvd
Reston, VA 20189
Home telephone number: (888) 888-8888
Work telephone number: (777) 777-7777

EDUCATION   **Associate's degree in Supervisory Leadership**, Southwest Missouri State University, Springfield, MO, 2002.

Foreign Language: Spanish   **Foreign Travel:** Guam, Haiti, and Mexico

EXPERIENCE   February 2003 to present: Full time. **Intelligence Analyst**, $45,000 per year, Central Intelligence Agency, CST Division PO Box 4605, Reston, VA 20195. Keith D. Pallace (666) 666-6666. Assist the Intelligence Supervisor, managing personnel and physical, information and automation security as well as security education programs, providing intelligence in support of organizational level activities.

- Process security clearances for six employees deploying to Iran in only 72 hours and personally oversee personnel security information and passports for 368 personnel.
- Conduct classes on Operations Security in preparation for a major exercise and train personnel on Information Security, resulting in zero security compromises.

April 1996 to February 2003: Full time. **Air Patrol Instructor,** $62,000 per year, Civil Air Patrol Great Lakes Region, Detroit MI, Corey Leonard, (555) 555-5555. As a member of the elite Great Lakes Patrol, I performed precision aerial demonstrations in support of the organizations public relations and recruiting efforts as well as training new team members.

- Supervised four personnel while traveling for performances worldwide; assisted the Team Leader in making operational and safety decisions.
- Trained 18 new members of the Great Lakes Patrol, instructing them in specific techniques of precision aerial demonstration as well as in public speaking.
- Performed with a consistent emphasis on safety consciousness and responsibility has resulted in 35,850 free fall parachute jumps conducted by my unit with no accidents.

Other experience in the US Army:
September 1996 to April 2000: Full time. **Artillery Observer**, $25,000 per year, HHC, 5 224th Field Artillery, Fort Sill, OK. SFC Lionel R. Carlson (444) 444-4444. Provided supervision and training to personnel in a forward observer team conducting reconnaissance to determine locations, create terrain sketches and visibility diagrams, and verify the accuracy of map data. Observed assigned sector of responsibility, detecting targets and requesting artillery, mortar, close air, or naval gun fires as appropriate.

HONORS
& AWARDS   Recognized for my exemplary performance with two Army Commendation Medals, eight Army Achievement Medals, and two Good Conduct Medals.

MILITARY
TRAINING   Intelligence Analyst Basic Non-Commissioned Officers Course (BNCOC; Intelligence Analyst Course (Distinguished Graduate); Battle Staff Non-Commissioned Officer's Course Jumpmaster Course; U.S. Army Special Operations Command Security Manager's Course Primary Leadership and Development Course (Commandant's List)

WEAPONS
QUALIFICATIONS   Skilled in the operation of various types of weapons, including M-16 rifle, 9mm semi-automatic pistol, M-203 grenade launcher, M-60 machine gun, and M-249 machine gun.

OTHER
INFORMATION   Hold a Top Secret security clearance with SCI.

Familiar with many popular computer operating systems and software, including, Windows.

LOGISTICIAN

Date

Exact Name of Person
Exact Title
Exact Name of Company
Address
City, State, Zip

Dear Exact Name of Person: (or Dear Sir or Madam if answering a blind ad):

   With the enclosed resume, I would like to make you aware of my background as an accomplished young professional with natural leadership abilities who offers exceptional organizational and training skills as well as a track record of excellence as a U.S. Army officer. It is my desire to embark upon a career with the Central Intelligence Agency, and the military intelligence field especially interests me.

   As you will see from my resume, I am working in a captain's job although I hold the rank of first lieutenant. I am excelling after being specially selected to hold the position as Senior Logistician in the Headquarter's Chemical Battalion. In this job, I have transformed a substandard budget management system into a model of efficiency with strong controls in place. This organization is preparing to relocate to Fort Hood, TX and I am handling the details of planning logistical support for this project which involves moving personnel and equipment. I was selected for this job on the basis of my effectiveness as the Chemical Officer for a chemical unit where, in my first active-duty assignment, I quickly earned attention for my exceptional planning, communication, analytical, and leadership skills.

   The son of an Army Lieutenant Colonel, I have lived and traveled overseas and graduated from high school in Italy after living there while in elementary and middle school. I am known as an aggressive self-starter and have consistently earned evaluations as someone who can be counted on to work at a higher level than expected based on my age and actual years of experience. Able to handle the stresses of high operations tempos, I offer a keen analytical mind and ability to handle multiple simultaneous tasks and complete each one above expected standards. While attending college full-time, I was an ROTC student and served in leadership roles emphasizing training and logistics management support for U.S. Army National Guard units.

   Although I am earning top-notch evaluations and on the "fast track" for promotion with the military, I am at a point where I feel my analytical, organizational, and leadership skills would be best used in other environments within the U.S. Government. With a degree in History, a minor in Political Science, and a background in international settings, I believe I could make valuable contributions to any agency in need of physically and mentally tough leaders. I hope you will contact me to suggest a time when I might meet with you personally to discuss your goals and how my background might serve your needs. I can provide outstanding references.

                                        Sincerely,

                                        Oscar S. Thellman

Name: Oscar S. Thellman
Citizenship: U.S.
8888 Shannon Road
Fort Rucker, AL 99999-9999
Home telephone number: (222) 222-2222 **Work telephone number:** (111) 111-1111
E-mail: OSThellman@hotmail.com

EDUCATION	**B.A., History** and a minor in **Political Science**, University of Kentucky, Lexington, KY, 1995.

- Was voted to the office of Junior Class Vice President.
- Financed my college education through employment with JCPenney department store.
- Held membership in Kappa Phi Theta fraternity and was elected Scholarship Chairman: devised an educational study program which resulted in improving the fraternity's average GPA and was adopted by the Honors Society for implementation campus-wide.
- Was captain of the rugby team; played on intramural flag football, softball, and soccer teams.
- Was member of the Political Debate Club.
- Was captain of the University of Kentucky's Soccer Team during my junior and senior years.
- In community service, participated in building houses with the Multicultural Community Development organization. Graduated from W. J. Morgan High School, Lexington Kentucky, 1990.
- Played on the school basketball and rugby teams.

Skill Summary: Developing and implementing training programs; analyzing and planning operations within tight time constraints; exceptional written and verbal communication skills; mentally and physically tough; well-organized and focused; highly proficient both technically and tactically; detail oriented.

Foreign Language: Speak French and Italian at conversational levels.

Foreign Area Knowledge: Very well versed in world events and an avid reader of international publications covering world news. As the son of a U.S. Army Lieutenant Colonel, traveled extensively worldwide and lived in Italy from fifth-ninth grades.

Foreign Travel: Italy, France, and Kosovo

EXPERIENCE	January 2004-present. Full time. **LOGISTICIAN.** $42,000.00 per year, U.S. Army, HHC, 3-147th Chemical Battalion, Fort Rucker, AL, MAJ William Sullivan, (777) 777-7777. As **Senior Logistician,** supervise ten supply and logistical professionals while ensuring the more than 350 soldiers in five chemical companies are fully supplied in case of war.

- Act as the **Budget Officer** with control of in excess of $475,000 including holding an JPOA credit card used to make purchases outside the normal military supply channels.
- As the battalion's movement officer, plan logistics support for units from other states participating in joint exercises such as the large-scale event Operation Anaconda and handling planning for unit movements overseas to Kosovo.
- Prepare budget spreadsheets and cost estimates for a unit which is currently preparing to relocate to Fort Hood, TX with all personnel and equipment and am overseeing all aspects of planning logistical support for this large and detailed project.
- On my own initiative, designed a new spreadsheet in Excel which transformed a budget management system lacking in adequate controls into a successful and cost-effective one.

September 2000 to January 2004. Full time. **CHEMICAL OFFICER.** $35,000.00 per year, U.S. Army, 2-229th Chemical Battalion, Fort Monroe, VA, SSG Benson K. Kinnard, (666) 666-6666. As the advisor to the battalion commander on NBC (Nuclear/Biological/

LOGISTICIAN

Chemical) operations, supervised five NBC technicians as an S-3 action officer planning and conducting evaluations of individual unit NBC training and operations.

- Coached and mentored personnel to a prestigious honor as the "NBC Room of the Quarter" which meant being selected over 42 other departments in 14 battalions.
- Prepared and presented reports and briefings to the Commanding General of the Chemical Battalion, including Unit Status Reports (USR), Commander's Readiness Conference (CRC), and Quarterly Training Briefs (QTB).
- Qualified as a tactical operations center officer and handled this managerial responsibility during exercises and deployments in a battalion with a no-notice worldwide mission.
- Officially evaluated a **"an exceptional officer—bright, articulate, and mature,"** was cited for having joined this unit during a period when the operations tempo was high, quickly integrating myself into operations and becoming a positive force toward unit effectiveness.
- On my own initiative, revitalized the inspection program and implemented changes in training and operational procedures which included ordering new masks and protective suits.

March 1997 to September 2000. Full time. STUDENT. Executive Development Program, $30,000.00, Officer Basic Course, U.S. Army Chemical School, Fort Riley, KS, SFC Theodore G. Macon, (888) 888-8888. Earned high ratings in the areas of oral communication, written communication, and in contributing to the quality of group work.

March 1995 to March 1997. Part-time, **ASSISTANT PLATOON LEADER.** $6,000.00 per year, US Army, 72nd Air Defense Artillery, Fort Bliss, TX, Michael Tresvant (999) 999-9999. While attending college full-time, assisted the platoon leader and platoon sergeant in a unit with as many as 40 people.

- Provided leadership while accounting for more than $500,000 worth of property.
- Planned and carried out group and individual training.

Other experience:
February 1992-March 1995. Part-time, **SALES REPRESENTATIVE.** JCPenney, 1348 Hazel Street, Lexington, KY, Thomas Kellar, (333) 333-3333. While attending college full-time developed public relations and customer service skills. Through patience and persistence, built a loyal client base through word-of-mouth; sold nutrition and health supplies.

HONORS & AWARDS

Recognized for my exemplary performance with two Good Conduct Medals, Army Achievement Medals, and a Service Ribbon, National Defense, Reserve Component.

MILITARY TRAINING

Air Movement Operations
Loadmaster Operations
Chemical Battalion Corps Budget Officer Course
Chemical Officer Basic Course
Infantry Advanced and Basic Individual Training

Hazardous Material Handlers Course
Chemical Warfare Training (worked with live chemical agents) Radiation Protection Officers
Course

FIREARMS
SKILLS

An Expert Marksman, am proficient with most U.S. small arms.

OTHER
INFORMATION

Hold a Secret security clearance.

Familiar with many popular computer operating systems and software, including full proficiency with Windows 95/98; Microsoft Word, Excel, Access, PowerPoint, and Outlook.

Offer skills with Radio Controlled Miniature Aerial Target Operations and Smoke Screening System.

Excellent personal and professional references are available upon request.

OPERATIONS OFFICER (CAREER CHANGE)

Date

Exact Name of Person
Exact Title
Exact Name of Company
Address
City, State, Zip

Dear Exact Name of Person: (or Dear Sir or Madam if answering a blind ad):

With the enclosed resume, I would like to make you aware of my background as an accomplished young professional with natural leadership abilities who offers strong organizational skills and a background of solid performance in the U.S. Army. It is my desire to embark upon a career in law enforcement with the Central Intelligence Agency (CIA) as an Operations Officer.

As you will see from my resume, I am working as a Military Policeman at Fort Polk, LA, where I provide leadership for two junior team members. I am known for my adaptability in a unit which supplies a variety of support services to this large military installation and support for the 62nd Military Police Company in its short-notice worldwide rapid response missions.

A graduate of the U.S. Army Military Police School in Fort Wainwright, AK, my training has also included courses in fingerprint classification and combat lifesaving as well as a unit armorer course. I have also completed six college credit hours in English and Criminal Justice courses at Alvin Community College in Alvin, TX.

I have been given the opportunity to work in a versatile organization where I carry out patrols, conduct investigations, instruct and train subordinates, and respond to 911 calls in a large military community as well as being involved in responding to international situations. My company also provides peacekeeping, reconnaissance, and security services around the world. In October of 2000, I was a member of a company which deployed to German in support of U.N. peacekeeping efforts.

Recognized as an aggressive self-starter, I have become known as someone who can be counted on to handle the stresses of high operations tempos. I also offer the ability to handle multiple simultaneous tasks and complete each one above expected standards.

With my background and training in law enforcement, I believe I could make valuable contributions to any agency in need of physically and mentally tough leaders. I hope you will contact me to suggest a time when I might meet with you personally to discuss your goals and how my background might serve your needs. I can provide outstanding references.

Sincerely,

Don E. Turner

Don E. Turner
Citizenship: U.S.
Current Address: 62nd Military Police Company, Ft. Polk, LA, 68634
Permanent (Parents') Address: 6474 Python Lane, Alvin, TX 77445
SSN: 000-00-0000
Birthdate: 30 April 1985
Home telephone number: (999) 999-9999
Work telephone number: (888) 888-8888
Permanent (parents') telephone: (777) 777-7777
E-mail: Dturner@ec.tx.us

Job Title Applying for: Operations Officer
Grade Applying for: GS/00/00

Veteran's Preference: 10 points

EDUCATION	Completed six college credit hours: English III Expository Writing in June 2002, English Composition in 2000, and Criminal Justice in 1999, Alvin Community College, Alvin, TX. **U.S. Army Military Police School,** Ft. Wainwright, AK, 1998. Graduated from **Woodland High School,** Baton Rouge, LA, 71489. Graduated 1990.
MILITARY TRAINING	Completed military training programs which included the following: Combat Emergency Lifesaver Course Unit Armorer Course Fingerprint Classification O.C. Spray Law Enforcement Orientation Course **Skill Summary:** Law enforcement, military policeman, conducting patrols; investigating crimes; handling stress and pressure calmly and with control; good verbal and written communication skills; physically and mentally tough; detail oriented. **Foreign Language:** Working knowledge of Spanish **Foreign Area Knowledge:** Very well versed in world events and an avid reader of international publications covering world news **Foreign Travel:** Germany, Panama, Italy, and Korea
EXPERIENCE	**September 1999 to present.** Full time – approximately 65 hours a week (on call 24 hours a day). **Military Policeman,** $1,700 per month, U.S. Army, 62nd Military Police Company, Ft. Polk, LA, 68634 Supervisor SSG Benjamin Davidson, (666) 666-6666 **(You may contact my supervisor).** Serve in a unit which trains and is "on call" at all times to respond rapidly with airborne capabilities to carry out responses to contingencies and provide security for the Commanding General of Ft. Polk and his staff at the headquarters of the 5th Special Operations Corps. Provide leadership for two junior team members as a Team Leader with arrest authority providing installation security at the nation's largest military base worldwide.

- Was an important contributor to the efforts which led my company to win the prestigious "Leadership Award" as the best Military Police company in the U.S. Army worldwide for 2002.
- Lead team members in responding to 911 calls on a rotating schedule which calls for my team to spend one to two months out of every four on daily patrol duty based on the number of missions being carried out and number of personnel available who are not deployed on other assignments.
- Carry out patrol duties which include traffic control, animal control, and processing criminal and traffic offenders.

OPERATIONS OFFICER

- Investigate a wide range of crimes from assaults, to domestic disturbances, to shoplifting, to trespassing, to responding to fights or disturbances.
- Provide investigation of other matters such as larceny or damage to government property or apprehending personnel who are AWOL (absent without leave).
- Instruct and train subordinates in professional skills as well as providing regular monthly counseling on job performance.
- Contribute to the effectiveness of humanitarian aid and peacekeeping efforts as a member of my company which was deployed to Germany from May to October 2000 to provide support for "Operation Mission Control."
- In field environments, serve as an MK-19 and M-60 Gunner and Driver where duties included area and zone reconnaissance, enemy prisoner-of-war operations, battlefield circulation control, airborne operations, area security, and refugee resettlement operations support.
- Serve in a unit called on to conduct MP Ammunition Inspection about one month out of every four.

November 1994 to February 1999. Part time: 25 hours a week. **Dietary Student Aide,** $500/week, Memorial Hospital, Baton Rouge, LA. Supervisor's name: William Harrison, phone: (555) 555-5555. While still attending high school, handled duties which included food tray preparation, cleaning, and transporting food to patients.

HONORS & AWARDS

Recognized for my exemplary performance with a Peace Time Service Medal from Special Operation duty in Panama, a Humanitarian Service Medal, and a Good Conduct Medal. Have also earned a Joint Meritorious Service ribbon, the Motor Vehicle Driver's Badge, and a National Defense Ribbon, Army Achievement Medal.

FIREARMS SKILLS

An Expert Marksman, am proficient with most U.S. small arms. Offer experience as an Armorer which includes cleaning and maintaining small arms such as:

Marvel .22	M-60 machine gun	MK-19
Grenade Launcher	M16A2 rifle	M-4 carbine rifle
Ruger Revolver		

CLEARANCE

Secret security clearance

OTHER SKILLS

Through training and experience, provide operator level maintenance on military trucks and patrol vehicles.
Have knowledge of most infantry basic light fighter skills:

conducting and reacting to ambushes	reading maps
providing route reconnaissance	conducting raids
conducting convoy escorts	setting up checkpoints

searching vehicles and personnel
conducting hasty and permanent built-up fighting positions
jumping from military high-performance aircraft for airborne operations

REFERENCES

Excellent personal and professional references on request.

PARAMEDIC (CAREER CHANGE)

Date

Exact Name of Person
Exact Title
Exact Name of Company
Address
City, State, Zip

PARAMEDIC

Dear Exact Name of Person (or Dear Sir or Madam if answering a blind ad):

I would like to take this opportunity to make you aware of the skills, experience, and knowledge I have gained while proudly serving my country in the U.S. Army in Special Forces and Ranger units where I contributed to the success of missions vital to national security.

As you will see from my enclosed resume, I have been serving with distinction as a Special Forces Medical Sergeant, based out of Bosnia, for approximately two years. Earlier in my military career I was stationed at Fort Jackson, SC, and served in 2-16th Ranger Battalion, where my jobs were focused on training and leadership. Throughout my military career, I have been selected to receive extensive training which has led to certification in several areas in the Medical Technician field.

Currently focusing on training both American and allied forces personnel in emergency, routine, and long-term care issues, I am known for initiative, knowledge, and the ability to pass that knowledge on to others in an effective manner. One of my greatest accomplishments has been as part of a team which gave me the ability to maximize our resources and reduce medical hazards while in combat.

With the proven ability to work under intense pressure and deadlines, I am combat tested and was a member of a Ranger battalion which received the Valorous Unit Award for "gallantry in action" during operation Desert Shield. I earned a prestigious awards such as the National Defense Service Medal and the Expert Infantryman's Badge for my contributions during a period of intense urban combat against a "well armed and numerically superior enemy" in a battle considered to be among the ten most important in American military history.

If you can use a versatile and adaptable professional in the CIA with well-developed leadership abilities, I hope you will call or write me soon to suggest a time when we might have a brief discussion of how I could contribute to your organization. I can provide excellent professional and personal references at the appropriate time.

Sincerely,

Kevin Y. Upton

Name: Kevin Y. Upton
Citizenship: U.S.
1212 Southview Hwy
Columbia, SC 22222-2222
Home telephone number: (222) 222-2222　　　**Work telephone number:** (111) 111-1111
E-mail: KevinUpton4534@yahoo.com

OBJECTIVE　　To offer a track record of accomplishments, honors, and experience to an organization that can benefit from my thorough knowledge of operational and security issues as well as from my expertise in training others in and personally providing medical care.

EDUCATION　　**College:** Completed 18 semester hours of General Studies, University of South Carolina,
& TRAINING　　**Columbia, SC;** was named to the **Chancellor's Honor List** in recognition of a perfect 4.0 GPA one semester.
Highlights of military training: Consistently placed at the top of each course and was named an **Honor Graduate** of nearly every military training program attended, which included the following:

- **Special Forces** Medical Skills Sustainment, Malaria Prevention and Control for Field Operations in Bosnia, Combat Tracking, Diver Medic Training and Emergency Medical Procedures, Special Forces Diving Medical Technician, and Military Freefall Parachutist Courses, 2001
- **Individual Terrorism Awareness** and **German and Spanish Language** Courses, 2000
- Basic NCO Course **(leadership training)**, 2000
- **Special Forces** Medical Sergeant Course Phase II, 2000, and Phase I, 1999
- **Special Forces** Assessment and Selection and Land Navigation, Ranger Team Leader, and Infantry Basic Refresher Training and Specialist Skills Courses, 1999
- **Assault Climbing,** Jungle Warfare, Toxic Agent Training, Jumpmaster Courses, 1998
- **Operator/Unit Level Maintenance** on the Improved Remotely Monitored Battlefield Sensor System (I-REMBASS), M1030 Military Motorcycle, Primary Leadership Development Course (PLDC), Advanced Firearms Tactics (U.S. Department of Treasury), and Pathfinder Courses, 1997
- **Mountain Warfare,** 1996
- **Ranger School,** Scout Swimmer, Pre-Ranger, Airborne, and Infantry Training, 1996

LICENSES &　　National Registry of Emergency Medical Technicians certification as an EMT and
CERTIFICATIONS Paramedic, 2003
Paramedic License, valid till May 2003
Open Water Diver
FAA Student Pilot License
Diver Medical Technician, valid till September 2001
United States Parachutist Association (USPA) certified
PALS, current through August 2001
ACLS (Advanced Cardiac Life Support), valid until August 2001
BLS, valid till September 2000

EXPERIENCE　　*Have consistently been singled out for recognition for my initiative and dedication as well as for my skills in training and mentoring others, E. F. Jackson Veterans Hospital, Columbia, SC:*
MEDICAL TECHNICIAN. 2002-present. Am receiving extensive advanced training while building a reputation as a knowledgeable, proficient, and dedicated leader and model of professionalism while planning and carrying out medical training assignments throughout the facility.

- Received a Certificate of Achievement for my efforts during a drug and narcotic rehabilitation training initiative and was cited for "dynamic efforts crucial to the successful creation and training of rehabilitation and restraint procedures."
- Train and supervise other technicians, and carry out emergency, routine, and long-term medical care for drug rehabilitation patients.
- Perform initial assessments to determine if patients were asymptomatic; determined the adequacy of respiration and cardiac function prior to treatment.
- Control medical equipment and supplies valued in excess of $85,000.
- Played a vital role in the development of a 90-day program of instruction which received praise from senior physicians and other nursing personnel to master critical drug and narcotic rehabilitation training techniques.

SPECIAL FORCES MEDICAL SERGEANT. US Army, Camp Tattum, 2-16th Ranger Battalion, Sarajevo, Bosnia (2000-02). Recruited to give the medical and training support for a Ranger Battalion with its no-notice worldwide response mission.
- Cited for my medical, technical, and tactical knowledge, organized and two small-scale medical facilities while overseas in Bosnia.
- Assisted in establishing a program which provided in 79% of all candidates much needed medical support.
- Received an Army Commendation Medal for my efforts in saving thousands of dollars by using internal resources for a live-fire complex construction project.
- Accounted for more than $75,000 worth of medical equipment and training aids and was cited for my ability to maximize resources and reduce medical hazards in combat.
- Was officially evaluated as a "flawless" performer who was "extremely intelligent, resourceful, and dependable" as well as "completely focused" on training and the most effective use of resources.

TEAM LEADER. US Army, Delta Company, 4-23rd Infantry Division, Fort Hood, TX (1996-2000). Supervised, trained, and counseled members of an airborne rifle team charged with responding worldwide within 18 hours.
- Provided the leadership for numerous successful activities which included coaching all team members to "expert" scores in marksmanship, producing a 282 average in physical fitness testing, and training 60 people who became licensed on land rovers and motorcycles.
- Received **The National Defense Service Medal** and gained significant combat experience as a member of a unit participating in a battle considered one of the ten most important in American military history. **Received Expert Infantryman's Badge for "gallantry in action" in Operation Desert Shield,** while executing a mission "of the highest national priority under the most austere and challenging circumstances" in intense urban combat against a well-armed and "numerically superior enemy."

- Advanced to this leadership role on the basis of my abilities and potential shown as a Machine Gunner, Automatic Rifleman, and Grenadier.

HONORS

Have been awarded numerous honors which have included:
The National Defense Service Medal
Military Freefall Parachutist Badge
Master Parachutist, Senior Parachutist, and Parachutist Badges
German Parachutist Badges
Pathfinder Badge
Ranger Tab
Special Forces Tab
Expert Infantryman's Badge
Combat Infantryman's Badge
The Bronze Star Medal
Armed Forces Expeditionary Medal
Army Commendation Medal (three awards)
Army Achievement Medal (two awards)
Army Good Conduct Medal (two awards)

CLEARANCE

Secret security clearance.

LANGUAGES

German and Spanish.

COMPUTERS

Operate databases and spreadsheets; highly skilled in using PowerPoint, Excel, Word.

WEAPONS

Consistently qualify as Expert with M-16/M-4 rifle and hand grenade and received U.S. Customs Service certification as a Sharpshooter.

PERSONAL

Current military and civilian passports. All vaccinations up-to-date. Am extremely flexible, prepared to relocate globally, and fully capable of frequent or long-term travel. Have traveled to 15 countries. Am considered an expert in mountaineering and rock climbing.

BIOCHEMICAL ENGINEER ANALYST

Date

Exact Name of Person
Exact Title
Exact Name of Company
Address
City, State, Zip

Dear Exact Name of Person (or Dear Sir or Madam if answering a blind ad):

With the enclosed resume, I would like to initiate the process of being considered for the Federal Bureau of Investigations Trainee Program. I feel I have much to offer the FBI.

As you will see from my resume, I am currently employed at Rice University in Houston, TX as a Agroecology Teaching Assistant so that I can complete my Master of Science degree in Biology. I served my country with distinction for nearly seven years while working in the intelligence field. I also held a **Top Secret/SCI security** clearance while serving in the U.S. Air Force. I was specially selected as NCO in Charge, Intelligence Systems, while deployed to Bogota, Colombia. I conducted critical briefings and debriefings in support of several Drug Enforcement missions while in South America.

After leaving the U.S. Air Force, I became a full-time student in order to earn my B.S. degree in Biology. I am in the process of completing my M.S. degree in Biology and have been selected for a prestigious teaching assistantship by an agroecologist. My medical and biological training has included courses in microbiology and chemistry. My senior year thesis while completing my undergraduate degree was on "Amino Acid Development Studies." While in the Air Force, I won a prestigious medal for my leadership in providing intelligence support to over 62 aircrews, often in full chemical protection gear while under a special operations mission in

I am confident that my background in both the intelligence and biological areas would make me a useful asset to the FBI, and I hope you will contact me to suggest the next step I should take in pursuing my goal of seeking employment with the Federal Burea of Investigations. I can provide outstanding references at the appropriate time.

Sincerely,

Eunis Quattelbaum

EUNIS QUATTELBAUM

713 Highland Road

(333) 333-3333 (Home)

(444) 444-4444 (Work)

SSN: 000-00-0000

Source: EXT

Highest Grade Held: N/A

OBJECTIVE To obtain a position in which I can utilize my knowledge of nuclear, biological, and chemical (NBC) materials as well as my extensive experience in the intelligence field.

EDUCATION **Bachelor of Science in Biology**, North Harris College, Houston, TX, 2003; GPA 3.52.
- Was named to the Dean's List.
- Was inducted into Sigma Si Theta in recognition of "conspicuous attainment and service in collegiate activities," 2001.
- Was inducted into Sigma Si Theta Biological Honor Society, 1998.

Working toward completion of a **Master in Science in Biology**, Rice University, Houston, TX, degree anticipated in 2005.

EXPERIENCE **AGROECOLOGY TEACHING ASSISTANT & BIOLOGY GRADUATE STUDENT.** Rice University, 6852 Gillespie Circle, Houston, TX 77989, Patrick Mosley, Supervisor, phone: (222) 222-2222. (2004-present). Enrolled in Rice University in order to complete a Master's degree in Biology, and was offered an assistantship by a Ph.D. and Agroecologist who recruited me to teach a course and lab in the Department of Interdisciplinary Studies.
- Courses in 2002 include Communities in Ecosystems, Taxnoma of Vascular Plants, and Independent Study of Agroecology.
- Previously was enrolled at University of Houston from 2000-2001; however, I transferred to Rice University in order to undertake a more rigorous program of study. At University of Houston, completed courses in Endocrinology and Entymology.
- In order to refine my knowledge of biology as it is applied in medical environments, completed courses through Fraley's Medical Services related to Medication Technician and Clinical Medical Office Assisting.

COLLEGE STUDENT, BIOLOGY MAJOR. North Harris College, 2753 Upchurch Dr, Houston, TX 79022, George E. Claxton, Supervisor, phone: (333) 333-3333. (2001-04). After leaving military service, I decided to pursue my undergraduate as a full-time student. Excelled academically with a 3.52 GPA.
- Courses included Chemistry, Microbiology, Organic Chemistry, Biochemistry, Medical Microbiology, and Immunization.
- As my senior project, completed a senior research project on "Amino Acid Development Studies."

U.S. Air Force experience: Served my country with distinction as an INTELLIGENCE OPERATIONS SPECIALIST.

2000-01: 225th Squadron Special Operations Group, Eglin AFB, FL, SGT Delvon Collins, phone: (444) 444-4444. For four years and 11 months, acquired experience in the intelligence and NBC fields. As a Staff Sergeant, was selected for a position as Assistant Noncommissioned Officer in Charge, Intelligence Systems, Intelligence Flight, 31st Operations Support Squadron, 4th Wing. Deployed to Osan Air Base, Korea, to provide support in air simulation procedures.

**BIOCHEMICAL ENGINEER
ANALYST**

- Conducted critical permission briefings and debriefings in support of over 500 combat missions flown over Kosovo in the coalition effort to maintain nation sovereignty.
- Received an Air Force Achievement Medal, and was described in writing as "instrumental in keeping commanders and pilots informed in a fluid environment."

1999-00: Received an Air Force Achievement Medal for outstanding achievement while assigned to the 31st Operations Support Squadron, 31st Operations Group, 4th Wing, Eglin AFB, FL. Was a member of the first air combat team which deployed in support of a drug enforcement operation, and provided direct support to the humanitarian airlift operation as part of the 325th Tactical Airlift Control Element operating in Bogota, Colombia.

- Conducted more than 100 aircrew debriefings, collecting an disseminating critical time-sensitive intelligence on tactical threats and airfield conditions throughout Colombia. Information I collected was utilized by the Headquarters Air Mobility Command Directorate of Intelligence and were instrumental in the success of a major relief mission.

1997-99: Received an Air Force Achievement Medal for outstanding achievement while working with the 92d Air Refueling Wing, Colombian International Airport. On the formal citation for the medal, was commended for "outstanding initiative and superb technical knowledge" while providing "top-notch intelligence support to the wing staff and over 75 aircrews, often in full chemical protection gear."

- Delivered several hundred wartime pre-mission briefings to aircrews, and was frequently requested specifically to be the official briefer.
- Enhanced aircrew comprehension of the enemy electronic threat, and on my own initiative constructed a chart to reflect enemy early warning/ground control intercept and signals intelligence capabilities.
- Assisted in the construction of an enemy surface-to-surface missile order of battle chart which became known as the SCUD tracking board. This board provided insight into how the where the enemy possessed the ability to launch missile strikes.

Other Air Force Experience:
1994-97: Flight Combat Squadron, Intelligence Flight, 8th Wing, Charleston AFB, SC, CPT Lance Cambridge, phone: unknown. Received two Air Force Commendation Medals for distinguished service as an **Intelligence Specialist** with the Intelligence Division, 258TH Commander Wing, and as **Noncommissioned Officer in Charge.** In a formal citation for the award, was described as "an invaluable asset and talented communicator who has given countless intelligence briefings which were thoughtfully and meticulously prepared and presented."

- Because of my can-do attitude, was specially selected to manage tanker intelligence for a two-month period while awaiting a supervisor.

- Was commended for "an uncanny ability to anticipate future requirements and find solutions before the problem arises.
- Ensured that my organization was receiving all essential documents and materials.
- On my own initiative, instituted new procedures in handling intelligence documents, message traffic, and visual aids which greatly facilitated the retrieval and accountability for classified material. Procedures which I instituted saved numerous man-hours.

TRAINING & Received numerous Certificates of Training from U.S. Air Force courses including these:
CERTIFICATIONS **Air Combat Command Quality Awareness Training,** 2001.
Combat Survival Training Course, 2001.
Constant Source (CS) Operations Course, U.S. Air Force, 2001.
JDISS/SIRAD/XLAMPS, J2/N2 Intelligence Data Handling System, 2000.
Introduction to Mini IDHS, J2/N2 Intelligence Data Handling System, 2000.
NCO Preparatory Course, 2000.
Intelligence Operations Specialist Course, U.S. Air Force, 1999.
MAC Affiliation Airlift Planners Course, 1999.
Medical and biological training Courses, 1998.
Survival, Evasion, Rescue, and Escape (SERE) Course, 1998.
Courses included these:

Microbiology/Cell Biology	Chemistry	Advanced Microbiology
Medical Microbiology	Cellular Physiology	Plant Morphology

HONORS/AWARDS Received numerous medals, awards, certificates of achievement, and certificates of appreciation for exemplary performance. Received a Joint Service Commendation Medal and a Defense Meritorious Award in 2000.

CLEARANCE Held **Top Secret/SCI** security clearance while serving in the Air Force.

PERSONAL Excellent personal and professional references are available upon request.

INTELLIGENCE OFFICER

Date

Exact Name of Person
Exact Title
Exact Name of Company
Address
City, State, Zip

INTELLIGENCE OFFICER   Dear Exact Name of Person (or Dear Sir or Madam if answering a blind ad):

The purpose of this letter is to initiate the process of being considered for an appointment as a Special Agent with the FBI.

I presently serve my country as a U.S. Army officer. With a background in Military Intelligence, I have proven that I possess strong abilities in analyzing and tracking real-world activities, combining attention to detail with excellent planning and organizational skills. Since my first days as an officer, I have quickly earned the respect of my superiors for my physical and mental toughness. I have been described as an individual who will find a way to get the job done whether I am providing training, supervising intelligence gathering activities, planning and carrying out exercise and crisis response actions throughout the world, or controlling multimillion-dollar inventories of equipment.

Since joining the military, I have met the challenges of working with a vast array of people from newly assigned technical personnel, to supervisors and managers, to senior executives. I have earned the reputation as an articulate, self-motivated professional with exceptional communication and motivational skills. I am a proactive manager and an aggressive, result-oriented professional who possesses sound judgment, keen analytical ability, and persuasive speaking skills.

I am confident that the qualities which helped me excel as a military officer would easily translate to success with the Federal Bureau of Investigation. From my experience in various duty stations such as Fort Greely, AK, have gained experience in preparing units to deal with U.S. contingency operations deployments to Spain, Turkey, and Egypt. I have developed an ability to converse in Spanish, Turkish, and Arabic.

I believe my background will prove to be a tremendous asset to the Federal Bureau of Investigation. I appreciate the opportunity to meet and discuss the Bureau's requirements, needs and goals and will provide outstanding references at the appropriate time.

Sincerely,

David L. Johnson

David L. Johnson
SSN: 000-00-0000
INTERNAL
4444 Broadstreet Blvd
Atlanta, GA 34545
Home: (222) 222-2222
Work: (111) 111-1111
E-mail: dljohn@hotmail.com
ANNOUNCEMENT NUMBER: 999ABCD9999

OBJECTIVE   To obtain a position as a Special Agent with the FBI.

EDUCATION   **B.S. in Biological Anthropology**, Emory University, Atlanta GA, 2000.
Honor Society Scholarship, Biological Science Department of Emory University, 1999.
President's Award from the Biology Department for A and B Honor Roll Emory University.
Merck Corporation Honorary Awarded Scholarship for Outstanding Academics, Marietta High School, Atlanta, GA, 1994.

EXPERIENCE   **INTELLIGENCE OFFICER.** US Army, 12nd Special Operations, Fort Greeley, AK 99914, MSG Nathaniel C. Bell, Supervisor, phone: (333) 333-3333 (2002-present). Was handpicked for this job as "second in command" of a 78-person company which is an element of the Special Operations Division and must be ready to respond to crisis situations and carry out operations throughout the world. Manage operating seaports through which moved personnel and assets throughout Turkey, Egypt, Jordan, and the Eastern Mediterranean area.

* Supervise a Department of Defense (DoD) "common user" port and became an expert on port handling operations, customs clearance, and cargo documentation. Control an annual operating budget of $4 million.
* Manage two Vehicle Processing Center. Was successful in directing port operations which moved 100,000 million tons of cargo and 700 privately owned vehicles.
* Save $150,000 yearly through my initiative in closing down a facility in Iskenderun and relocating the operation to a more efficient site. During a 60-day strike against US forces, provide leadership to assure the safety and life support needs for employees at two facilities 750 miles apart.

PLATOON LEADER. US Army, 77th Aviation, 445 Scottsdale Road, Ft. Benning, GA 39514, SFC William Parks, Supervisor, phone: (444) 444-4444 (1999-2002). Officially evaluated as "an aggressive young officer who excels under pressure ... clearly head and shoulders above her peers," was selected for advancement to a higher managerial level after changing to an aviation MOS based on my performance as supervisor of helicopter units Supported the Delta Company Aviation Battalion in its short notice worldwide response mission.

* Deployed 13 soldiers to five different command posts throughout Iran to support U.S. efforts in "Operation Noble Eagle."
* Tailored the type and level of support needed in contingency missions to supported units in response to the operation's status as deliberate or crisis action.
* Managed AH-1 Helicopter Technical Inspectors which determined maintenance requirements and insured that appropriate maintenance has been performed on each attack unit.
* Controlled two CGS systems as well as helicopters and generators with a total value in excess of $12 million while supervising 35 people.
* Earned praise for my ability to manage multiple simultaneous tasks while prioritizing

and allocating resources and following up to ensure complete success of each task.

- Developed a Common Ground Station CGS and Ground Control Approach Radar Repair (GCA) certification program and internal competitions which allowed my team to improve professional skills, knowledge, and a more cohesive spirit.
- Maintained an operational readiness rate above 95% as Maintenance Officer.
- Selected above all brigade Senior Avionic Mechanics to serve as the Primary Avionic Mechanics.
- Scored 360 points on an extended scale for physical fitness testing (the standard perfect score is 300) and motivated my platoon to bring average scores up to 270.

INTELLIGENCE OFFICER

INTELLIGENCE OFFICER. US Army, 94049 Wilkenson Road, Ft. Carson, CO, Lt. Derrick Bixley, phone: (555) 555-5555 (1995-99). As Intelligence Officer for the Ft. Carson Military Police battalion, prepared, analyzed, and assimilated tailored intelligence products to the Battalion Commander to ensure all necessary information was available for sound decision making.

- Earned a reputation as a "truly outstanding officer ... who continues to excel in every area" and as one who made "immeasurable contributions."
- Advised the battalion commander, subordinate company commanders, and staff members on issues related to physical security, personnel, information, and information systems security as well as on security management and crime prevention.
- Controlled $35 million inventory of sensitive equipment.
- Cited for my ability to pass knowledge on to others while training and supervising personnel in intelligence support and security operations procedures.
- Played a vital role in preparing one Ft. Carson unit for service in Colombia by providing them with timely, accurate, and detailed intelligence reports as well as by briefing personnel in antiterrorist and force protection procedures and providing "host country" information.
- Created realistic "opposition forces" scenarios for external and battle staff exercises.
- Consistently scored above 300 in physical fitness testing.
- Was cited for my ability to identify potential problem areas, assess the situation, and develop effective corrective actions.

TRAINING

Avionics School, inspecting/approving equipment for airborne operations, 1999
Airborne School, how to exit and land from a high-performance Army helicopter, 1999
Security Manager's Course, providing security for physical assets and information systems, 1997
Motor Officer Course, procedures for managing vehicle maintenance operations, 1997
Physical Security Manager's Course, regulations of arms rooms

and crime prevention measures, 1996
Military Intelligence Officer's Course, military decision making process, 1996

AWARDS	U.S. Army Commendation and Achievement Medals and three Good Conduct Medals
CLEARANCE	Top Secret/SCI security clearance
LANGUAGES	Offer basic working knowledge of French and Spanish
TECHNICAL KNOWLEDGE	Ground Control Approach Radar (GCAR) Repair and Common Ground Station (CGS) certification programs.
COMPUTER SKILLS	Familiar with Word, Excel, and PowerPoint

RESEARCH SPECIALIST

Date

Exact Name of Person
Exact Title
Exact Name of Company
Address
City, State, Zip

Dear Exact Name of Person (or Dear Sir or Madam if answering a blind ad):

With the enclosed resume, I would like to make you aware of my interest in exploring employment opportunities with your organization.

At the present time, I am working full-time as a Detective for the Los Angeles Police Department. I have excelled in a track record of promotions while organizing Human Intelligence information, developing a language maintenance program, and providing other officers with definitive language training activities.

As you will see from my resume, I served my country with distinction in the U.S. Army, and I was entrusted with a **Top Secret/SBI** security clearance. With strong analytical, communication, organizational, and research skills, I have also served as an Operations NCO, Supervising Interrogator, and Language Instructor in the US Army. As an Operations Specialist, I trained and supervised other individuals while supporting missions in Ft. Eustis, VA. As a Supervising Interrogator, I created an intelligence collection plan which enabled an organization to process interviews at much higher efficiency. I also took the lead in cross-training counterintelligence soldiers in interrogation tactics and techniques. As a Language Instructor for the National Endowment for the Humanities, my teaching and communication skills played a key role in improving the student success rate by 25%, and I was chosen as Assistant Coordinator of the Teaching Team.

I am proficient in listening, reading, and writing German and Spanish, and I am certified as a Foreign Linguist. I have a Master of Science degree in English and Language Studies from Santa Clara University, here in California. I also completed the Basic German Course at the Multi-Cultural Language Institute, Portland, OR. I offer strong weapons skills and extensive computer knowledge. While serving my country, I received 9 medals and awards for exceptional performance including the Defense Meritorious Service Medal, the Joint Service Achievement Medal, and the Army Achievement Medal.

If you can use a dedicated young professional, I hope you will contact me to suggest the next step I should take in the employment application process. Thank you in advance for your time.

Yours sincerely,

Lynn A. Lucas

Lynn A. Lucas
000000000
INTERNAL
1587 Whitehead Circle
Santa Clara, CA, 87645
Home: (111) 111-1111
Work: (222) 222-2222
Email: lynnalucas@aol.com

ANNOUNCEMENT NUMBER: 999ABCD9999

OBJECTIVE	To obtain a position as an Intelligence Research Specialist with the FBI.
EDUCATION	**Master of Science degree in English and Language Studies,** Santa Clara University, Santa Clara, CA, 2001. **Bachelor of Science in Liberal Arts**, Christopher Newport University, Newport News, VA, 1995.
TRAINING	Basic **Arabic Course**, Foreign Language Center, Middle East Division, Saudi Arabia, 1999. **Intelligence Basic Noncommissioned Officer Course**, Saudi Arabia, 1998. **Counterintelligence Force Protection Source Operations (CFSO) Course**, Fort Eustis, 1998. Basic **Arabic Course**, Multi-Cultural Language Institute, Portland, OR, 1997. **Primary Leadership Development Course,** Fort Eustis, VA 1996-1997. **Basic Interrogator Course,** Fort Eustis, VA, 1996. Basic **Spanish Course,** Multi-Cultural Language Institute, Portland, OR, 1996.
LANGUAGES	Highly proficient in listening, reading, and writing Spanish and German (scored 3/3 on Spanish Defense Language Institute Proficiency Test). Certified as a Basic Linguist in the Modern Standard Arabic Language.
EXPERIENCE	Excelled with a "track record" of promotions within the Los Angeles Police Department: **2004-present: DETECTIVE.** Los Angeles Police Department, 5592 Wade Park, Los Angeles, CA 92256-5586, Carlos Santana, Supervisor, phone: (444) 444-4444. Train and supervise 12 police officer under my direct command while organizing Human Intelligence collection efforts. Successfully lead numerous missions which provides valuable Human Intelligence information.

- **Program development:** Develop and organize a language maintenance program which increased proficiency among all hispanic linguists assigned to the organization. Am praised in writing for "providing definitive and thorough instruction" which greatly aided language training activities.

2002-2004: POLICE OFFICER. Trained and supervised other officers while supporting missions throughout the inner city communities.

- **Honors:** Was selected from among 20 other linguists to work with the Drug Enforcement division. Excelled while performing as a transcriber in support of DEA operations which resulted in the apprehension of high-profile drug dealers in Los Angeles and Oakland.
- **Automated reporting proficiency:** Quickly learned the new computerized report format, and became the organization's inhouse expert on the new report which was designed to improve reporting. Trained staff counterparts and subordinate organizations on new computer capabilities.

- **Counterintelligence activities:** Conducted liaison with agents of the FBI and the Mexican Police as a Counterintelligence/Interrogation team member associated with the LAPD. Was publicly praised for producing 36 reports which significantly enhanced the 1999 murder investigation of a LA police officer.
- **Administration:** Improved reporting accuracy of the Precinct Status Reports to above 90% through my persistent attention to detail. Was commended for my strong leadership qualities.

LANGUAGE INSTRUCTOR. National Endowment for the Humanities, 2116 Dobbin Drive, Santa Clara, CA 87645, Parker Miller, Supervisor, phone: (333) 333-3333 (1999-2002). Was specially selected for this position teaching English to Hispanic, Chinese, and German immigrants entering the country. Developed and revised instructional materials and tests.

- **Honors:** Received the Performance Awards for my excellent performance in this job. Was selected as **Assistant Coordinator** of the Teaching Team. **Initiative and dedication:** Played a key role in the 25% improvement of the student success rate in the Spanish Department as the success rate increased from 80% to 96%. Was praised for spending many volunteer hours tutoring 40 at-risk students; their eventual success contributed significantly to the institute's improved success scores.
- **Special projects:** Was chosen to conduct a German and Spanish language-training course for 30 California Police Department officials in August 2001. The aim was to improve high-intensity drug trafficking. Was chosen as Language Coordinator for the European and Latin American School's Arabic and German contribution to the 2001 Worldwide Language Olympics, 2001.
- **Program development:** Developed and implemented a safety program recognized as "the best on the installation" in 2000.

SUPERVISING INTERROGATOR. US Army, I-345 Support Battalion, Saudi Arabia, APO AP 5487, SSG Edward Diocia, phone: (444) 444-4444 (1995-1999). Trained and supervised three personnel on an Analysis and Control Team and was selected as a NATO Survival School Interrogator. Received a prestigious National Defense Service Medal for my exceptional performance in this job.

- **Leadership:** Took the lead in crosstraining counterintelligence soldiers in interrogation tactics, techniques, and procedures.
- **Special projects:** Competed against native linguists in the World Wide Language Olympics.
- **Knowledge of counterintelligence investigative and operational concepts:** Demonstrated outstanding human intelligence (HUMINT) collection abilities. On my own initiative created an intelligence collection plan which provided the Detachment the ability to process interviews at a much higher efficiency. Crosstrained counterintelligence soldiers in interrogation tactics, techniques, and procedures, and was evaluated in writing as "a superb instructor." Completed numerous Arabic interrogations.
- **Project management:** In preparation for an assignment in Egypt, set the example by scoring highest on the foreign language exam.

OPERATIONS SPECIALIST. US Army, 156th Special Operations, Ft. Eustis, VA 87946, SFC Eric Stanton, Supervisor, phone: (555) 555-5555 (1993-95). For 3 years, acquired experience in the intelligence and NBC fields.

1993-95: As a Staff Sergeant, was selected for a position as Assistant Noncommissioned Officer in Charge, Intelligence Systems, Intelligence Flight, and Air Defense Artillery. Deployed to Saudi Arabia twice for desert missions.

- Conducted critical permission briefings and debriefings in support of over 500 combat missions flown over Iran in the coalition effort to maintain Kosovo sovereignty.
- Received an Armed Forces Expeditionary Medal, and was described in writing as "instrumental in keeping commanders and pilots informed in a fluid environment."

SPECIAL SKILLS   Offer strong skills in the following areas:

- **Analysis:** Proven ability to apply inductive and deductive principles to resolve a problem, question, or issue. As a **Military Language Instructor** and Teaching Team Assistant Coordinator, analyzed student performance and identified student deficiencies with regard to listening, reading, writing, and speaking. Developed training strategies which helped students succeed. As **NCO in charge of the Operational Control Element for Intelligence**, analyzed intelligence priorities and planning intelligence collection efforts in order to meet those needs. As a **Supervising Interrogator,** analyzed Human Intelligence collections needs and obtained needed information.
- **Weapon skills:** killed and qualified in the use of .40 caliber semi-automatic pistol, Heckler & Koch MP5/Colt AR15/Olympic Arms .45 caliber rifle, and 12-gauge shotgun.
- **Research skills:** As **NCO in charge of the Operational Control Element for Intelligence**, created and managed an intelligence database, and was responsible for researching political, military, social, and cultural situations. Researched archived reports. As **Los Angeles Police Officer,** analyzed previous problems associated with the Precinct Status Reports and identified key ingredients for assuring that the reports were completed accurately. Developed and implemented a plan to improve reporting which resulted in the first error-free report in the organization's history.
- **Written communication skills:** Display my exceptional written communication skills while preparing a wide range of report, employee evaluations, and operating updates. As an **Operations NCO and Police Officer**, produced a variety of reports for the Intelligence and Securities Command (INSCOM).
- **Oral communication techniques:** Adept at using communication skills to draw information vital to the investigation from the interview subject. Trained in the psychology of the criminal mind and in detecting leads during the interview and interrogation process. Have performed with distinction as a **Language Instructor** in the prestigious Defense Language Institute. As **Operations NCO**, developed the briefing which was given to all visiting VIPs visiting DOD civilians or other governmental personnel. Served as a Platoon Sergeant in a Training Unit.
- **Organizing/planning/prioritizing skills:** Have frequently been selected to handle multiple responsibilities because of my ability to multi-task. As NCO in charge of the Operational Control Element for Intelligence, planning and prioritized collections needs. As Language Instructor at the National Endowment for the Humanities, organized the efforts of the Spanish Language Instructors at the 2000 World Language Olympics.

CLEARANCE   Top Secret security clearance with SBI.

COMPUTER
SKILLS   Familiar with popular computer operating systems and software, including Windows; proficient with Word and Excel.

SPECIAL AGENT

Date

Exact Name of Person
Exact Title
Exact Name of Company
Address
City, State, Zip

Dear Exact Name of Person (or Dear Sir or Madam if answering a blind ad):

With the enclosed resume, I would like to initiate the process of being considered for an appointment as a Special Agent with the FBI.

As you will see from my resume, I offer approximately nine years of experience with the Boston Police Department in Massachusetts. After excelling in earlier jobs requiring strong investigation, communication, and training skills I was selected to receive additional training and certified as a K-9 handler. Since 2003, I have been filling dual roles as a K-9 Officer and Police Specialist. Presently leading the department in the number of criminal apprehensions by K-9 teams for the year to date, I am also considered highly effective in training and supervising new officers in areas which include police safety, criminal enforcement, traffic enforcement, public safety, crime prevention, investigation techniques, and report writing.

Since joining this police force in 1994, I have met the challenges of working with the public and my fellow officers while earning a reputation as an articulate, self-motivated professional with exceptional communication and organizational skills. I am known as a patient and persistent investigator who will follow all leads and pursue a case to its conclusion. A persuasive speaker, I have been effective in giving testimony when my cases come to trial.

I am confident that the qualities that have made me effective as a representative of this city's law enforcement community would easily translate to success with the Federal Bureau of Investigation. I appreciate the opportunity to meet and discuss the Bureau's requirements, needs, and goals and how my background might serve them. I can provide outstanding references at the appropriate time.

Sincerely,

Paula Quincey

Paula Quincey
000000000
INTERNAL
1107 Birch Circle
Boston, MA 11231
Home: (111) 111-1111
Work: (222) 222-2222
Email: pquincey@msn.com
Announcement Number: (888) 8888-888

OBJECTIVE   To obtain a position as a **Special Agent** with the **FBI**.

EDUCATION   **Bachelor of Arts in Visual Arts Management**, Suffolk University, Boston, MA, 2002.
- Graduated with a 3.33 GPA.

EXPERIENCE   *Am earning a reputation as a quick learner and skilled trainer who relates well to others and offers a strong ability to work with the public as a member of the Boston Police Department, Boston, MA:*

2003-present: K-9 OFFICER and **POLICE SPECIALIST.** 5ᵗ Precinct, 1326 Sapona Road, Boston, MA 11231, Andrew Lewis, Supervisor, Phone: (333) 333-3333. Have quickly become recognized as a highly effective dog handler and am leading the department in the number of criminal apprehensions for the year to date while also contributing through my knowledge and experience in the capacity of training specialist.
- Completed training which allows me to work as a team with my dog in areas including narcotics searches of vehicles, buildings, and interdiction.
- Have learned that well-trained K-9 officers are useful in calming scared children.
- Work with my dog during tracking and trailing lost children or law violators, land and water cadaver recovery, and for handler protection such as during building searches.
- As a Police Specialist, train new officers who are recognized for their efficiency in accident investigations and report writing.
- Provide training in officer safety, criminal enforcement, traffic enforcement, public safety, crime prevention, investigative techniques, and report writing.

1998-2003: POLICE INVESTIGATOR. 14ᵗʰ Precinct, 8010 Bonanza Drive, Boston, MA 11734, Eleanor Bell, Supervisor, Phone: (444) 444-4444. Was offered an opportunity to become a homicide investigator on the basis of my skills displayed while investigating serious criminal acts.
- Oversaw cases from conducting the investigation, through charging the criminal, to presenting evidence in the case before a court of law.
- Led the department with most arrests resulting in closed cases over an eight-month period.

1996-1998: POLICE SPECIALIST. 1292 Alamac Avenue, Easton, MA 11854, Kyle Willis, Supervisor, Phone: (555) 555-5555. Recognized for my outstanding ability to communicate both verbally and in writing as well as for my skill as a trainer in passing on my knowledge to others.
- Produced effective officers while involved in internal training in areas which included officer safety, criminal investigation, crime prevention, criminal enforcement, traffic enforcement, public safety, and report writing.
- Created a new city citation book for the City of Boston. Applied my communication skills to sell the city on the idea of issuing glove pouches to all officers.

1994-1996: POLICE OFFICER. 210 Blue Street, Springfield, MA 11264, Lester Banks, Supervisor, Phone: (666) 666-6666. Gained a strong base of experience in crime prevention and detection, criminal enforcement, traffic enforcement, patrolling, and investigation.

- Was recognized as a persistent and patient investigator who would not give up until all leads were followed and the case closed.

Highlights of earlier experience: Learned to work with the public and provide valuable customer service in the food service industry as well as applying my creativity as a visual merchandiser for a major department store.

SPECIAL AGENT

TRAINING & PROFESSIONAL CERTIFICATIONS

Attend continuing education courses at Springfield Technical Community College, Springfield, MA, 1994; completed classes including the following:

Boston Basic Law Enforcement Training: Traffic & Criminal Enforcement, Criminal Apprehension, Weapons: .357 Caliber Handgun, 12-Gauge Shotgun.

- **Boston Advanced Law Enforcement Training:** 500 hours of in-service training and six years of patrol experience, culminating in a four-year college degree.
- **Police Law Institute:** course of study included units on search & seizure, search warrants, and surveillance.
- **K-9 Certifications:** North American Police Work Dog Association, 2003 and Certificate of Training, Police K-9 Patrol, 2003.
- **Radar Certifications:** Radar Operator Certification Training, 2003; Operator Certification for Radar, 2000; re-certification, 2002.
- **Intoxilyzer Certification:** (40 hours), 1997; recertification, Intoxilyzer Recertification (16 hours), 2002.
- **Search and Seizure Certification:** (80 hours), 1996; recertification, sponsored by the Boston Law Enforcement Institute (8 hours), 2002.
- Interview and Interrogation certification, 1998.
- Advanced Defensive Handgun/Defensive Urban Rifle/Shotgun, 1998.
- Legal In-service Training in DWI Enforcement, 1996.
- DCI Statewide Mobile Certification Class, 1996.
- Street Level Drug Enforcement for Patrol Officers, 1996.
- Hazard Communications Training, 1995.
- CPR Refresher: 1995, 2003.
- Field Training Officer Course, 1994.
- Emergency Medical Services First Responder Re-Certification, 2001.
- Investigating Child Abuse and Neglect, 1994.
- Law Enforcement Wellness, 1993.
- Defensive Tactics Refresher (Aikido), 1993.
- Basic Criminal Investigation for Patrol Officers, 1993.
- State Certification; Criminal Justice Education and Training Standards Commission, 1992.
- Glock Transition Training and Qualification, 1992.
- Hazardous Materials for Law Enforcement Parts 1 and 2, 1992.

SPECIAL SKILLS Attend continuing education courses at Springfield Technical Community College, Springfield, MA, 1998; completed classes including the following:

- **Analytical Skills:** Analyze information from automotive accident scenes in order to reconstruct events and draw conclusions; perform detailed analysis of hostage situations to secure the area until hostage negotiators arrive, stationing officers in strategic locations to provide reconnaissance and security to the crime scene.
- **Crime Scene Investigation:** Extensive knowledge in this area includes: identifying potential witnesses and suspects, securing the crime scene to ensure that no evidence is removed or damaged, and collecting physical evidence such as latent fingerprints; hair, skin, and fiber samples; or items dropped or handled by victims or suspects.
- **Computer Skills:** Computer literate and familiar with many popular computer operating systems and software, including but not limited to Windows 95, Corel WordPerfect, and the Mobile Data Terminal systems utilized by the Boston Police Department.
- **Communication Skills:** Display my exceptional written communication skills while preparing a wide range of incident, accident, and other police reports. Have built a reputation as an articulate communicator capable of verbally disarming tense situations while responding to domestic disputes and traffic/criminal enforcement calls.
- **Defensive Tactics:** Completed training which included preventing an assailant from obtaining my weapon during a struggle, as well as officer safety, and protection of the public.
- **Drug Investigations:** Skilled in apprehending criminals, detecting clues and securing evidence, as well as conducting surveillance operations.
- **Interview and Interrogation Techniques:** Adept at using communication skills to draw information vital to the investigation from the interview subject. Trained in the psychology of the criminal mind and in detecting leads during the interview and interrogation process.
- **K-9 Use:** Experienced in recovering cadavers and conducting searches of buildings, as well as tracking and trailing potential suspects using trained police dogs.
- **Leadership Skills:** Selected as a Field Training Officer and Advanced Field Training Officer, in addition to serving as Acting Lieutenant for a one-month period and Acting Sergeant for three weeks.
- **Staff Development & Training:** Accepted into Instructor Certification class for 1999; served as Training Officer – Advanced, instructing law enforcement personnel in officer survival, investigative techniques, and the application of criminal and traffic laws.
- **Stress Management:** Demonstrate ability to direct stress in a positive manner and make quick, effective decisions in stressful situations.
- **Weapons Skills:** Skilled and qualified in the use of .40 caliber semi-automatic pistol, Heckler & Koch MP5/Colt AR15/Olympic Arms .45 caliber rifle, and 12-gauge shotgun.

PERSONAL Received a Good Conduct Medal in recognition of five years of service to the Boston Police Department with no disciplinary actions, April 2003. Excellent personal and professional references are available upon request.

PART THREE
RESUMES FOR DIRECT COMMISSION, ARC PAGE
FORMATS, & WARRANT OFFICER JOBS

In this section you will find samples of resumes used to apply for specialized career situations. A couple of these resumes were used by individuals in the military who sought specialized advancement opportunities. For example, you will see the resume of a young military enlisted soldier seeking a direct commission to become an officer, and you will see an enlisted soldier seeking to advance into warrant officer ranks.

COMMISSIONED OFFICER

Date

Dear Exact Name of Person: (or Dear Sir or Madam if answering a blind ad):

With the enclosed resume, I would like to express my deep desire to become commissioned as an officer in the U.S. Army. I am presently serving as a proud member of the Infantry Paratrooper Division, and I feel I have much to offer my country as an Army Officer.

COMMISSIONED OFFICER

Here is a resume and cover letter of an individual who was successful in his application to become a commissioned officer in the U.S. Army. He has been serving his country as an enlisted soldier. Use the cover letter and resume as a sample, only. Please note that you should follow precise instructions on how to address a letter such as this one. Military procedures will provide you with precise guidance in this area. Although this letter and resume worked in the past, procedures and requirements can always change, so make sure you follow the procedural requirements of your particular branch of the service.

Extensive educational background

As you will see from my resume, I hold both a Master's degree in Counseling Psychology and a Bachelor's degree in Sociology with a secondary concentration in Social Work. In one internship related to counseling, I worked as a Counselor and Drug Treatment Specialist for Hastings Behavior Therapy facility in Baton Rouge, LA. In an internship related to my Bachelor's degree program, I worked as an intern for the City of Baton Rouge's Police Department.

ROTC background and management experience. For nearly one year while earning my undergraduate degree, I was a member of the Reserve Officer Training Corps (ROTC). I received "Outstanding" evaluations of my performance as a Company Commander, Platoon Leader, Squad Leader, and Team Leader. Although I excelled as a ROTC member and received the Henderson Award, I made the decision to exit the ROTC Program and earn my Master's degree (M.S.E.D.) in Counseling Psychology immediately after college.

Excellent communication skills and leadership ability. After completing Advanced Individual Training (A.I.T.) in 1998, I was selected to become the company's new Training NCO where I played a role in training 95 soldiers in a six-week cycle. Subsequently I served the goals of the U.S. Army by becoming a Home Town Recruiter for one month in July 2002, and I exceeded all recruiting quotas while communicating the advantages of a military career to high-quality high school students. While "selling" young people on the advantages of a military career, I realized with certainty that I wish to make a career in military service as an Army officer.

Language and communication skills, certifications, and firearms. With a working knowledge of German, I am CPR and First Aid qualified and I am a certified Ocean Front Lifeguard. I am considered an Expert Marksman and can operate and maintain numerous military weapons. I am physically fit and am confident that I could pass the most rigorous background investigation.

After graduating college, I made a commitment to serve my country as a military officer, and I am confident I could be an asset to the officers' corps. I come from a family with a long tradition of military service: my father was in the Marine's and my brother has been in the Coast Guard for 12 years. With extensive training and experience in behavioral counseling, I feel I could serve my country in even greater capacities as an officer. I respectfully request that you consider me for a direct commission.

Sincerely,

Aaron I. Ortiz

Name: Aaron I. Ortiz
Citizenship: U.S.
2424 Bishon Lane
Fort Carson, CO 84849
Home: (999) 999-9999
E-mail: aortiz@bellsouth.net

OBJECTIVE	I want to be commissioned as a U.S. Army officer.
EDUCATION	**Master of Science in Education (M.S.E.D.) Counseling Psychology,** University of Southern Colorado, Pueblo, CO, GPA 3.2 approximately, 2003.
	Bachelor of Arts (B.A.) in Sociology with secondary concentration in Social Work, Southern University & Agriculture College, Baton Rouge, LA, 1998; became a member of ROTC in Fall 1998; received "outstanding" evaluations in these positions:
	Company Commander: Commanded 125 people. **Platoon Leader:** Managed 25 people. **Squad Leader:** Managed 14 people. **Team Leader:** Managed 8 people. As an ROTC Cadet, earned the Leaders & Achievers Scholarship; received the prestigious Truitt-Henderson Award.
TRAINING	Joint Readiness Training Center, Fort Eustis, VA, 1999.
	Advanced Individual Training and Basic Training, Fort Hood, TX, 1998.
EXPERIENCE	**INFANTRY SOLDIER.** U.S. Army, 32nd Infantry Division, Fort Carson, CO 84849, (2002-present). Am a proud member of the U.S. Army with a Specialist rank. I wish to make a career in the military, and believe that I can serve my country to my fullest capacity as an officer. **MOS:** Infantry Paratrooper. Perform with distinction in field environments.
	HOME TOWN RECRUITER. U.S. Army Recruiting, 3479 Baulding Drive, Baton Rouge, LA (July 2002). Was assigned as a recruiter for one month, and excelled in communicating the advantages of a military career to high school students in and near my home town.
	• Exceeded all goals for recruiting, and became known as an articulate individual who truly believes in the Army values and value of serving one's country.
	TRAINING NCO. U.S. Army, 15th Training Corp Division, Fort Jackson, SC (2000-02). After a distinguished performance in Advanced Individual Training (A.I.T.), was selected to play a role in training 95 soldiers in a six-week training cycle; known as an excellent communicator.
	Other experience:
	COUNSELOR (INTERN). Hastings Behavior Therapy, 843 Callahan Road, Baton Rouge, LA (1997-1998). In an internship related to my Master's degree program, performed as a Counselor and Drug Treatment Specialist in a medium/maximum security facility incarcerating several thousand prisoners.
	POLICE DEPARTMENT INTERN. City of Baton Rouge Police Department, Baton Rouge, LA (1996-97). Worked with homicide investigations, narcotics investigations, and street patrols as I worked in an internship which refined my knowledge of law enforcement.
TECHNICAL SKILLS & PERSONAL	**Computers:** Familiar with many popular software programs.
	Firearms: Expert marksman. Operate and maintain M4 carbine, M16, M240B, M249 AR.
	Clearance: Can pass the most rigorous background investigation.
	Certifications: CPR and First Aid trained and qualified. Ocean Front Lifeguard Certification.
	Languages: Working knowledge of German.

ARC: ELECTRICAL POWER SUPERVISOR

Name: Ben M. Yancy
SSN: 000-00-0000
INTERNAL
888 Fullenstone Road, Madison, WI 97987
Home: (555) 555-5555
Work: (111) 111-1111
Email: byancy@hotmail.com
Announcement Number: 11JAN339385

ARC FOR ELECTRICAL POWER PRODUCTION SUPERVISOR

Here you will see an example of a specialized kind of resume referred to as an ARC. Often the ARC can be up to five pages long, although you must consult the job vacancy announcement for precise specifications.

EXPERIENCE SUMMARY

Extensive knowledge of total quality management methodology, tools, and techniques. Knowledge of directives pertaining to The Boeing Company disaster preparedness programs and activities to project, plan, and manage disaster preparedness programs. Knowledge of Air Field Operability program, governing directives and methods and procedures for program implementation. Extensive technical and supervisory experience related to all aspects of the repair, maintenance, and operation of power plant equipment in accordance with manufacturer's specifications, technical orders, and shop operating procedures. Highly resourceful and technically expert troubleshooter and problem solver in testing and emergency situations. Extensive background in personnel supervision, industrial maintenance, preventive maintenance, and electrical power production.

EXPERIENCE

Jan 2003 - present. 40+ hours per year. **Electrical Power Production Supervisor.** The Boeing Company, 9774 Paulsen Rd, Madison, WI. **Supervisor's name and phone:** Joseph Buchanan (111) 111-1111. Supervise, inspect, maintain, operate, and repair mobile, gas, and diesel power generators ranging in size from 5kw to 750kw. Maintain all associated equipment such as portable load banks. Utilize power tools and precision measurement equipment. From 2 Jan 2003-present, deployed to the 18th Special Operations Squadron (SOS) in support of Operation MOUNTAIN SEARCH at Shem Bali Army Camp, located 85 miles from the Iraq border. Maintained over $6 million worth of electrical power generation and ground support equipment. Was Key Control Operator for a 6 megawatt, 4160 volt, prime power plant consisting of eight Mobile Electric Power-012A (MEP) generators supporting 95% of the base electrical requirements. Professionally performed several 300-hour Preventive Maintenance Inspections (PMIs) on various MEP series and commercial generator sets while also providing well-maintained generators for reliable electrical power. Performed daily inspections on 11 generators providing prime electrical power to remote locations. Was evaluated as "an outstanding performer and a tremendous asset to the civil engineers at Shem Bali." Was commended for "superior technical knowledge which allowed training of less qualified technicians on mission-critical emergency generators." Became known for my strong troubleshooting and problem-solving skills: on numerous occasions, performed rapid maintenance actions on broken generator engineers. On a routine basis, install and operate electrical power plants, mobile generators, distribution equipment, automatic transfer panel, airfield lighting, and aircraft arresting systems. Modify and repair equipment utilizing a wide range of technical publications. Post entries on operation inspection and maintenance records. Inspect work performed by other electrical power production assistants in order to verify quality and compliance with policy, regulations, and appropriate publications. Assure the mobility readiness of six gasoline and four diesel generator sets. On a formal performance evaluation, was praised by the group commander for my enthusiasm and expertise. Was credited as being responsible for the idea of installing lights in overhang to use for squadron functions and as loadbanks for testing generators.

Sep 1999 – Jan 2003. 40+ hours per year. **Electrical Power Production Mechanic**. Applied Industries, 4134 Buchanan Lane, Madison, WI. Supervisor's name and phone: Frances Bailey (222) 222-2222. Inspected, maintained, operated, and repaired mobile, gas, and diesel power generators ranging in size from 5kw to 100kw. Maintained all associated equipment such as air compressors, pumps, and portable load banks. Utilized power tools and precision measurement equipment. On a formal performance evaluation, was praised in these words: "SSgt Pruitt performs all assigned duties in a professional manner and sets the standard for others to follow." Was described as "a multi-skilled individual capable of handling and completing any type of task." Utilized my background as a civilian electrician while teaching new recruits basic knowledge of wiring and trained others in the fundamentals of DC magnetism as well as the characteristics of both AC and DC circuits and parallel generators.

May 1997 – September 1999. 40 hours per week. **Diesel Mechanic**. Longley Maintenance Company, 459 Leeds Avenue, San Antonio, TX
Supervisor's name and phone: Donald Coach (333) 333-3333. Perform inspection and maintenance/repairs on vehicles ranging from one-half ton trucks to large over-the-road tractors, trailers, and school buses. Perform Department of Transportation inspections. Perform maintenance and repairs on Recreational Vehicles ranging from small travel trailers to large motorhomes and General settings. Am Level Two Gregory Poole Generator Certified.

May 1995 - May 1997. 40 hours per week. **Mechanic and Inspector**. Hardin, Inc, 741 Faber Hwy, San Antonio, TX. Supervisor's name and phone: Peter Cumberland (444) 444-4444. Perform preventive maintenance and repair work on vehicles ranging from small passenger cars (imports and exports) to heavy diesel trucks and trailers. Perform Department of Transportation inspections. Held Mobile Air Conditioning Society License.

Feb 1993 – May 1995. 40 hours per week. **Sorter**. Federal Express, 7764 Conner Hwy, San Antonio, TX. Supervisor's name and phone: Leonard Johnson (555) 555-5555. Checked and sorted 1800 packages an hour which were directed or sent to other hubs in the United States and North America.

Jul 1990-Feb 1993. 40 hours per week. **Maintenance Mechanic and Operator**. Southwestern Airlines, 5551 Shelby Drive, San Antonio, TX. Supervisor's name and phone: Eric G. Jameson (666) 666-6666. Maintained a fleet of 34 trucks and vans ranging in size from one-half ton GM trucks and vans used for environmental clean up. Qualified on industrial vacuums and Sewer Jet Trucks.

Mar 1987-July 1990. 40 hours per week. **Power Plant Operator/Mechanic**. U.S. Army, Delta Co. 159th, Ft. Carson, CO. Supervisor's name and phone: Franklin Thomas (777) 777-7777. Operated, maintained, and inspected six prime power generator sets rated at 3,000 kilowatts each while operating and maintaining a prime power plant providing power for the Ft. Carson area. Trained and supervised six personnel in the daily operation of the plant. Monitored the electrical load demand for both utility and technical bus. Operated electrical switchgear components such as remote control switches, power transfer controls, circuit breakers, and voltage regulating rheostats. Controlled the distribution of electrical power to bus and feeder circuits. Observed and analyzed readings from instruments such as ammeters, voltmeters, frequency meters, temperature and pressure indicating devices. Operated, maintained, and inspected auxiliary equipment such as air compressors, cooling water pumps, pre-lube pumps, fuel oil pumps, and centrifuges. Monitored the waste heat recovery system and made adjustments as necessary. Applied my technical knowledge in numerous emergency situations. For example, averted a possible power outage and avoided loss of life and property by the actions I took after I noticed loud recurring noise emanating from the engine area on number three generator. On another occasion, assisted in lowering unusually high boiler temperature caused by a malfunctioning boiler diverter valve.

Dec 1985-Mar 1987. 40 hours per week. **Depot Maintenance Supervisor.** U.S. Army, Camp Casey, South Korea. Supervisor's name and phone: Christopher Lionels (011) 11-1-111-1111. Supervised 10 personnel in the inspection, maintenance, operation, and repair of 82 mobile gas and diesel, 5kw to 800kw power generators. Supervisor of the only heavy maintenance shop for generators in Camp Casey, South Korea.

Aug 1984-Dec 1985. 40 hours per week. **Generator and Maintenance Mechanic.** U.S. Army, 3-59th Battalion, Ft. Benning, GA. Supervisor's name and phone: Saul Jernigan (888) 888-8888. Inspected, maintained, operated, and repaired fixed and mobile gas and diesel power generating nits which supported operation, instrumentation, radar surveillance, computer, closed circuit TV, POL distribution systems, and airfield lighting systems. Operated, maintained, repaired, and troubleshot emergency power generators (gasoline and diesel power, 1.5 through 450kw) that provided backup electrical power for critical base facilities as well as four fire deluge pump engines. Utilized power tools and precision measurement equipment. Assisted with the installation of the Tracer fuel leak detection system base wide. Used existing training plans to train base personnel on proper operation of standby generators reducing user downtime. Played a key role in the prevention of fuel contamination in the environment. Inspected, maintained, operated, and repaired fixed and mobile, gas, and diesel power generators ranging in size from 5kw to 450kw. Maintained all associated equipment such as air compressors, pumps, and portable load banks. Utilized power tools and precision measurement equipment. Performed additional duties including Bench stock monitor. Demonstrated my resourcefulness and initiative by designing and fabricating guide pins to allow for quicker installation of AC alternators in Mobile Electric Power generator sets. During one emergency situation, worked with interior and exterior electric standby personnel during a power outage at the base fire department and played a key role in restoring power and preventing any hindrance to the fire department's mission. Utilized newly established training plans to train using organization personnel on the proper installation of emergency standby equipment.

Dec 1981 - Aug 1984. 40 hours per week. **Depot Maintenance Supervisor and Shop Safety Monitor.** U.S. Army, 2-459th C Company, Honolulu, HI. Supervisor's name and phone: Martin Roberts (999) 999-9999. Was promoted to supervise six people as supervisor for the Main Engine Rebuilt Section, Main Component Rebuilt Section and the Cylinder Head Rebuild Section. Supervised 18 people in the inspection, maintenance, and repair of power generators and support equipment for all military bases in Hawaii. Performed additional duty as Safety Monitor. Earned respect for my ability to perform inspection and repair activities to the depot level overhaul and maintenance of both prime and standby power generating units at 15 remote installations throughout Hawaii. Disassembled, cleaned, visually inspected, repaired, assembled, and tested diesel electric generating systems, air compressors, aircraft arresting barriers, and all mechanical components utilizing the latest test equipment and procedures. Repaired, modified, and overhauls power plant equipment in accordance with manufacturer's specifications, technical orders, and current shop procedures. Was evaluated on a formal performance evaluation as "a highly motivated and dedicated NCO who continuously produces excellent results from his every tasking." Was praised for my outstanding performance in correcting numerous mechanical problems in order to keep generators in service. Was praised in a formal performance evaluation for "initiative and versatility" while working as part of team at the Honolulu Airport repairing the prime power plant's commercial buss breakers. The repairs enabled the base to transfer the commercial power source when available without interference to base missions. During one assignment as manager of the Small Engine Repair Section, implemented procedures which improved productivity and efficiency.

EDUCATION

Associate of Applied Science Degree in Automotive/Diesel Technology, San Antonio Technical College, San Antonio, TX, Jan 1994.
Master Mechanic Course, San Antonio Technical College, San Antonio, TX, Jan 1993.

TRAINING

Completed training in Electrical Standards, The Boeing Company, Occupational Health and Safety Seminar, Madison, WI, Jan 2003.
Electrical Power Production Technician Course, The Boeing Company, Occupational Health and Safety Seminar, Madison, WI, May 2003.
Gregory Poole Generator Qualification Certification Course leading to Gregory Poole Generator Qualification, Longley Maintenance Company, San Antonio TX, Apr 1997.
Hazardous Material Pallet Loading Course, Southwestern Airlines, San Antonio, TX, Aug 1992.
Total Quality Management, Southwestern Airlines, San Antonio, TX, Nov 1991.
Diesel Engine Overhaul and Generator Set Operation Course, San Antonio Technical College, San Antonio, TX, May 1992.
Non-Commissioned Officer Leadership School, U.S. Army Ft. Carson, CO, Nov 1990.

**LICENSES &
CERTIFICATES**

Certified as a Level II Gregory Poole Generator Mechanic, Jun 2000.
Certified Service Technician, Jun 1995. Mobile Air Conditioning Society License, Oct 1993.

AWARDS

US Army Training Ribbon, 1995
Small Arms Expert Marksmanship Ribbon, 1995
NCO Professional Military Education Graduate Ribbon, 1994
US Army Longevity Service Award Ribbon, 1993
National Defense Service Medal, 1991
US Army Good Conduct Medal, 1990

CLEARANCE

Secret security clearance

WARRANT OFFICER

NAME: Ralph Ormand
ADDRESS: 10296 Giles Road, Fort Belvoir, VA 44549
RANK: E-7
SSN: 000-00-0000
UNIT: C-353rd Maintenance Shop, Fort Belvoir, VA 44598

OBJECTIVE: To obtain an appointment as an ARNG warrant officer, in MOS 745B Unit Maintenance Tech (Light).

PERSONAL DATA:

DATE OF BIRTH: 3-03-03	**HEALTH:** Good	**MOS:** 55B87
HEIGHT: 68"	**MARITAL STATUS:** M	
WEIGHT: 190	**DEPENDENTS:** 3	

SUMMARY

I feel I am qualified to be appointed as a warrant officer based on my civilian and military training and experience. I am confident that the leadership skills that I have obtained through my military as well as my civilian training will be invaluable to me as a warrant officer. My experience as an Electronic Measurement Technician for the C-353rd Maintenance Shop, Fort Knox, KY has provided me with a sound basis for the responsibilities of a Tank System Mechanic at Fort Belvoir, VA. I am certain that I can fully perform the duties of an Army NG Warrant Officer and I will uphold the dignity and integrity of the office. I am physically and mentally fit.

MILITARY EXPERIENCE PERTINENT TO MOS 09W

Jun 04-present. **Electronic Measurement Equipment Technician.** US Army, C-353rd Maintenance Shop, Fort Knox, KY. Perform various functional electronic, physical, and radioactive testing involving interpretation and analysis of measurement data in accordance with cyclic inspection requirements, to insure correctness of instruments undergoing certification. Analyze and isolate component malfunctions. Calculate and determine tolerances. Assist supervisor with technical data for inclusion in reports as well as recommending equipment improvements and offering solutions to problems related to the testing of precision measuring equipment.

Jun 01-Jun 04. **Electronics Mechanic.** US Army, 78th Motor Pool Fort Campbell, KY. Duties included troubleshooting components of the M1A1 tank and Bradley power unit system using the STEM-1/ FVS. Removed and installed power packs and a variety of mechanical, electrical, and pneumatic parts. Referred to published guidance to include manufacturer's repair manuals, technical manuals, blueprints, vehicle schematics, and wiring diagrams. Served as a member of the Maintenance Assistance and Instruction Team (MAIT). Issued heavy mobile armament and automotive equipment. As Alternate Waste Site Manager for the 78th Motor Pool in Kentucky, became familiar with the Army and National Guard Series 385 Regulations regarding safety and Hazmat communications standards and was responsible for finding innovative ways to minimize and discard waste.

Sep 99-Jun 01. **Material Handler.** US Army, Training Squadron Maintenance Shop, Fort Carson, CO. Duties included receiving and ordering organizational tools and parts as well as controlling the maintenance status of the parts. Was always prepared to display the operational readiness of the equipment to include inspecting, sight firing control systems, and load testing various equipment. Maintained equipment files on 19 NCNG units. Assisted in the scheduling, shipping, and receiving of equipment delivered to the MATES for distribution to various units or rebuild facilities. Acted as customer liaison, which included preparing files, setting up 100% inventory appointments, and sending out letters to supported units.

Apr 96-Sep 99. **LWV Mechanic (M48).** US Army, 34th Motor Pool Division, Fort Hood, TX. Carry out duties which include performing testing, diagnostic testing, fault isolation to the circuit card assembly, troubleshooting, wire tracing, module replacement, and repair of light wheeled vehicles.

Dec 88-Apr 96. **Tank System Mechanic.** US Army, MATES, Fort Belvoir, VA.
Supervised and followed the guidelines of the facility's standard operating procedures. Ensured safety protection was being worn, assigned jobs to my subordinates, and set the pace so that tasks were started and completed in a timely manner. Commanded M48, M60A3, M1, and M1A1 tank crews at MATES. As an Electronic Mechanic, I diagnosed, removed, and installed ignition switches and electronic control assemblies and aligned Stab and GHS switches.

CIVILIAN EXPERIENCE PERTINENT TO MOS 09W

May 85-Dec 88. **Electronics Mechanic.** 159th Transportation Division, Ft. Hood, TX. Analyzed engine misfires on a diagnostic machine. Troubleshot electrical circuits using digital and regular multimeters. After rebuilding engines, performed function checks using dynamometer testers. Also installed engine controllers and repaired/replaced HEI ignitions and automotive computers as well as installing various control modules and sensors.

CIVILIAN EDUCATION

Bellarmine College, majored in **Fire Protection and Planning,** Louisville, KY, 2003. Kentucky Fire Academy, majored in **Fire Control and Inspection,** Louisville, KY, 2002. Tidewater Community College, majored **Auto Mechanics,** Portsmouth, VA, 1996. Diploma, Whatcoma High School, 1984.

MILITARY EDUCATION

BNCOC-RC NCMA, Fort Campbell, KY. Scope of training concentrated on leadership skills. PNCOC-RC NCMA, Fort Knox, KY. Scope of training concentrated on leadership skills. M1A1 DET CRS, Fort Hood, TX. MOS training that taught the basic skills in MOS 09W M1 Trans, Gowen Field, Fort Belvoir, VA. Training. Scope of training concentrated on track vehicle maintenance. M1A1 Trans. Training, Fort Belvoir, VA. Scope of training concentrated on track vehicle maintenance.

Although the purpose of this book is to show you samples of federal resumes and the resumix, we wanted to include another application which is often used to apply for federal positions. The Optional Form (OF) 612 is an application which you may choose to prepare instead of the resumix. We are not recommending that you choose the 612 instead of a federal resume as your method of applying for federal jobs. We just wanted to provide an example of what the 612 looks like when it is completed correctly. Please note that your job experience can be shown on continuation sheets, instead of being squeezed into the space on the form itself.

Another form sometimes used to apply for federal government jobs is the Standard Form (SF) 171. We are not showing an example of the SF 171 in this book, but you can find examples of the SF 171 in PREP's book entitled "Government Job Applications & Federal Resumes."

OF 612 for a PROGRAM COORDINATOR

Job title in announcement: PROGRAM COORDINATOR
Grade(s) applied for: GS-
Announcement number:

PROGRAM COORDINATOR

Here you see an example of how to prepare an application called an Optional Form (OF) 612, which is sometimes used instead of a resumix.

4.

Last Name	First and Middle Name	
SUTTON	PAUL	GERARD

5.

Social Security Number
000-00-0000

6.

Mailing Address
2509 Callie Lane

City	State	Zip Code
Evansville	IN	46237

7.

Phone Numbers (include area codes) and e-mail:
Home: (999) 999-9999
Work: (888) 888-8888
E-mail: psutton@earthlink.net

WORK EXPERIENCE

8.   See attached continuation sheets.

PARK GUIDE, PROGRAM COORDINATOR, & OPERATIONS ASSISTANT
From: 11/2003
To: present
Salary: GS-0000-00
Hours per week: 40
Employer's Name and Address: Lance B. Washington Colonial Gardens, 2934 Winter Lochen Rd, Savannah, GA 31416
Supervisor's Name and Phone Number: Teresa Miller, (888) 888-8888

Overview of responsibilities:
Have received the highest evaluations of my performance while excelling in a position which requires outstanding planning, communication, and operations management skills. Have refined my public relations and customer service skills while serving as a public spokesman for an urban park (Lance B. Washington Colonial Gardens) which is comprised of 13 park buildings encompassing eight city blocks and which is visited by two million people annually.

Extensive responsibility for program development and database creation:
Extensive creativity combined with strong written and oral communication skills are required in order to excel in my position. I have utilized my strong analytical and communication skills in the process of creating numerous new programs and demonstrations which have contributed to the success of the urban park I represent. I have analyzed, researched, and created multiple programs which are now ongoing park programs. Programs of particular interest to an adult population include the following programs which interpret Savannah's involvement in the Civil War and its prominent political and social history. Created the databases related to these programs.

- **Savannah College of Art and Design (SCAD):** Developed a program 25 minutes in length which I present to groups of up to 135 people who are curious about the art museum and performance theatres on the campus.
- **African Heritage:** Developed a program which is a 30-minute gallery tour of the First African Baptist Church and Credit Union which highlights the architecture as the earliest example of African art and culture in the U.S.
- **Savannah Squares:** Researched, developed, and now present a 30-minute program to as many as 45 people on the architectural design and historical significance of all the Savannah Squares within the city.
- **Midnight in the Garden of Good and Evil:** Developed and now present a program discussing the successful movie and novel "Midnight in the Garden of Good and Evil" written by John Berents. The movie was mostly featured at the Mercer House in heart of Savannah.

Also created—after extensive analysis and research—the databases and programs which resulted in three popular new children's programs within the vast urban park known as Lance B. Washington Colonial Gardens. I present those programs, which last up to 30 minutes in length, to groups of up to 22 children.

- **Hands-on History:** Present a program which allows children to play Civil War games, musical instruments, and period toys which allow children to experience a taste of colonial life.
- **A Civil War Soldier's Life:** Present a program which encourages children to imagine what it would be like to be a soldier during the Civil War by permitting children to interact with items a soldier would have possessed during that time period.
- **Brush with History:** Present a program through which children learn history through participating in an historical treasure hunt.

Strong oral and written communication skills:

My formal evaluations have praised the effectiveness of my written documents, and my written work has been described as "clear, relevant, concise, well organized, grammatically correct, and appropriate to audience." My oral communication skill have been praised in writing as "persuasive, tactful, and appropriate to audience" and I have been commended for demonstrating courtesy and respect for other points of view when working with the general public. In addition to performing extensive oral communication in presenting the programs above as well as others, I communicate extensively with the public while informing visitors of public transportation routes and locations. I also communicate orally while providing directions to other attractions and museums within Savannah. As a service to the public, I provide accurate and detailed information pertaining to other historic area sites. I communicate orally as I make orientation movie announcements.

- Was specially chosen for the responsibility of recruiting at area colleges, and I have been commended for my articulate explanation of the Savannah Squares and specifically Lance B. Washington Colonial Gardens. Utilize a PowerPoint presentation during these formal presentations.

Outstanding customer service skills:

On formal performance evaluations, I have earned the highest possible evaluations of my performance in the area of customer service. A formal written evaluation praised me as "delivering high quality services to customers" and I was described as "initiating suggestions for improving service." I was commended in writing for maintaining customer service as my highest priority.

Demonstrated ability to handle multiple simultaneous tasks and to adjust to constantly changing priorities:

I have demonstrated an ability to adjust to rapidly changing priorities while articulately communicating with the public and representing numerous individual sites at these vast parks. On my own initiative, I maintain my knowledge of multiple sites so that I am always prepared to answer detailed questions from the general public about numerous facts, events, people, and structures which include the following:

Savannah Squares	First African Baptist Church
City Market	The Mercer House
Tybee Island Beach	Savannah River Bridge Run
The Chestnut House	Forsyth Park

Operations management and building security responsibilities:
Am entrusted with the responsibility of opening and closing park buildings in accordance with Standard Operating Procedures (SOPs). On my own initiative, I have contributed numerous suggestions which have enhanced security at individual program locations and sites. Maintain an attitude of "attention to detail" at all times in order to maintain a safe environment for visitors. Remain alert to people and situations which potentially pose a threat to public safety. I help to assure public safety as I carry out the responsibility of conducting inspections of park buildings to ensure visitor and facility safety. I also help to maintain control of the urban park's assets by taking periodic inventories of historical artifacts in various buildings throughout the park. As needed, I provide crowd control at the Savannah College of Art and Design in accordance with SOPs. I also monitor crowd behavior at those sites, and I make accommodations for individuals with disabilities.

Involvement in cash control and financial accountability:
Monitored the payment of user fees for park resources. Handled cash and check transactions in the sales area at the Mercer House. Was responsible for drawer reconciliation at the opening and end of my shift, and completed daily revenue paperwork totaling sales.

Administrative duties and responsibilities for training other employees:
Have been entrusted with the responsibility of training new incoming guides on the local tour sites. Was selected to serve on the Washington Garden's Annual Event Committee, and provided oversight for the process of granting leave for six-month periods.

Computer skills:
Utilize my proficiency with various software programs in order to maximize my job effectiveness. Have trained other employees in the use of PowerPoint, and especially in improving their use of a PowerPoint presentation which is used for recruiting purposes at area colleges.

PROCESSING INTERN
From: 10/2000
To: 09/2003
Salary: Intern

Hours per week: 40
Employer's Name and Address: Indiana State Archives, 11932 Curren Drive, Evansville, IN 57328
Supervisor's Name and Phone Number: Frances Curle, (777) 777-7777
Assisted the Financial Management Staff with tracking, inventorying, labeling, packing, and transporting archival materials. Played a key role in the development of an automated access system along with data entry in that system. Assisted researchers in the Archives public search room with historical, legal, and genealogical research. Instructed and assisted researchers in the use of microfilm equipment.

CLASSROOM AIDE
From: 07/1998
To: 10/2000
Salary: NA
Hours per week: 40
Employer's Name and Address: Kindred Care—North, 890 Peterson Lane, Indianapolis, IN 50388-4253.
Supervisor's Name and Phone Number: Maria Byrnes, (666) 666-6666
Supervised daily activities and provided support to mentally disadvantaged children, ages 12 to 18. Assisted teacher with planning, organizing, and presenting information and instruction to help students learn subject matter and skills that contributed to their educational and social development. On my own initiative, mastered bodies of knowledge which helped me communicate with mentally disadvantaged children: Discrete Trials, Picture Exchange Communication Systems (PECS), and American Sign Language.

SERVICE STAFF MEMBER
From: 12/1996
To: 07/1998
Salary: NA
Hours per week: 25
Employer's Name and Address: Harvest Moon Café Gallery, 1219 15th Street Suite 2-A, Indianapolis, IN 52016.
Supervisor's Name and Phone Number: Tamara Shumate, (555) 555 5555
Gained experience in working with the public, peers, and management while learning to work as part of team committed to the highest quality customer service.

9.   May we contact your current supervisor? **YES**

EDUCATION

10.   Highest level completed – **Bachelor of Arts**

11.   Last High School or GED. Give the school's name, city, ZIP Code and year diploma or GED received.
            Hillcrest High School, Indianapolis, IN 55816
            Year received: 1995

12.   Colleges and universities attended. Do not attach a copy of your transcript unless requested.

Name	Total Credits Earned	Major(s)	Degree	Year
Butler University	122	History	BA	1999
Indianapolis, IN				

OTHER QUALIFICATIONS

13.   **Job-related training** courses. **Job-related skills** (other languages, computer software/hardware, tools, machinery, typing, speed, etc.) **Job-related** certificates and licenses. Job-related honors, awards, and special accomplishments, publications, memberships in professional/ honor societies, leadership activities, public speaking, and performance awards). Give dates, but do not send documents.

Computers:
Proficient with Word, PowerPoint, WordPerfect, Excel, PowerPoint, Microsoft Works, Adobe PageMaker; am adept at utilizing the Internet with various search engines. In my current position, function as a PowerPoint "coach" and train other individuals in maximizing their effectiveness using PowerPoint during formal presentations to large groups.

Honor:
Was selected to represent my employer at Savannah College of Art and Design. Give speeches to large and small groups about careers in the Lance B. Washington Colonial Gardens.

Certifications:
Standard First Aid
Adult CPR

Training:
U.S. Department of Commerce Community Awareness Training, 2003
The National Rail Passenger Service Seminar, 2001
Equal Opportunity Employment Training, 1999

GENERAL

14.   Are you a U.S. citizen? **YES**

15.   Do you claim veterans' preference? **NO**

16.   Were you ever a Federal civilian employee? **YES**
For highest civilian grade give:

Series	Grade	From	To
GS-0000	08	10/2000	09/2003 (present)

17.   Are you eligible for reinstatement based on career or career-conditional Federal status? **NO**

APPLICANT CERTIFICATION

18.   I certify that, to the best of my knowledge and belief, all of the information on and attached to this application is true, correct, complete

and made in good faith. I understand that false or fraudulent information on or attached to this application may be grounds for not hiring me or for firing me after I begin work, and may be punishable by a fine or imprisonment. I understand that any information I give may be investigated.

SIGNATURE   **DATE SIGNED**

_____

Paul G. Sutton

ABOUT THE EDITOR

Anne McKinney holds an MBA from the Harvard Business School and a BA in English from the University of North Carolina at Chapel Hill. A noted public speaker, writer, and teacher, she is the senior editor for PREP's business and career imprint, which bears her name. Early titles in the Anne McKinney Career Series (now called the Real-Resumes Series) published by PREP include: *Resumes and Cover Letters That Have Worked, Resumes and Cover Letters That Have Worked for Military Professionals, Government Job Applications and Federal Resumes, Cover Letters That Blow Doors Open,* and *Letters for Special Situations.* Her career titles and how-to resume-and-cover-letter books are based on the expertise she has acquired in 20 years of working with job hunters. Her valuable career insights have appeared in publications of the "Wall Street Journal" and other prominent newspapers and magazines.

PREP Publishing Order Form

You may purchase any of our titles from your favorite bookseller! Or send a check or money order or your credit card number for the total amount*, plus $4.00 postage and handling, to PREP, 1110 1/2 Hay Street, Fayetteville, NC 28305. You may also order our titles on our website at www.prep-pub.com and feel free to e-mail us at preppub@aol.com or call 910-483-6611 with your questions or concerns.

Name: _____

Phone #: _____

Address: _____

E-mail address: _____

Payment Type: ☐ Check/Money Order   ☐ Visa   ☐ MasterCard

Credit Card Number: _____ Expiration Date: _____

Put a check beside the items you are ordering:

☐ Free—Packet describing PREP's professional writing and editing services
☐ $16.95—REAL-RESUMES FOR RESTAURANT, FOOD SERVICE & HOTEL JOBS. Anne McKinney, Editor
☐ $16.95—REAL-RESUMES FOR MEDIA, NEWSPAPER, BROADCASTING & PUBLIC AFFAIRS JOBS. Anne McKinney
☐ $16.95—REAL-RESUMES FOR RETAILING, MODELING, FASHION & BEAUTY JOBS. Anne McKinney, Editor
☐ $16.95—REAL-RESUMES FOR HUMAN RESOURCES & PERSONNEL JOBS. Anne McKinney, Editor
☐ $16.95—REAL-RESUMES FOR MANUFACTURING JOBS. Anne McKinney, Editor
☐ $16.95—REAL-RESUMES FOR AVIATION & TRAVEL JOBS. Anne McKinney, Editor
☐ $16.95—REAL-RESUMES FOR POLICE, LAW ENFORCEMENT & SECURITY JOBS. Anne McKinney, Editor
☐ $16.95—REAL-RESUMES FOR SOCIAL WORK & COUNSELING JOBS. Anne McKinney, Editor
☐ $16.95—REAL-RESUMES FOR CONSTRUCTION JOBS. Anne McKinney, Editor
☐ $16.95—REAL-RESUMES FOR FINANCIAL JOBS. Anne McKinney, Editor
☐ $16.95—REAL-RESUMES FOR COMPUTER JOBS. Anne McKinney, Editor
☐ $16.95—REAL-RESUMES FOR MEDICAL JOBS. Anne McKinney, Editor
☐ $16.95—REAL-RESUMES FOR TEACHERS. Anne McKinney, Editor
☐ $16.95—REAL-RESUMES FOR CAREER CHANGERS. Anne McKinney, Editor
☐ $16.95—REAL-RESUMES FOR STUDENTS. Anne McKinney, Editor
☐ $16.95—REAL-RESUMES FOR SALES. Anne McKinney, Editor
☐ $16.95—REAL ESSAYS FOR COLLEGE AND GRAD SCHOOL. Anne McKinney, Editor
☐ $25.00—RESUMES AND COVER LETTERS THAT HAVE WORKED. McKinney. Editor
☐ $25.00—RESUMES AND COVER LETTERS THAT HAVE WORKED FOR MILITARY PROFESSIONALS. McKinney, Ed.
☐ $25.00—RESUMES AND COVER LETTERS FOR MANAGERS. McKinney, Editor
☐ $25.00—GOVERNMENT JOB APPLICATIONS AND FEDERAL RESUMES: Federal Resumes, KSAs, Forms 171 and 612, and Postal Applications. McKinney, Editor
☐ $25.00—COVER LETTERS THAT BLOW DOORS OPEN. McKinney, Editor
☐ $25.00—LETTERS FOR SPECIAL SITUATIONS. McKinney, Editor
☐ $16.00—BACK IN TIME. Patty Sleem
☐ $17.00—(trade paperback) SECOND TIME AROUND. Patty Sleem
☐ $25.00—(hardcover) SECOND TIME AROUND. Patty Sleem
☐ $18.00—A GENTLE BREEZE FROM GOSSAMER WINGS. Gordon Beld
☐ $18.00—BIBLE STORIES FROM THE OLD TESTAMENT. Katherine Whaley
☐ $14.95—WHAT THE BIBLE SAYS ABOUT... *Words that can lead to success and happiness* (large print edition) Patty Sleem

_____ **TOTAL ORDERED**

_____ **(add $4.00 for shipping and handling)**

_____ **TOTAL INCLUDING SHIPPING**

PREP offers volume discounts on large orders. Call us at (910) 483-6611 for more information.